THE WORLD OF
MASKS

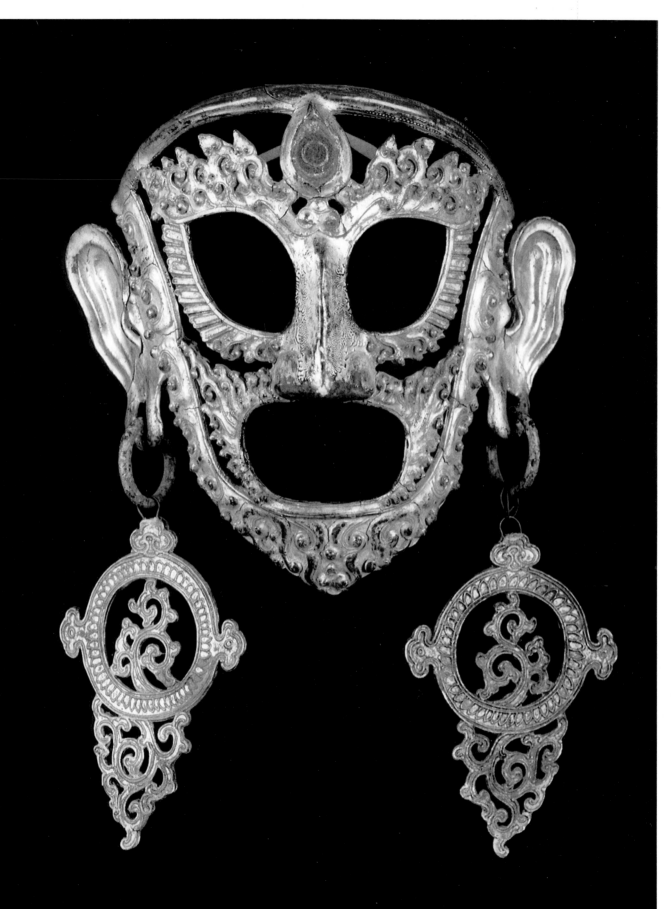

THE WORLD OF
MASKS

Erich Herold

HAMLYN

Text by Erich Herold, Libuše Boháčková,
Olga Kandertová, Hana Knížková and
Stanislav Novotný
Translated by Dušan Zbavitel
Photographs by Jan Pícha
and Hana Knížková
Line drawings by Ivan Zpěvák
Graphic design by František Prokeš
Designed and produced by Aventinum

English language edition first published 1992
Hamlyn is an imprint of Octopus Illustrated
Publishing, Michelin House, 81 Fulham
Road, London SW3 6RB,
part of Reed International Books

Copyright © 1992 Aventinum, Prague

ISBN 0 600 57442 3
Printed in Czechoslovakia by Polygrafia,
Prague
2/09/12/51-01

Contents

Introduction

The mask, as a means of the dramatic transformation of one person into another identity, perhaps ranks among the oldest manifestations of human culture. There is evidence of the use of masks long before people started to cultivate the soil, and certainly before they discovered about the extraction and use of metals. One of the best-known examples of Palaeolithic art is a painting found in the Trois Frères Cave in southern France (Fig. 1). A dancing figure wears reindeer antlers on his head and what is perhaps a mask on his face. His hands are hidden in bear's paws and his body in an animal skin provided with a horse-tail. Other parts of the figure may also be interpreted as parts of various animals' bodies. This is the first time we come across an image that could be interpreted as a complete mask, although the surrealistic juxtaposition of incongruous animal elements could also have been a representation of a mythical figure, a dream or a shaman in a state of trance.

Images of this kind are known to exist among many non-European peoples of the recent past and it is impossible to know exactly what the Trois Frères painting represented. Nevertheless, a mask is one possible interpretation.

The oldest extant mask, in the sense of a 'second face', originated in present-day Palestine. It was part of the renowned archaeological collection of Moshe Dayan, the former Israeli Minister of Defence, and is now kept in the Israeli Museum in Jerusalem (Fig. 2). The age of the mask, which is made of hard limestone, is estimated at approximately 9,000 years. It is convex and perfectly elliptical in outline, representing a stylised human face with large oval holes for the eyes, a small nose and an open mouth with two rows of teeth, reduced in number. Nothing is known, of course, about the purpose served by this mask, nor by whom it was

Fig. 1
A Palaeolithic dancer wearing an animal mask, from the Trois Frères Cave, southern France.

used. However, the rounded holes, placed along its edge at regular intervals, suggest that it was part of a costume and was worn to cover someone's face. It may have been worn on the head of a living man or of a dead one. Its purpose may have been the protection of its wearer against evil spirits, or the petrification of the face of a man buried in the earth in expectation of eternal life, as occurred in some of the developed cultures of later ages, for example ancient Egypt.

Whatever the purpose of this mask may have been, it undoubtedly impresses us as a mature piece of art and we cannot but admire the perfection of its execution. The elliptical eyes repeat the ellipse of the mask's outline in a rhythmical and harmonious reiteration. The way they are set into the concave areas, suggesting eyelids, renders this unique stone artefact lively in expression; we can hardly resist feeling that its very author is looking at us through the unmoving eyeholes.

Since its ascertainable beginning, the mask thus bears marks of an art and is intrinsically connected with it, representing one of its greatest subjects. This is essentially the theme of the human face. Even in the so-called animal masks, except the most realistic ones, attempts at an anthropomorphization of their expression are observable. It is this anthropomorphization which raises the mere animal to the level of a supernatural being, turning it into a powerful spirit in the eyes of the observer. On the other hand, however, it brings the animal closer to the man by expressing, in purely artistic terms, the underlying totemistic idea of the kinship of the human race with its mythical animal ancestor. In the mask, the subject of which is the human face, the artist found a useful field for experiment. His mastery of his craft enabled him to apply his skills to the broader subject of the entire human

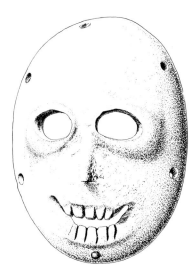

Fig. 2
Early Neolithic mask made of limestone, from Palestine.

figure. This is why the faces of the human figures representing ancestors, for instance among many African tribes, are treated in the same way as the human masks of the respective tribes, with the result that we are sometimes in doubt whether the figure is a stylised portrait of an ancestor, or a man wearing a well-known type of the tribal mask on his face. In a similar way, masks of the communities which have reached a higher level of structure, for example in India, do not at all deviate from the dominant art style of the given society, but fully accord with it.

The almost universal use of masks bears testimony to the fact that the idea of making them was reached by mankind in many places of the world independently, thus being in a way characteristic of humanity in general. We may even surmise that man, in his ideal evolution, inevitably had to reach such an idea at the time when he started to believe in supernatural beings affecting his life either in a positive or negative way. He undoubtedly tried first to influence their activities by entreaties and sacrifices, by endeavouring to gain their favour or to divert their anger, whenever he felt that he might have aroused it by his conduct. However, this was only the first step to the logically ensuing efforts to acquire the very qualities and power of those supernatural forces. On the ground of the general concept of the so-called sympathetic or imitative magic offering the possibility to reach the desired aim by imitating certain phenomena or qualities, he believed he could attain success by adapting that appearance of them which he fancied in his mind or saw in his dreams. Besides this active mental process, yet another, passive and defensive in character, may have played a role at the birth of the concept of masking. The appropriation of a different face was aimed at changing the identity of the man, thus protecting him against supernatural beings, confusing them in their search for a target of their anger, or even frightening them off.

The belief in the existence of supernatural beings and their power of affecting the life of man also resulted in the necessity of some sort of communication with them. Out of the members of primeval communities, specialists were sorted out very soon, predestined for this particular task by their extraordinary qualities. The

latter undoubtedly included a higher sensibility, imagination and sometimes even an ability to fall into a trance with a temporary loss of consciousness. Unusual sounds made in this state may have been considered to be voices of spirits, demons, etc. Primeval man, closely connected with nature, must also soon have discovered natural hallucinogenic means of creating such a state. Although not aware of the true basis of their psychological effects, he regarded them as a means of manipulating supernatural beings. The knowledge of these means raised an individual to the status of a powerful magician, shaman etc. in the eyes of his fellow-tribesmen. The social exclusivity resulting from it inspired him to guard his knowledge as an invaluable secret. Although this individual, as he himself believed, was more than anyone else able to make contact with supernatural forces and even to exert influence upon them, he did not lose his weak human nature. On the contrary, this was endangered to a higher degree, and it was the mask which was intended to protect him against this danger by concealing his vulnerable human identity.

Probably similar was the motivation of the rise of many other masks used in most varied situations, whenever man was convinced that supernatural forces were near by, or that it was necessary to protect himself against their emanating power, even if they were not out to harm anybody. Such situations arose at the birth of child, at an illness or death of a man or animal connected with the man through the totemistic ties of kinship, at the initiation of a young man into the secrets of life, which he had to possess both as a mature individual and as a member of the community, at the preparations for a hunt, at sowing, harvesting, etc. For such situations, every community tended to create, strictly to maintain and to obey certain rules of conduct and activities, the breach of which could threaten the existence of the whole community and each of its members. Their original 'reasoned' motivation, however, gradually fell into oblivion, especially under changed conditions of life, leaving behind only a 'meaningless' ritual holding in a firm grip the life of a member of both the primeval society and of the tribal community preserved in some areas of the world until today. The ritual mask is usually part of such a rite.

7

The more a ritual withdraws from the conditions which gave it birth, the more mysterious it seems to be. The fact that such a ritualisation is not always necessarily a long-termed process but may be achieved within an unbelievably short period of time, can be verified even by the contemporary man in many social processes taking place around him, the length of which can be measured by much less than the duration of an entire human life. The ability and necessity of the ritualisation of vital behaviour is a characteristic of the animal world, too, and man may have inherited these qualities from the time preceding the stage at which he separated himself as the only species endowed with reason.

Since man credited the mask with such a power, it is not surprising to see that he also explained it as resulting from the hidden presence of the spirit who was the source of this power. This is the only explanation of the high regard and ritualised care for the masks as well as various taboos concerning their making and use. And this is also the only way how to explain the survival of this regard for the mask, even after the latter has long ceased to be a requisite of a magic ritual and fully entered the service of the dramatic art in some areas of the world. Though the theatre also derives its origin from magic mysteries, it was soon liberated from the bonds of ritual servitude in stratified societies of the Eurasian continent, and was turned into a means of entertaining, heightening the prestige and satisfying aesthetic needs, especially, at first, of the sophisticated power élite. The mask as a product of plastic arts entered a new phase of its development here. The fact that this art thus acquired a new dependence accords with the general laws of development and does not concern our subject any more.

*

The aim of this book is to present a survey of masks in the pre-colonial traditions of societies in Africa, Oceania and America and in the countries of some of those parts of Asia which had a complicated social structure. The book does not form an exhaustive survey, as its limited extent could not permit this. An informed reader, already possessing a deeper knowledge of the masks of one particular area, will undoubtedly miss some known types in this book. This is especially true of the masks of 'tribal' societies of Africa and Oceania, the Lamaistic masks, and those of Sri Lanka. These omissions were inevitable, however, to allow enough space for the masks of areas which have been rather neglected hitherto, such as India, Japan and Korea. Furthermore, anyone specialising in the masks of Africa has, today, at his or her disposal an almost inexhaustible number of books and articles devoted to African arts and even to masks in particular, while in other regions of the world art literature has so far been rather uninterested in the phenomenon of masking.

Nor can the present book cover the whole field as far as the masks of Asia are concerned. The authors have omitted the rare but extant masks of small ethnic communities of the northern part of the Asian continent, as well as those of China (Plates 137 and 143). In these territories masking is a closed book, offering the would-be collector practically no possibilities of acquiring any piece.

To those wishing to set out on the exciting journey of collecting the masks of the world, this book will offer advice as to suitable areas to study. In many cases, this journey is very expensive, since a large number of the masks discussed here have long ceased to form part of a living culture, being only accessible on the curiosity market with its ever-rising prices. The journey is also often risky; the exhausted sources of the original materials and their high prices represent an irresistable temptation for the producers of copies and fakes. These fakes, often very skilfully made, appear especially in those countries in which the much sought-after materials originated. Purchases should only be made by those who have acquainted themselves thoroughly with reliable collections and have studied the cultural heritage of the area in question.

Those who merely wish to learn the basic terms, to understand what a mask is and what its significance has been in the complicated structure of human culture will find the answers here.

Africa

Although the principle of masking was known in all the continents, Africa is the continent that perhaps comes to mind first due not just to its sculptural genius but also to the publicity given to these objects by artists in Paris at the beginning of the Modern Art movement. The French writer and one-time Minister of Culture André Malraux compared the significance of the mask in African culture to the importance of the cathedral in Europe. This comparison may seem exaggerated, but the broad application of the mask in the social, spiritual and cultural life of the African continent from antiquity until today confirms these words.

Few documents record the existence of masks in the African past. Their existence is, however, so indisputable and they are found in places so remote from each other that we are fully justified in assuming that masking was an integral part of the culture of most of the African continent perhaps before the first century BC.

The oldest examples are rock-paintings of masked figures found in Tassili in Algeria (Fig. 3) and Fezzan in Libya, and the so-called Bushmen paintings from South Africa (Fig. 4). The paintings from the Algerian mountains, discovered in the 1950s by French expeditions headed by Henri Lhote, originated at a time when this part of Africa was not yet as deserted as it is today, but still offered bearable conditions of life to herdsmen possibly around 3500–1500 BC.

Equally as uncertain as their dating is the interpretation of the purposes served by these masks. The Fezzan paintings might reproduce hunting masks, the aim of which was to enable hunters to come as close to their prey as possible without being noticed. Hunting masks were used in northern Nigeria and Chad even in this century, examples being preserved in museum collections. These depict the heads of the long-necked *calao* horn-bill. The hunters attached the masks to their heads by means of a band tied around their foreheads (Fig. 5). Hidden in high grass, the crawling hunter imitated the movements of the bird which he intended to catch.

The purpose of the horned animal mask depicted in the famous Bushmen painting, however, was probably different. This particular painting shows a recumbent man supporting his head on one arm which is bent at the elbow; in the other hand he holds an object which looks like a shield, raising it high above his head. The legs of the man are bent at the knees

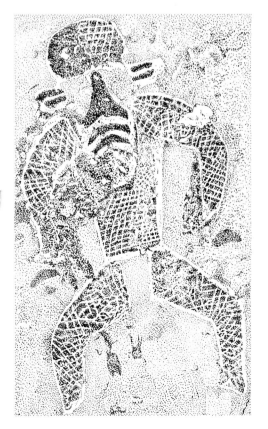

Fig. 3
A rock-painting of a dancer waring a mask, from Tassili in Algeria.

9

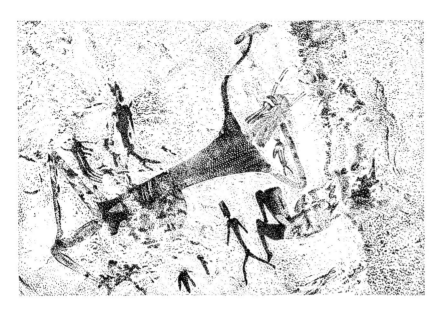

Fig. 4
A rock-painting of
a recumbent man wearing an
animal mask, from South
Africa.

Fig. 5
A hunter in a hornbill-head
mask, from Nupe, northern
Nigeria.

at a sharp angle as in a comfortable and relaxed sleeping position. This painting is usually held to be a 'royal funeral', but this interpretation does not seem correct. The position of the figure is in no respect reminiscent of a dead body; in spite of its recumbent posture, it breathes life. Horizontal stripes on the chest hardly represent the 'wrapping up of a corpse' (only known in Africa in ancient Egypt), but are much more probably the painting of the body or the coloured patterning of a costume. Also very unlikely is the use of an animal mask as a funeral mask. In Africa funeral masks were probably confined

to ancient Egypt, and the misinterpretation of this figure seems to be directly influenced by a knowledge of ancient Egyptian funeral customs as well as a common tendency to discover echoes of the great Egyptian culture in Africa's cultura heritage. In fact this picture is probably a case of a mask being used in a similar way as animal masks were used, until recent times, in western and central Africa.

All of the masks depicted in the rock-paintings of Algeria are face masks, similar to those used in most of the rest of Africa. However, the scenic context of these paintings is not clear enough to allow us to deduce the purpose served by the masks. Nor do we know anything more about the ethnic origin of the artists who made these paintings (Fig. 6).

The oldest extant African masks are ceramic heads, six belonging to men and one to an animal, excavated in Lydenburg in eastern Transvaal in the 1960s (Fig. 7). They were dated by means of a modern method called thermoluminescence, which assigned them to the fifth century AD. We do not know for certain, however, that they actually are masks. The two largest heads are hollow cylinders more than 30 cm in height, with the sides carved into human faces. The upper part of the cylinder is closed by a dome representing the top of the head and surmounted by the figure of an unidentifiable quadruped. The heads display stylistic features which are well known in much later African carvings, and especially in masks. For example, the stylisation of the eyes in the form of cowrie shells is probably an exact reproduction of tribal scarification. The size of the masks, making it possible for a person to wear them on the head, eye-slots allowing the wearer to see out, and a striking similarity to contemporary African masks justify us in supposing that they really are masks, even though the vast separation of time and space does not admit any direct link with the known arts of present-day ethnic elements. The remaining heads of the Lydenburg find, smaller in size, may represent dance headpieces, tied to a covering robe or to some kind of base on the top of the dancer's head. This use is suggested by two holes drilled into the necks of the heads. In this case, too, parallels may be found in the artistic and ritual repertory of contemporary African peoples.

1   A face mask made of
wood and sheet brass.
Marƙa, Mali; now in
a private collection in
Prague. Height 32 cm.

The oldest extant African artefact which is undoubtedly a mask belongs to a set of relics from the Ife city-kingdom of Nigeria (Fig. 8). These relics, mostly consisting of brass and pottery heads of the *oni*, the rulers of the kingdom, represent the apex of naturalistic art in Africa. Both these heads and the mask, cast in copper and almost 30 cm high, bear the marks of an idealised portrait and are endowed with all the stylistic peculiarities of Ife art, such as the upper eyelid overlapping the lower one in the inner corner of the eye, or a groove running parallel with the edge of the upper eyelid. Rows of rounded holes are drilled into the upper lip, face and chin, probably to hold strings of beads, perhaps representing whiskers; another row of holes on the upper edge of the forehead was probably used for attaching a crown or some other royal insignia. There is an oral tradition which sug-

Fig. 6
A cave painting of three masks, from Tassili in Algeria.

gests that the mask represents the *oni* Obalufon, who is believed to have introduced bronze-casting in Ife. Its style, the material used and the perfection of the casting place the mask in the peak period of Ife art, the twelfth to fifteenth centuries. Nothing is known about the circumstances in which the mask was used. It may have been put over the face of a deceased *oni*, although the slots placed under the eyes suggest that the mask was more probably used by living people, possibly at court ceremonies.

By the fifteenth century, bronze-casting seems to have been developed in the Ben-

in kingdom, about 200 km to the south east. Here it served the needs of the court, being used to make the royal altar furniture and chiefly regalia needed for its complicated ceremonies. It was only in Benin that bronze-casting grew in terms of quantity, particularly after 1500, due to overseas trade with Europeans who supplied Benin with copper alloy in exchange for various goods.

In 1897, a British 'punitive expedition' seized several thousand artefacts of brass and other material in Benin. Among these artefacts were a couple of masks in the form of human heads. They were worn on the top of the head, the face and also probably the body of the wearer being covered by a robe or plant material fringes tied to holes drilled into the edges of the mask. The Benin bronze pieces reflect the artistic development of some four or five centuries, but the masks date only from the eighteenth century (Fig. 9). They were used at a court ceremony called *odudua*, which, according to tradition, was only taken over by the Benin king, or *oba*, from Uzala, which was less than 30 km away, in the mid-eighteenth century.

Of course, Benin artistic relics include older masks, too. These, however, are not a means of masking, but are the insignia of individual grades of Benin court hierarchy. They were worn hanging over the chest or attached to the waist. These are bronze masks, representing human or animal faces, and somewhat reduced in size.

A few such hierarchic human masks, carved from ivory and originating from the sixteenth century, rank among the most outstanding art relics of Benin. Such a mask, worn at the waist, formed part of the ceremonial costume of the *oba* him-

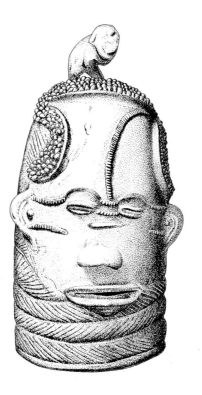

Fig. 7
A clay helmet mask from Lydenburg, South Africa. Height 38 cm.

12

self. The best-known mask of this kind, preserved in the London Museum of Mankind, has a diadem consisting of 11 bearded Portuguese heads from the sixteenth century, the stereotyped form of which remained an element of ornamentation in Benin art in later centuries.

Apart from these historic examples, most of which are now kept in European, American and African museums, all known African masks which have been collected were probably made during the nineteenth and twentieth centuries. Nevertheless, we can be reasonably certain that these masks represent a very long tradition of mask use in Africa. In the masks collected during the more recent decades, we may notice, when comparing them with earlier examples, apparent alterations, and new elements or ornamentation, such as figure superstructures, sometimes even of alien origin. Some of these innovations were made possible by a general slackening of old social and religious bonds and rules as late as the twentieth century, which resulted in the secularisation of many types of African masks.

*

What we usually call a mask is, in fact, only one of its parts. The face or head, whether human or animal, which is most frequently the object of art collecting, will often have had a robe attached to it, and sometimes fringes and collars made of raffia. The masking robe frequently pushed that part which we call the mask to the background. It is often apparent that, from the ritual viewpoint, the masking robe was more important, the carved or otherwise executed face part being missing altogether among some peoples. Interesting in this respect is the practice of the *egungun* secret society of the Nigerian Yoruba, whose members perform at rituals to commemorate dead ancestors. In terms of carving, this cult brings forth a rich iconographic repertory of masks and dance headpieces of various types, characteristic of certain areas of Yorubaland. While performing, the dancer is always entirely veiled by a fantastic costume made of many-coloured textiles. What is sometimes missing, however, is that very part, carved from wood, which we consider to be of the utmost importance, and yet the spiritual force of the 'mask' is in no way diminished.

2   A face mask of the *lo* society, made of wood stained black with vestiges of red pigment. Senufo (Siena), Ivory Coast; now in Náprstek Museum, Prague. Height 27 cm.

13

3　A face mask of
black-stained wood.
Kulango, Ivory Coast; now
in Náprstek Museum,
Prague. Height 37 cm.

Such 'masks without masks' may be
found in many places in Africa. In some
cases, they have the appearance of
a living stack of grass moving on human
legs (e.g. in Senegal), or a living stand of
vertical rods tied around the head of the
dancer (e.g. in South Africa). The best-
known example of a masking costume
lacking any special carved face mask is
a tight covering made of raffia and palm
fibres which covers the head too; the face
is merely suggested by two tube-shaped
holes for the eyes. Such masks may be met
with among a number of southern Zaire
peoples.

Although masked performances are
common all over the vast territory of Africa, from the Atlantic coast in the west to

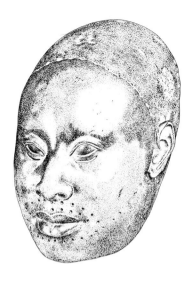

Fig. 8
Copper mask of the *oni*
Obalufon, from Ife, Nigeria.
Dated from the twelfth to the
fifteenth century. Height
29.5 cm.

the Indian Ocean in the east, masks in the European sense of the term, carved from wood, are not necessarily the most common form. Nevertheless, it is only these masks that we shall cover in the following paragraphs, since they are one of the main parts of the art tradition of Africa.

*

African masks are often made of wood. Their maker is thus mostly a carver, sometimes specialising in this genre, sometimes also satisfying other needs of his community. In western Sudan the carver's profession is often combined with that of a smith. However, not all wooden masks are made by professional carvers, taught through apprenticeship to a master. Some communities have only self-taught carvers who mostly work for themselves, and occasionally to order for their neighbours. This is true, for instance, of the dance masks of the Kalabari who live in the Niger delta.

Various ritualistic rules, concerning the work of carvers in general, are doubly valid in the case of masks, because they represent the personification of deities, in this case spirits inhabiting nature. Such regulations include, for instance, sacrifices offered to the spirit of the tree of whose wood the mask is to be made, the upholding of various taboos concerning the eating of food before the work starts and during its execution, sexual abstinence, etc. In some areas, the carver must work in seclusion from the rest of the villagers, in others they are allowed to watch him at his work, except perhaps during certain stages. Thus, among the peoples dwelling on the Cross River in eastern Nigeria, the carver is allowed to carve a head-shaped dance head-dress (Plate 17) in public, but he must execute the final stage, which is covering it with antelope skin, secluded from any onlookers.

The preparation of a mask does not end with its carving. Its surface is usually stained with plant juices, saturated with palm oil, or painted in several colours, originally with natural pigments, sometimes including kaolin, but since the end of the last century also with imported synthetic paints (Plate 18). Among the Satlampasu in Zaire or the Marka in Mali the surface of the mask is covered with copper sheets (Plate 1). This initial preparation is followed by further additions; sometimes a special cover is made for the top of the dancer's head and the nape of his neck. The eyes may be enlivened by set-in slivers of tin or driven-in nails. Animal and metal teeth or wooden strips are set into the mouth, and so on, according to local tradition. Finally the mask is sometimes spiritually activated, for example by driving in an iron nail (Plate 19), because iron is believed to be endowed with magic power; a chicken or an egg is sacrificed to the mask, or some other magic element is added. In some places, this ritual is performed by the carver personally, in others by the user of the mask.

In exceptional cases, ivory is used for making masks. Such is the case among the Lega of eastern Zaire. In contrast with this precious material, a material which is easi-

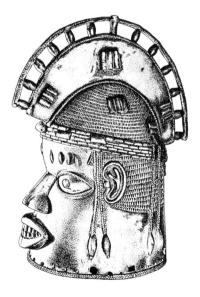

Fig. 9
Eighteenth-century *odudua*
mask in bronze, from Benin,
Nigeria. Height 35.5 cm.

15

ly accessible everywhere in Africa may be used. This is the calabash shell, whose convex form literally asks to be turned into a rudimentary depiction of a human or animal face. Masks were made of this material by the Nilotic Shilluk in southern Sudan and they also occur, albeit rarely, among the Makonde in Tanzania and Mozambique, who otherwise normally use various types of soft pale wood for making their masks.

The metal found in some historic masks was obviously always exceptional, its very preciousness emphasising the social prestige of the rulers' courts. Beside the masks from Ife and Benin, this is also true of a few bronze masks of the Abron people from the inland area of Ghana, which are probably finds from undocumented excavations. It was only in the twentieth century that new metal masks were added to the historic ones. These were the masks made by the Yoruba iron-founder Ali Amonikoyi who lived in the then German colony of Togo, in the city of Kete Kratchi, in 1907—09. He was asked to make the masks by a German official. These masks, lacking any functional roots in local tradition, are reminiscent of some types of Yoruba masks, but they appear to have been partly inspired by pictures of the Benin bronze pieces which the official had shown to Ali Amonikoyi.

After World War I the German colony of Cameroon was divided between the French and the British. The French colonial administration concentrated bronze casters in Fumban, the capital of the small Bamum kingdom — until then the brass casters had been making prestigious objects such as large ceremonial pipe-bowls, handles for fans, knife-handles and orna-

Fig. 10
A pair of *gelede* dancers wearing identical masks, from Yoruba, Benin.

4 A face mask of painted wood. Ashira/Bapunu, Gabon; now in Náprstek Museum, Prague. Height 27 cm.

ments for the rulers of small states in the so-called Cameroon Grasslands. An influx of new European customers created a demand for new goods as various souvenirs. Among other items, massive brass masks were executed in the style of the wooden masks traditional to that area, but treated in a more realistic way and sometimes provided with complicated figure superstructures. The development of these masks was made easier perhaps by the application of a different technique, i.e. modelling the object to be cast in wax (Plate 20). Cast by the same method, called lost-wax casting, are the Senufo masks which appeared on the art market and in collections towards the end of the 1950s and during the 1960s. As early as the 1930s, however, miniaturised exact metal replicas of the wooden Senufo masks were sold in the Ivory Coast. We even cannot exclude the possibility that they were also made in Europe. It might even have been these replicas which in-

17

spired the later production of the Senufo masks of the *kpelie* type in brass.

Lastly let us mention the various vegetable materials out of which African masks were made on a larger scale than can be documented today, due to the fragile nature of these materials, and to the real impossibility of collecting such artefacts. We have literary testimony, dating from the beginning of the 1930s, to the existence of basketwork masks, formerly used by the Jukun in the Benue River ba-sin in Nigeria, although the Jukun are, first of all, the authors of well-known but iconographically problematic wooden masks. Since the publication of the first monograph especially devoted to African masks, Leo Frobenius's *Die Masken und Geheimbünde Afrikas*, in 1898, we know of basketwork masks used by the Mandingo tribe in Gambia. These cover the entire head like huge helmets. On both sides of a sharp ridge placed on the top of the head, antelope horns are attached, the fa-

Fig. 11
Guardians of an initiation camp clad in masking costumes. Chokwe, Angola.

18

cial side being provided with characteristic tube-shaped eyes.

The basketwork masks of the Salampasu of Zaire are also remarkable. The use of very thin and elastic plant material strips made it possible for the producers to maintain all the stylistic principles of the wooden masks of this people. The masks made of these two different materials represent two different social groups. The very rare basketwork masks, which originated in the clan complex of the Dan-Ngere in the western Ivory Coast, tried to maintain the iconographic and stylistic peculiarities of their current wooden models, albeit with less success.

Related to the basketwork masks in technical terms are those constructed from rods and covered with sheets of bark cloth hammered from the bark of certain trees. Details of a face are either painted on this cover or cut from cloth and pasted on. These masks, known particularly among the Chokwe (Plate 21), also often occur among other peoples of southern Zaire, western Zambia and northern Angola. For decades non-traditional materials have been used too. Thus, instead of bark cloth, the masks are sometimes covered with sackcloth or even mere brown paper; the white clay is replaced by glossy paints (Plate 22), etc.

A rod construction for a mask covering the entire head is also used by the Yaka people of the Kwango River basin in Zaire. Here, the mask itself, carved and painted in several colours, is attached to a rod construction, and sometimes figure ornaments surmount the top of the head. Yaka masks may thus be called composites as far as the materials used in their production are concerned.

Let us conclude this survey with masks made of cotton or imported fabrics, which flow down on to the chest and the back of the dancer in long, wide strips. These include the elephant masks worn by the members of the Elephant Society in the Cameroon Grasslands at various ceremonials. The long strip falling to the front was obviously meant to suggest the trunk and the large disc-shaped objects sewn onto the sides represent the ears of an elephant. The visual effectiveness of these masks is enhanced by rich ornamentation consisting of sewn-on glass beads.

*

The basic and most frequent type of Afri-

5 A ceremonial mask for *bedu* dances, made of wood with a painted surface.
Nafana, Ivory Coast; now in Náprstek Museum, Prague. Height 121 cm.

6 A face mask of wood
with a brownish-black-stained
surface and tree bark. Bete,
Ivory Coast; now in
Náprstek Museum, Prague.
Height 27 cm.

can mask is the face mask, usually carved from wood (Plates 2, 3 and 38). Such a mask represents a human or animal face (Plate 9) and is most frequently fixed in front of the face of the dancer wearing it, although sometimes it is shifted to the top of his head, its eyes being thus turned upwards (Fig. 10). The masks worn in this way have no holes for the eyes and the wearer will have to peer through the weave of the attached costume. Masks of this type are most frequently found in southern Nigeria.

Face masks are sometimes doubled. In such cases they represent two more or less identical human faces placed side by side (e.g. among the Senufo or Ngere in the Ivory Coast), or a human face and an animal one (the Baule in the Ivory Coast). In some face masks, besides the face the top of the head and the hairstyle are also carved from wood (e.g. among the Baule, Plate 34, or the Gabon, Plate 4); the top of the head may also be made of raffia with the hairstyle represented by raffia strings or sewn with blackened raffia (the Pende in Zaire).

Among a number of peoples living in Mali and Burkina Faso (formerly Upper Volta), the top of the face mask is provided with a high, flat, blade-shaped protrusion, in exceptional cases up to several metres in height (the Dogon in Mali and Bwa in Burkina Faso), carved, together with the mask, out of a single piece of wood. The protrusion may be decorated with carved or painted geometrical ornaments, or profiled ornamentally. It is this decoration which shows the iconographic significance of the mask, in accordance with which the mask proper, covering the dancer's face, is usually much stylized or even schematised, containing no semantic function in itself. This is true of the masks of the Dogon, Mossi, Kurumba and other peoples.

The tendency towards a flat representation of the subject is also observable in other types of masks to be found in western Sudan. Some masks are surmounted by a human or monkey figure (Bambara, Dogon), or a figure smaller in size may be placed in front of the protrusion (Mossi, Gurunsi). However, human figures carved above the forehead of the mask occur in other areas, too, especially in the more recently made masks of the Guro in the Ivory Coast or the masks of the Ibibio,

7 A male face mask of wood with vestiges of paint, iron nails and sheet iron strips. Ibo, Nigeria; now in Náprstek Museum, Prague. Height 59.5 cm.

21

painted in several bright colours and produced in large quantities in the city of Ikot Ekpene in south-eastern Nigeria.

The majority of African face masks are attached to the wearer's head by means of strings threaded through holes along the edge of the mask; sometimes the mask is held in position by cloth tied to its edge and covering the nape of the neck, or by an elastic basketwork part (Plate 40) connected with the masking garment (e.g. among the Chokwe in Zaire). Among the Guro and Bete in the Ivory Coast and the Ibibio in south-eastern Nigeria, a wooden stick is inserted through holes drilled into the sides of the mask, which the dancer grips in his teeth (Plate 9). A supplement of the face masks representing women, although worn by men, is sometimes a large wooden shield or breast plate with breasts carved on the chest (especially among the Makonde in

8 A face mask of painted wood. Teke, People's Republic of Congo; now in a private collection in Prague. Height 33.2 cm.

9 An elephant mask of
stained wood and white clay
pigment. Baule-Yaure, Ivory
Coast; now in Náprstek
Museum, Prague. Height
44.5 cm.

Mozambique, but also among the Nigerian Yoruba), and in other cases artificial breasts are directly attached to the woven masking robe (the Ibo in eastern Nigeria and the Chokwe in southern Zaire).

Another basic type with many variants is the so-called helmet mask, formerly also defined as a bell-shaped mask or pot-mask. These are large wooden masks in the form of hollow cylinders, closed and rounded at the upper end, in which the entire head is hidden, the edge of the mask resting on the dancer's shoulders. The sides of the cylinder are carved in relief into the likeness of a human face and the top into a head-dress. A classic example of this type is the *sowei* mask of the women's *bundu* or *sande* secret societies in Sierra Leone and Liberia, for instance the Mende, Temne and others (Plate 11). In terms of technique, the helmet masks also include the basketwork masks of the Mandingo from Cassamance and the Yaka masks. Wooden helmet masks are sometimes supplemented with a carved figure on the top of the head (Plate 38). This is either merely a human or animal head placed on a high column (in the Mende of Sierra Leone), an entire figure of an animal (among the Suku in Zaire), or man (among the Bobo-Fing in Burkina Faso, or the *epa* cult masks of the northeastern Yoruba in Nigeria, Plate 37). Less frequent are two or more faces carved in a helmet mask of the Gabon Fang or some of the peoples in the Cross River basin in Nigeria.

A transitional type between the helmet

10   Mask of the *gelede* society, made of wood with traces of paint. Yoruba, Nigeria; now in Náprstek Museum, Prague. Height 30 cm.

24

11 A helmet-shaped initiation mask of the *bundu* female secret society, made of stained wood. Mende, Sierra Leone; now in Náprstek Museum, Prague. Height 40 cm.

mask and the so-called dance head-dress is represented by the masks of the *gelede* secret society and some masks of the *egungun* society of the Yoruba in Nigeria and Benin (formerly Dahomey). These are made of wood and represent an entire human head. Their dominant part is the face, the top of which is much lowered and the nape shortened, so that the mask rests fully on the dancer's head. It is slight-ly tilted towards the forehead, the eyes looking obliquely upwards. A cloth robe is attached to the edge of the mask. The lowered tops of these masks are often richly decorated with figure carvings, sometimes depicting various scenes, or an elaborate hairstyle or hat is carved on the top (Plate 10).

The third fundamental, albeit very he-terogeneous, group of African masks is represented by the so-called dance head-dresses. These masks are worn on the top of the head, thus optically increasing the height of the dancer. They lack the part masking the face which is mostly covered with a masking costume provided with inconspicuous holes through which the dancer can see out. Without the masking robe such a head-dress often does not look at all like a mask, but is more reminiscent of a free figure sculpture. The dance head-dress may have an entirely abstract form rather like a tower-shaped object (among some peoples in north-eastern Nigeria).

In some cases, however, these head-dresses are reminiscent of helmet masks in the form of human heads, although their interior is not large enough to hold the entire dancer's head, the head-dress resting on his shoulders (Fig. 12). This is the type of some of the masks of the Makonde in Mozambique, often wrongly called helmet masks, and those of many peoples from the Cross River area in eastern Nigeria; their masks are sometimes provided with two faces, a male and a female one, looking in opposite directions. The latter are called masks of the Janus-head type, after the ancient Roman god of that name, and in terms of their size they often rank among actual helmet masks. By contrast, other dance head-dresses from the same area are in the form of human or animal heads, covered with skin and provided with a slender neck, to which a rounded basketwork support is attached in order to enlarge the base of the head-dress and thus to fix it more firmly to the top of the dancer's head.

Unique in their manner of wearing are the head-dresses of the Kuyu in the inland of the Republic of Congo, called *kebe-kebe* (Plate 12). They have the appearance of human heads reduced to approximately half natural size and represent mythical ancestors of the people. Together with the head, a cylindrical neck is carved and provided with a deep groove to which a long robe, made of white cloth and veiling the entire figure, is tied. Also attached to the neck is a 30-cm-long pointed handle, by means of which the dancer holds the head-dress above his head. The so-called *yoké* masks of the Wurkun from the Benue River basin in Nigeria are another variant of this particular type.

The most remarkable figure dance head-dress, called *chi-wara*, was created by the Bambara (or Bamana) living in the Republic of Mali. These are highly stylized figures of antelopes, attached to a small basketwork cap which is tied on to the dancer's head by strings fastening under the chin. Long strings, covering the dancer's face in an illusory way, flow freely down from the edge of the cap. The *chi-wara* head-dresses are of two kinds. The vertical type, from the area between the cities of Bamako and Sikasso, is flat, being a highly stylised carved contour to be looked at in profile, rather than a three-dimensional statue.

The dancers perform in pairs. The

Fig. 12
A dancer wearing a helmet mask from the Grasslands, Cameroon.

12 *Kebe-kebe* dance
head-dress of painted wood.
Kuyu, People's Republic of
Congo; now in Náprstek
Museum, Prague. Height
50.5 cm.

head-dresses representing males have
bow-shaped horns, a huge carved mane
and sexual organs. The female masks have
straight horns and no mane, and a calf
standing behind the mother, or directly on
her back, is carved together with her.

The second, horizontal type originated
in the Bamako area and is lower and more
massive, its three-dimensional character
being more prominent. The horns of this
type are horizontal. Horizontal head-

dresses are always carved out of at least
two pieces of wood, the horned head and
the body being made separately, both
parts being joined with iron clamps,
a leather ring or a tin collar at the neck.

Besides these *chi-wara* head-dresses,
which are well known and much favoured
by collectors, another head-dress, called
sonni-senni, also belongs to the mask
repertory of the Bambara. Instead of an
antelope, the dancer's basketwork cap is

provided with a superstructure having the form of a stylized winding body of one or two erect serpents, with a miniature long-eared human head. Both the antelope and the serpent play a significant role in Bambara mythology.

Very similar to the Bambara *chi-wara* of the horizontal type, both in form and the method of wearing, are the *sa-saidu* head-dresses made by the smiths of the Kurumba in Burkina Faso, but they in no way match the formers' artistic qualities. They represent a recumbent antelope with bow-shaped horns, whose body is covered with geometric ornaments. These are, again, contours meant to be looked at in profile, but they are stereotyped and lack that rich stylistic inventiveness which characterises the *chi-wara.* As well as these rather small dance head-dresses, the Kurumba also have large ones, in the form of long-horned and high-necked

Fig. 13
The wooden mask of an Ijo water spirit. Kalabari, Nigeria; now in the Museum of Mankind, London. Height 35.5 cm.

antelope heads. These coloured dance head-dresses, called *numtiri,* are usually attached to the head by means of a basketwork cap.

Among the dance head-dresses, we may also rank one of the largest African masks. This is the mask made by the Baga people in Guinea and representing the goddess of fertility, Nimba. The mask takes the form of a stately female bust with a large head and large flat breasts. The heavy bust rests on four 'legs' which fit around the dancer's shoulders. This is why it is often called a shoulder-mask or simply a dance bust. A smaller variant of the same head-dress is the bust of a young girl performing at the initiation rites of this people (Plate 13). This mask is called *yoké, youkui* or *komoé,* has a smaller head than that of Nimba, smaller breasts and only two 'legs' which are, in fact, handles by means of which the dancer can manipulate the mask. A square hole is cut in the chest of both these masks, through which the dancer can see out.

The fourth type of African mask is defined as a dance helmet. This is, again, a kind of dance head-dress, whose base is formed by a 'helmet' in the form of the top of a sphere, carved from a single piece of wood. Unlike the helmet mask, the dance helmet does not cover the dancer's face. The top of the helmet is surmounted by a carved figure superstructure (among the Senufo in the Ivory Coast, the Tussian in Burkina Faso, or the Afo in Nigeria); its form may be adapted to that of a sitting bird or animal by adding a head and a tail (some masks from the Cameroon Grasslands or the antelope masks of the Kurumbra of the Sikomse group in Burkina Faso), or the surface carved into the form of an animal head (e.g. among the Bambara in Mali). Some larger animal masks are, in fact, dance helmets, especially the buffalo masks worn horizontally on the head (Fig. 13). They occur in several stylistic variants among many peoples from the Senufo in the west to peoples inhabiting the Benue River basin in Nigeria and small village chieftainships in the Cameroon Grasslands (Plate 14), to the Duala on the coast of Cameroon far in the east.

This technical typology is, of course, neither exact nor exhaustive, its aim being rather to explain the meaning of the terms

13 *Yoké* head-dress made of wood with a black-stained surface. Baga or Nalu, Guinea; now in Náprstek Museum, Prague. Height 78 cm.

used in current literature to describe African masks. Some iconographic types of masks belong to various types in terms of technology. For example, the buffalo masks, which we generally class with dance helmets, may sometimes be considered to be helmet masks, depending on whether the hollow space inside is large enough to hold the dancer's entire head, or whether his face remains uncovered by the mask. In some masks, such variants may exist even within the framework of a single people. Moreover, there are masks in Africa which cannot be grouped with any of the categories mentioned above. For instance, in western Sudan an animal mask may be found, attached to a large wooden construction covered with cloth, under which two dancers are hidden, just as in the famous *barong* masks of Bali, Indonesia, or in clown performances at a European circus. In an overwhelming majority of cases, however, the typology given is sufficient for a technical classification of African masks.

In terms of subject, the African masks belong to three basic types: first, masks with human features, sometimes defined as anthropomorphic — not human, since they seldom portray actual living people and are mostly personifications of the spirits of the dead (Plates 4, 35 and 42) or supernatural beings in human form; second, masks with animal features, for similar reasons not usually defined as animal (Plate 16), but as zoomorphic, since, although their actual meaning is known (monkey, hyena, antelope, buffalo, elephant, warthog, etc.), their form is often completely changed by stylisation. Cases are not rare in which the zoomorphic mask representing an actual animal species combines features of various animals. For instance, an antelope mask, or rather a mask of the spirit possessing the form of an antelope, is provided with the muzzle of an animal of prey, symbolising a certain quality which, though missing in the actual antelope, is nevertheless possessed by the powerful spirit portrayed by the mask. No less frequent are the masks of the third type, called theriomorphic, which combine the traits of a human face with attributes of various animals. The eyes and the nose are often a human trait in masks with other dominant animal features. It is this ability to create new organically united super-realistic entities out of

29

14 A buffalo mask of stained wood and white clay pigment. Bamileke, Cameroon; now in Náprstek Museum, Prague. Height 43.5 cm.

faces, their animal nature being shown by adding some small attribute typical of the animal in question (the Yaure in the Ivory Coast).

*

Most African masks are made within a given tradition and style. In the majority, however, we may notice great differences in the quality of artistic execution, even when their authors have respected iconographic stylistic tradition. These differences are apparent in the size of the mask, the choice of expressive means offered by the respective style, the degree of stylisation, the emphasis put on some elements, or the ability to set forth an individual concept, and the level of craftsmanship.

Moreover, thematic originality is not unknown to the authors of African masks; indeed, it is sometimes expected by the onlookers. This is true, for instance, of the initiation masks of the Yaka in Zaire or the Yoruba masks of the *gelede* secret society in Nigeria and the Republic of Benin. In both these cases, and particularly in Yoruba masks, the style of the face is standardised from one mask to another, but the figurative superstructure is highly variable in content, in an obvious effort to surprise the spectators and to amuse, delight or shock them. The comic aspect in African masks is not only expressed by the method of stylisation or by disproportions as in European caricatures, but by the very subject matter. Thus, in the faces of Yaka masks, the nose is sometimes elongated and upturned in such a way that its tip leans towards the face like a small elephant trunk. We do not know, and neither do the Yaka themselves, what the original model of such a concept was. Such a nose, however, although reminiscent of European caricatures, does not arouse mirth among the spectators. If, however, the top of this mask is surmounted by, for instance, a figure with disproportionately large sexual organs or holding a bottle in his hands, the spectators understand the satirical content of the mask and are obviously amused.

From the European point of view, the hairstyle or the scarification of the face in some masks make an impression of fantasy. In actual fact, however, both these elements are simply reproductions of reality, even if, as in the case of hairstyle, somewhat simplified. Both the scarification and the hairstyle are identification marks

heterogeneous elements which is one of the peculiarities of African artistic sensibility and one of the testimonies to the artistic talent of African people. By contrast, the masks representing animal spirits are sometimes provided with human

30

15   A miniature mask of stained wood covered with cotton fabric and cowrie shells. Gerze, Liberia; now in Náprstek Museum, Prague. Height 9.5 cm.

of membership of a social group (people, clan, etc.) and therefore must not be altered. This is why we meet 'tribal' scarification even in the zoomorphic masks of some tribes. In spite of considerable stylisation, anthropomorphic masks conform to the formal expectations of given areas, e.g. among the Dan in the Ivory Coast or the Makonde in Mozambique. In the latter case, this intention is emphasised by reproducing a lip peg in the masks, which alter the faces of the local populations in a characteristic way.

*

The ritual life of precolonial Africa offered many an occasion for mask performances. Undoubtedly of utmost importance in many areas was the admission of a young man or woman among the adult members of the community on attaining maturity. This admission was preceded by initiation into the practice of work, hunting, healing, etc. of the adults, sexual life, the local mythico-historical traditions, customary norms of law in the form of various taboos, etc. The initiation took place under conditions of strict isolation and sexual segregation in a special camp outside the village or in the bush. This is why this preparation is often re-ferred to as 'bush-school'. The length of the term differed, mostly lasting for several months. Its conclusion, connected with initiation rites, symbolises the transition from child to adult. In some places, it was preceded by the making of artificial scars on the face or other parts of the body, according to the local custom, circumcision of boys and the excision of girls (a surgical procedure by which the clitoris was removed), deformation of the teeth, etc. The officials responsible for these preparations and their rituals would appear in characteristic masks on various occasions. They are, for instance, the guardians of the camp (Fig. 11), preventing the uninitiated from entering it (as among the Chokwe in Zaire), or the functionaries maintaining communications between the school camp and the village from which they bring food (as in the Dan-Ngere complex in Liberia and the Ivory Coast). The boys leave the camp in masks, too, for example among the Yaka in Zaire. In the same country, the western Pende celebrate the conclusion of the initiation by farce-like plays performed by almost two dozen dancers wearing stereotyped masks (Plate 41).

Another frequent use of masks is by the

16 A buffalo mask of wood with a stained and painted surface. Guro, Ivory Coast; now in Náprstek Museum, Prague. Height 54.5 cm.

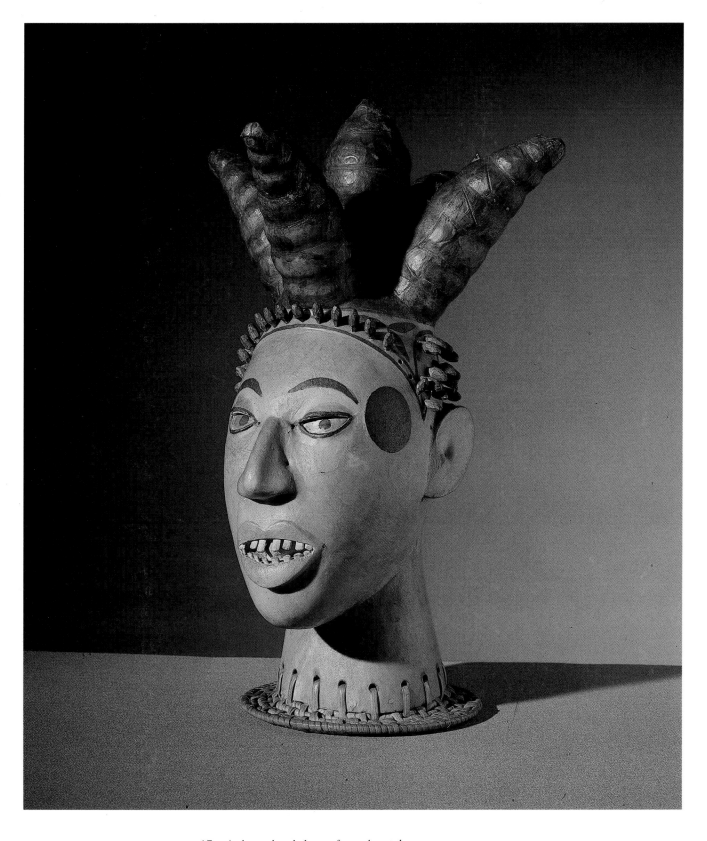

17 A dance head-dress of wood, antelope
skin, sheet aluminium, bone (teeth) and
a basketwork base. Ekoi (Ejagham), Nigeria;
now in Náprstek Museum, Prague. Height
44 cm.

18   A face mask of wood decorated with
synthetic paints, sheet iron, string, tow,
horsehair and brass cartridge cases. Ngere,
Ivory Coast; now in Náprstek Museum,
Prague. Height 32 cm.

19 A face mask of black-stained wood, sheet aluminium, red factory-made cloth, plant fibres (coloured blue) and an iron nail. Dan or Tura, Ivory Coast; now in Náprstek Museum, Prague. Height (without beard) 23.7 cm.

20 A mask with a figure superstructure,
made of brass cast by the lost-wax method.
Bamum, Cameroon; now in Náprstek
Museum, Prague. Height 43.6 cm.

21   The mask of a guardian of an initiation
camp, made of rod construction, sackcloth,
resin and textile cuttings, with an extension
made of strings. Chokwe, Zaire; now in
Náprstek Museum, Prague. Height 51 cm.

22 *M'kishi* mask made of rod construction
and bark cloth painted with latex paints.
Luvale, Zambia; now in Náprstek Museum,
Prague. Height 41 cm.

23 Initiation helmet mask of painted wood
with a basketwork construction, fabric and
raffia fringes. Yaka, Zaire; now in Náprstek
Museum, Prague. Height 52 cm.

24 A face mask of the *ekpo* society, made
of painted wood. Bini, Nigeria; now in
Náprstek Museum, Prague. Height 27 cm.

25 Miniature replicas of face masks, badges of initiation, made of bone. Pende, Zaire; now in Náprstek Museum, Prague. Height 4.7 and 5.2 cm.

so-called secret societies existing among many African peoples. Their secrecy does not concern membership; all of the adult members of the clan, or a certain age category, often being members. In Sierra Leone and Liberia even female secret societies may be found. The attribute 'secret' is given because of their external similarity with historical European secret societies, such as meeting in a special house with no access by non-members, admission after various tests of courage, etc., but whereas the European secret societies served subversive political purposes, organising resistance to the existing order, those of Africa were, first of all, religious in function, maintaining contact with supernatural forces and securing their favour for the tribal collective. In terms of politics, they were the very opposite of their European counterparts, their purpose being to maintain the existing order

and to prevent any disturbance of it. Their members appear in masks not only while carrying out their religious ritual functions, but also at the funerals of their co-members.

Much occasion for the growth of the richly structured secret societies was offered in areas politically segregated into small village chieftainships (e.g. in Liberia, the Ivory Coast and eastern Nigeria). This was also reflected in an unusual variety of mask types extant in these regions. Here the secret societies sometimes replace a higher political as well as moral authority and have even been able to defuse quarrels threatening to grow into armed conflicts. In some areas secret societies are also responsible for the initiations described above.

In the countries which reached the stage of creating states with a varied court life, hereditary offices and a complicated

41

property structure, such as the Yoruba city-states in Nigeria or small kingdoms of the Cameroon Grasslands, the secret societies, besides serving their religious purposes, also had the function of an additional or alternative political authority. The membership was selective here, conditioned by descent, property, heredity of functions, prowess tested in war, etc. Here, too, the mask is an indispensable part of public rites.

Apart from these two large spheres, that is the initiation ceremonies and religious and social functions of the secret societies, African masks are used on many other occasions. Thus, among the Dan of Liberia and the Ivory Coast, a special village functionary wearing the mask of a given type controlled whether fire was extinguished in huts after the villagers had left for the fields. Other Dan masked officials led people to war; others acted as judges; others entertained. Elsewhere, e.g. among the Pende in Zaire, the magician-healer appeared in a mask, and among the Asante in Ghana, who otherwise did not use masks; only an important agent of the royal court, the executioner, wore one.

*

The important part played by masks in many African cultures is suggested by the fact that in some areas people used to wear miniature replicas of masks as badges of the tests they had undergone. Such mask badges, carved from ivory, are known among the Pende in Zaire (Plate 25). Miniature wooden or clay masks, corresponding to various types of large masks, worn by the peoples living in the borderland between Liberia and the Ivory Coast, also served as badges of those who had passed through initiation ceremonies (Plate 15). They may also have represented a memento for a young man, reminding him of the grade which he was expected to attain in his secret society. Sometimes they were a substitute, a kind of reminder of a mask lost through the ravages of time.

The mask is also present in African art as a decorative or symbolic element of other kinds of object. Miniature replicas of the masks worn by dancers during their performances are carved either into the objects which they hold in their hands, such as dance shields or fly-whisks, or the musical instruments accompanying the dance. In the Ivory Coast, among the Senufo, the well-know kpelie masks are carved in relief into the wooden doors of sanctuaries, etc. All of this bears testimony to the extraordinary role of masks in the cultural life of African peoples.

42

Oceania

In terms of cultural geography, Oceania consists of four areas: Australia in the south east; Melanesia, consisting of a chain of islands situated to the north and north west of the Australian coast; Polynesia, inside a triangle between Hawaii in the north, New Zealand in the south west and Easter Island in the east; and Micronesia, comprising islands situated in the western half of the Pacific from the equator northwards. Masks were used particularly by the inhabitants of Melanesia. Although they may also be found in Australia, Polynesia and Micronesia, they are a rather exceptional phenomenon here.

AUSTRALIA

Australia was inhabited by hunters and food gatherers, who were constantly changing their hunting-grounds and looking for fresh sources of drinking water. Their products were confined to such objects as were indispensable for survival, and masks certainly did not belong to that category. This is not to say, however, that masks were unknown to the aborigines of Australia, but rather that as artefacts they were ephemeral with no possibility of an existence beyond the rite for which they were put together. Almost all over the continent, men glued birds down to their skin with blood for initiation rites and 'corroboree' rituals honouring mythical beings. This ground-layer was complemented with larger feathers so that the masked man would be as similar in appearance to the venerated mythical being as possible (Fig. 14).

Besides feather masks, masks made of palm leaves were also used in Australia. They are known from the northernmost headland of the Cape York Peninsula in Queensland, influenced, in respect of culture, by the Torres Strait islands. Three types, differing in form and used at initiation ceremonies, have been found. One of them portrays a human face and is provided with a nose made of beeswax with black and red stripes; the second has the form of a horizontally slanted crocodile's head; the third is formed by a kind of cone also surmounted by the head of a crocodile. As in the interior, the surfaces of the latter two masks were decorated with glued feathers of various birds, usually white in colour.

Fig. 14
The feather mask of the spirit of the desert grass. Aranda, central Australia. Dated from the second half of the twentieth century.

MICRONESIA

In Micronesia, we only know of the use of masks in the Mortlock Islands group forming the centre of the Caroline Islands archipelago. At one dance, the purpose of which was to drive away a cyclone, flat wooden masks called *tapuanu* were worn (Fig. 15). These are semi-oval, provided with a long straight nose, a small mouth little narrow eyes placed at the top of the nose and narrow hooked eyebrows carved in relief. The face is always white, except for the black or brown mouth and eyebrows. The same colour outlines the entire mask. A flat circular dark protrusion, representing the hairstyle, often sticks out from the more or less horizontal upper edge of the mask.

POLYNESIA

In Polynesia, we know of only one place where masks were made. This is New Zealand. These masks were rather flat and very schematised images of faces, carved from wood and provided with exact patterns of the tattooing which only chieftains were allowed to wear in Maori society. In spite of a simplification of the features, these were true portraits of actual personalities whose identity was not revealed by the likeness of the face but the pattern of the tattoo. The masks called *koruru* (Plate 26) used to be placed at the top of the front wall of the *whare whakairo* (meeting house).

It is virtually impossible to understand the historical and social conditions responsible for such different levels of mask use. Whereas in Australia the ephemeral character of masks may be understood in terms of the necessity to restrict the number of material artefacts, this does not apply in Polynesia and Micronesia. The local farmers and fishermen were settled in one place and, with more favourable environmental conditions, they developed more elaborate material equipment. The first Europeans who came to Polynesia and Micronesia were impressed by the forms of state organisation that they found there; but developed states making use of masks are found in Africa, e.g. Yoruba; so economic and political development in itself explains nothing.

MELANESIA

In Melanesia, however, cultural history developed in other ways. There are masks personifying supernatural beings who affect the harvest and fertility, and masks of secret religious societies. These were organisations of a religious and political character. The membership, which was open to every adult man after his initiation, was not secret, but rites connected with the cult of some important supernatural beings were secret. At the same time, the members of these societies watched over the non-members to make sure they obeyed all religious orders and prohibitions.

Fig. 15
Tapuanu masks used at a ceremony in the Lukunor Island in the Mortlock group of the central Carolines. Dated from the beginning of the twentieth century.

26 *Koruru* mask made of wood inlaid with mother of pearl. Northern New Zealand; now in Museo Nazionale Preistorico e Etnografico 'L. Pigorini', Rome.

Another group of Melanesian masks is connected with the ancestor cult. It is within the power of a deceased person to help living descendants, provided they hold the soul in due esteem. In some places there appear masks in the form of mythical totemic beings, from whom certain groups of people or clans derived their origin. The power and significance of totemic beings surpassed that of dead ancestors. Side by side with these types of masks, personifications of other supernatural beings may be found, but they are not universally widespread and we shall only mention them in individual cases.

The *sakaiba* masks were known in the coastal area of north-western New Guinea, but they were not common, their use being confined to a few places. These are flat face masks carved from pale, soft wood which is light in weight. They are roughly oblong in shape, with a straight, pointed nose ending in a dart, a narrow half-open mouth and relatively large eyes slanted horizontally. The hair and beard

are suggested by glued tufts of grass or feathers. The face, and sometimes also the forehead, are decorated with inexpressive dark brown or black painted ornaments in the form of mazes and labyrinths.

Information on their use is confined to statements that they appeared at wedding ceremonies. The faces were stylised in a similar way as the faces of the ancestors' figures, which suggests that they may also be portraits of deceased forefathers. The purpose of the masks was to indicate that the ancestors were also taking part in the wedding ceremony, thus guaranteeing that they would help the pair in future.

The area of the Sepik River basin and its tributaries in the northern part of the island and the adjacent coast is rich in masks. In spite of local differences, they have some common features. The most common type is represented by the wooden face masks used at the rituals of ancestor worship. The masks are oval and provided with elongated, narrow noses. The longest noses are to be found in the masks from the lower part of the basin. This nose usually extends beyond the bottom edge of the mask. Though it gets shorter the more one travels away from the coast, it still remains strikingly huge. On the upper Sepik, this trait also appears, although here the masks have lost their original function, only serving as portraits of ancestors and kept in the men's ceremonial houses.

When proceeding from the mouth of the river westwards, we reach the area around Aitape (Plate 43). Here the masks again have a more emphasised nose, but now it is not pointing towards the lower edge, but protrudes obliquely forwards.

The eyes of the coastal masks are narrow, placed at the top of the nose and obliquely directed towards the centre (Plate 51). Further from the coast, however, they become more rounded, and on the mid-Sepik they are circular in shape. The same is true of their convexity; the coastal masks are convex crossways, but their convexity diminishes towards the inland area, and they are entirely flat in the middle part of the basin.

They are no less different in colour. The masks from the mid-basin differ, by using expressive colours (white, brown, red, yellow and black), from the less-colourful coastal masks, the distribution of the colours changing, too. Whereas at the coast larger areas covered with a single colour predominate, patterns of concentric circles and dark-coloured spirals on a light background appear more frequently inland.

Less frequent is the occurrence of masks made of rotang, identical in shape to the wooden masks. In some villages, masks made of coconut shells have even been found, and on the upper Sepik mask-life portraits of ancestors are made of clay.

A separate group consists of helmet masks made of rotang. They are anthropomorphic, but the much elongated nose makes them appear like birds' heads. They served ritual purposes in a fertility cult.

From the centre of the Sepik basin, helmet masks are known, consisting of a basketwork skeleton covered with bark cloth, usually in the form of a fish or croc-odile. They are elongated horizontally in a striking way and represent totemic beings. Most remarkable are group masks in the form of a gigantic broad cone or an elongated roof; their length exceeds 7 m, the height is almost 1 m and the width fluctuates around 2 m. A single mask was able to house up to 20 people (Fig. 16). Their use is well documented in two villages in the middle part of the basin, but their purpose is not quite clear; probably they were personifications of totemic ancestors.

Their very opposite is the miniature masks from the lower Sepik, which are only about 10 cm long. These adorned the interiors of the ceremonial houses, while particularly small carvings were attached to spear shafts (Plates 27 and 28).

Among the Abelam people living on the slopes of Prince Alexander Mountains, north of mid-Sepik, masks made of rotang were used, wooden ones being much less frequent. They may be divided into two groups according to their form and use, irrespective of the materials they are made of. The first group is represented by cone-shaped or even semi-globular helmet masks. The eyes are decorated with concentric circles, separated from each other by open-work areas in the form of long triangles or bows placed one above the other in a row parallel to the emphasised nose. This nose is reminiscent of a parrot's beak, directed from the top of the mask towards its bottom edge in the form of a bow-shaped rib which is triangular in perimeter and highest in the middle of its entire length. The lower end of the nose is provided with a large circular and obliquely placed hole. The mouth is mostly missing and the ears have the shape of short broad cones, attached to the mask by their points. The surface of the mask is always decorated iln many colours. The individual hues (black, white, yellow and red) form concentric circles around the mouth. These masks were worn at rituals worshipping the female being *babatagwa*. During the ceremony they were decorated with young leaves of the sago palm.

The second group consists of flat face masks used at a fertility cult during the yam harvest (Fig. 17). Every man cultivated a few yams in a small sacred field, paying them much attention, including the enacting of magic rites, in order to in-

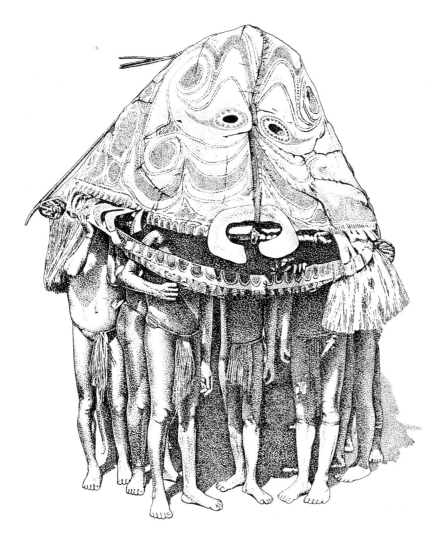

Fig. 16
A group mask consisting of a wooden construction covered with bark cloth, in the form of the mythical founder of the clan, from Angerman village, central Sepik basin, northern Papua-New Guinea. (From a photograph taken in 1912.)

27   A miniature mask of
pale wood and lime. Sepik,
northern New Guinea; now
in Náprstek Museum,
Prague. Height 17 cm.

vigorate their growth. The ripe tubers, sometimes up to 200 kg in weight, were kept in the ceremonial houses, where they were decorated with masks and various objects such as necklaces with large mother of pearl discs, belts and bracelets. The tubers decorated in this way were called *nimandu* ('big man') and considered to personify supernatural beings during the celebrations. The edges of the masks were adorned with open-work woven bands which were complemented with glued-on bird feathers during the ritual.

South-east of the mouth of the Sepik lies Astrolabe Bay. The inhabitants of this area used large *asa kate* face masks at their initiation rites and funerals. These masks are carved from hard wood, have a prolonged oval shape and are highly arched obliquely as well as lengthwise. The most striking element is, again, their long, relatively narrow, high nose, reaching almost to the half-open mouth which is thrust forward in relief. The eyes are drop-shaped, sticking out from the flat rounded face, and are always slanted horizontally. No less striking are the huge ears, each of which is formed by a protrusion curving upwards, under which another protrusion arching downwards is placed. The surface is processed in a rough way and covered with a thick layer of dark brown or black paint. The culture of the local inhabitants, once influenced by European missionaries in the third quarter of the nineteenth century, soon disappeared, which is why we so seldom come across Astrolabe masks in museum collections.

In the neighbouring Huon Bay, masks were worn by the members of the Kate, Yabim and Bukawa peoples and the inhabitants of Tami Island. The masks were connected with the *balum* rite, the purpose of which was to worship beings favourably inclined towards humans. The rites were concentrated on two occasions. One of them was an initiation, taking place only once in every 10—18 years. Apart from a number of ceremonies, its most important point was the circumcision, executed by a masked person representing the *balum* being.

In Tami Island, this being is called *kani*, and the same name is borne by the masks used at this ceremony (Plate 52). These are carved from a single piece of pale wood and are relatively flat, with a face in the form of a vertically elongated oblong or oval, with a low, flat, dart-shaped nose, narrow, horizontal eye-slots and an oval mouth with strikingly emphasised teeth. The surface is mostly white, but the area around the eyes and mouth is covered with ornaments, taking the form of large black or red triangles bordered by narrow grooves filled with white paint. The eyes, mouth, nose and decorative protrusions on the forehead are again black or red. The mask was complemented by large pieces of bark cloth veiling the body of the masked man. After contact with Europeans became more intensive, however, these masks ceased to be used in the old way and were hung on the walls of the ceremonial houses. The majority of the extant *kani* masks therefore have no holes at the edges, necessary for tying the mask to the face.

Another occasion when the inhabitants of Huon Bay used masks was at the rituals of the cult of the *tago* beings. Here they used egg-shaped helmet masks. The face is oval and white, the set-in wooden nose long, narrow and relatively high, the mouth half-open, with marked teeth. The forehead and the chin are decorated with a few coloured stripes or patches and doubled mother of pearl rings. The eyes are always narrow, horizontal and bordered with concentric black or red ovals, the last of which is drawn out in a sidewards way. Above the face, the entire perimeter of the mask suddenly broadens in a semi-globular way into a hairstyle, surmounted by a bunch of feathers and decorated with wood-carvings portraying the founder of the clan (e.g. a fish). Attached to the lower edge of the mask are long, dense fringes made of leaves, entirely covering the dancer's body.

Masks with two faces are quite frequent. Such masks are called *weman* and they also differ from the *tago* masks by their shape, their faces being not oval, but triangular with an upward tilt. However, they are only a variant of the *tago* masks and their purpose is identical. Similar to the basketwork *tago* masks are wooden *nausang* masks from the Kilenge region of the western coast of New Britain in the Bismarck Archipelago.

Two types of hood-shaped masks called *jipai* are known among the inhabitants of the Asmat coast in south-western New Guinea. Both are basketwork masks

28   A miniature mask of pale wood and lime. Sepik, northern New Guinea; now in Náprstek Museum, Prague. Height 20.4 cm.

49

made of twisted strips of the bark of a species of mulberry tree. The masks of the first type (Plate 29) are conical in shape, the base of the cone being provided with two short horizontal sleeves. The mask covers the entire head, shoulders and the upper part of the chest and back, the rest of the body being hidden by fringes made of sago-palm leaves. The surface of the basketwork mask is decorated with painted stripes or oblongs which are red or white in colour. Oval holes for the eyes and mouth are made in the face part, the eyes always being shown by a pair of flat decorative wood-carvings with a circular or oval hole in the centre. The nose and ears may also be made of wood, but in many cases the ears are missing altogether and the narrow nose is made of the same material as the mask. The top of the mask is surmounted vertically by a piece of reed decorated with beads made of seeds, or with feathers. The men performing in these masks represented the villagers who

had died since the preceding festival. They walked through the village to simulate their last visit to their living descendants.

The second type is a simplified version of this mask. This takes the form of a conical basket with a circular or oval base, without any holes for the arms and decorated with painted or carved wooden ornaments; thick fringes are attached to the bottom edge. These masks are connected with a fertility cult. After a festival lasting for several days, a masked man would pass through the village. The children would throw fruits almost as large as oranges at him. These symbolised testicles and enhanced the fertile power of the mask. On the following day the masked man would visit all the houses of the village in which families with small children lived. The father would stand in front of the house with his children, introduce them to the mask and the masked man would touch the boys' testicles and the

Fig. 17
Basketwork masks in the form of *nimandu* beings, used at a celebration of the yam harvest, from Abelam, northern New Guinea. Dated around the 1960s.

50

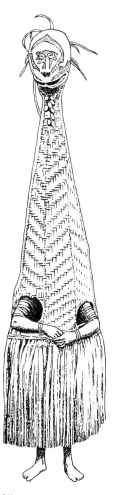

Fig. 18
A basketwork mask-hood from
Urama Island in the Era River
delta at Papuan Gulf on the
southern coast of Papua-New
Guinea. Dated from the
beginning of the twentieth
century.

girls' nipples in order to 'make them grow well'. The day afterwards, the masked man would receive gifts in the form of food from the inhabitants of the village. These would then be distributed in the ceremonial house, among all the members of the community. On the last day of the festival, the mask would once more be carried through the village and afterwards deposited in the ceremonial house which symbolised the world of the dead. Both types of the mask may also have been used further westwards, on the Mimika coast.

The inhabitants of the westernmost part of the Papuan Gulf wore masks at the *moguru* ceremonial cycle. This was connected with a fertility cult and its most important component was initiation rites. The cycle was organised every year and was divided into several phases. At the beginning of the entire cycle, boys at the age of puberty would form one group and girls of the same age formed another. One end of the *darimo* ceremonial house was assigned to each group. For a couple of weeks, both groups met at festive ceremonies, at which they were taught the

51

30 Painted *eharo* mask of bark cloth on a wicker construction. Elema, Papuan Gulf, southern New Guinea; now in Náprstek Museum, Prague. Height (without fringes) 90.5 cm.

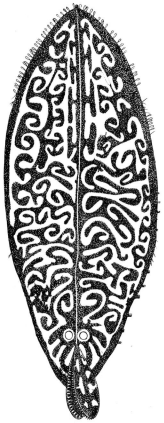

Fig. 19
A *sevese* or *semese* mask made of bark cloth stretched over a wooden frame, from the eastern part of Elema, Papuan Gulf, Papua-New Guinea.

duties of adults, among whom they were admitted after the conclusion of this part of the cycle. The meetings were sometimes also attended by masked dancers embodying supernatural beings and taking active part in the lessons. The respective masks are wooden, flat and oval or circular in shape and are provided with a strikingly long, narrow and low nose, dividing the area of the mask lengthwise into two halves. Small round eyes are placed in the middle of the entire length of the face and are emphasised by concentric circles painted around them. The small open mouth is placed close above the bottom edge.

The Gogodara, living on the left bank of the lower Fly River, used masks about 1 m in height. These are leaf-shaped or oval and are formed of bark cloth stretched over a wooden framework and decorated with painted geometric ornaments, using black, brown, white, red and yellow, and with feathers attached to the edges. Near the bottom edge, inside the area of the mask, there is a small rounded

head made of soft wood, with a large nose broadening from the top, and large eyes emphasised by wide concentric circles. The top of the head is sometimes provided with a conic protrusion. The masks personify the founder of the clan.

Eastwards from the mouth of the Fly River, along the coast up to the tiny Goaribari Island, ceremonies similar to the *moguru* cycle were held. However, they lacked any apparent connection with a fertility cult and concentrated upon the initiation of the tribe's members on attaining maturity, including their initiation into the sexual life of an adult. The initiates gathered in the ceremonial house. During the ceremonies, masks were used, the actual purpose of which is not known.

In the western part of the area, these were helmet masks made of rotang, relatively flat and almost circular in outline. A typical feature is the trunk-like nose protruding from the central part of the mask. In the close vicinity of the top of the nose, there are oval and horizontally slanted eyes, with a wide mouth near by, curved in parallel with the edge. The surface is covered with a thick layer of clay, decorated with red and black patches which are filled with tiny white dots around the eyes, inside the mouth and on the forehead. Long plant material fringes are attached to the mask's edge.

In the eastern part of this region, *avoko* masks were worn. These were helmet masks too, circular or oval in shape, but larger, and their strikingly long, narrow nose did not protrude from the centre of the mask, but from the area at the bottom edge. This nose is almost completely divided into two parallel parts placed one above the other, which gives it the appearance of a long, half-closed beak. The surface of the mask is not covered with a layer of clay and is often adorned with bunches of bright feathers. The eyes are rounded, relatively large and placed at the top of the nose. Their colouring is also different, coloured areas being replaced by simple geometric ornaments.

The inhabitants of the small Urama Island in the delta of the Era River, in the middle part of the Papuan Gulf, used hood masks around 3 m in height (Fig. 18). A cone made of rotang basketwork is decorated at the lower edge with fringes of plant material which veiled the masked person. The thin basketwork of

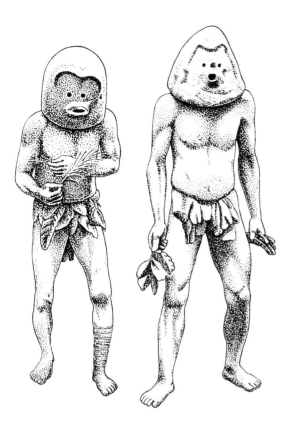

Fig. 20
Helmet masks made of clay covering a wooden or bark cloth construction. From the vicinity of the Asaro River, New Guinea. Dated from the second half of twentieth century.

31   A helmet mask of bark cloth on a bamboo construction. Baining, New Britain; now in Museum für Völkerkunde und Vorgeschichte, Hamburg.

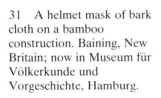

the cone above the fringes contains two holes for the arms, and the cone is surmounted by a round head made of bark cloth, with a half-closed mouth, a long nose and small oval eyes. The pale grey head is adorned with strips of reddish-brown bark cloth, making an irregular oval around the face. In each case, the decoration differs, a common feature being a small area with a ray-like border, to which grey eyes are attached. A thin striped tuft of leaves is usually to be seen on the top, and fringes of threaded brown seeds and berries hang under the chin. The name of the mask has not been preserved, but we know that it represented a guardian of tabooed coconuts.

In the same part of the Papuan Gulf the *keweke* masks were used, most probably at initiation rites. Their height is over 1 m. They have the shape of a long leaf, are flat, and the mouth protrudes from the lower part like a long and narrow open beak. The eyes are formed by large round holes. The mask is sometimes made of basketwork and sometimes of bark cloth, but in both cases, due to its large size, a wooden frame is indispensable. In the masks made of bark cloth, we find dark ornaments similar to plant motifs, placed in the lower half or two-thirds of the entire length. These ornaments are attached to the lower edge with fringes. Identical in form are the masks called *aiaimunu* from

Fig. 21
A dancer wearing a *lor* helmet
mask. From Tolai, Gazelle
Peninsula in the northern area
of New Britain. Dated from the
end of the nineteenth century.

Namau Island, *hevehe* from Orokolo situated further east, and the *sevese* or *semese* of the Elema people (Fig. 19). Their decorations and especially their size vary, the largest being those of the Elema, which may reach 3 m; they represent spirits of the dead or the spirit of the sea.

Around the mouth of the Purari River, *kanipu* masks were worn. They are cone-shaped and were made from a wooden frame covered with bark cloth. They are about 50 cm high and always have a half-open oval mouth just above the bottom edge, a relatively stout, but low nose and large round eyes. The surface of the cone is decorated with ornaments consisting of wide spirals, triangles and stripes with tendril-like projections made of dark bark cloth. These ornaments are always arranged symmetrically along the axis of the face. Another decoration may be seen on the top, e.g. a vertically or horizontally slanted bark cloth. The masks are used by the guardians of tabooed coconuts.

The *eharo* masks (Plates 30 and 53) of the Elema are similar to the preceding type, but their eyes, suggested by a few concentric circles, are always placed at about the middle of the nose and not at its top, as was the case with the *kanipu*. Their surface is also decorated with dark patterns (black and red on a white background), but the ornaments are simpler, the dark stripes, for instance, lacking the tendril-like projections. At the sides, the

Fig. 22
Masked men of the *duk-duk*
secret religious society. From
Tolai, Gazelle Peninsula in
northern New Britain. Dated
from the end of the nineteenth
century.

54

eharo are often provided with long triangular protrusions, or their top may be surmounted by an anthropomorphic figure
made of bark cloth. In some cases the
figure is bordered with a bow reminiscent
of a halo which, however, may sometimes
also be found in masks with no figures.
The top of other masks is surmounted by
an image of a clan ancestor (bird, fish),
or only a flat disc with a face. One case
was recorded in which a model of a
European sailing boat was placed on the

top. The top of the cone may also be rounded and undecorated. The *eharo* masks were not considered sacred, even uninitiated women and children being allowed to look at them, and they were used on various dance occasions.

The overwhelming majority of the inhabitants of New Guinea inland did not use masks. Masks were used, however, by peoples living in the vicinity of the Asaro River in the Eastern Highlands. These are helmet masks, shaped as spheres or round-topped cones, made of clay laid on a frame of bark cloth or branches (Fig. 20). Their eyes are large and rounded, their mouths oval and half-open

33 *Sisu* mask made of basketwork from strips of tree bark. Sulka, New Britain; now in Überseemuseum, Bremen.

and they are sometimes provided with a narrow, straight nose dividing the face into two approximately identical halves. In some of them we may meet strikingly large eyebrow arches and semicircular ears. A thin layer of clay always covered the whole figure of the masked man. The mask represented a dead person. This impression was enhanced by the grey colour of the clay and cracks in the drying surface, reminiscent of the appearance of a disintegrating human body. Intermittent movements of the hand holding a tuft of leaves drove away the imaginary swarms of flies encircling the rotting flesh. The local inhabitants believed they were able to personify the dead by this masking, thus also acquiring the supernatural power possessed by every deceased man.

The people inhabiting the islands in the Torres Strait, between New Guinea and Australia, commemorate people who have died since the preceding ceremony by a cycle of rituals, called *hóriómu*, which take place every year at the beginning of the monsoon. The cycle lasts for a couple of weeks and consists of dance and pantomime performances in which all adult men participate. The dancers represent not only those who have recently died, but also famous ancestors who left the world a long time ago, and a number of supernatural beings. The *kárara óboro* spirits appear at the performances every day, personified by large *kárara* helmet masks made of tortoise-shell. Their frontal part is usually formed by a horizontally slanted crocodile's head with open jaws. These are placed in such a way that the masked dancer can see out through them; the small eyes of the mask are not cut through. The back of the mask is horizontally elongated, usually acquiring the form of a fish. Rarer are cases in which the entire mask is shaped like a fish. The top carries wooden sticks adorned with the feathers of the bird of paradise. The mask only veils the dancer's head, his body being hidden by thick plant material fringes. During the celebrations of the yam harvest, anthropomorphic masks are used. These are wide and their ellipsoid horizontal eyes are placed at the top of a narrow, straight nose broadening towards the large half-open mouth which is provided with two rows of triangular teeth. Flat, oval ears are attached to the edges of the mask and a triangular cut-

34   A face mask of wood stained black and
white. Baule, Ivory Coast; now in Náprstek
Museum, Prague. Height 23.5 cm.

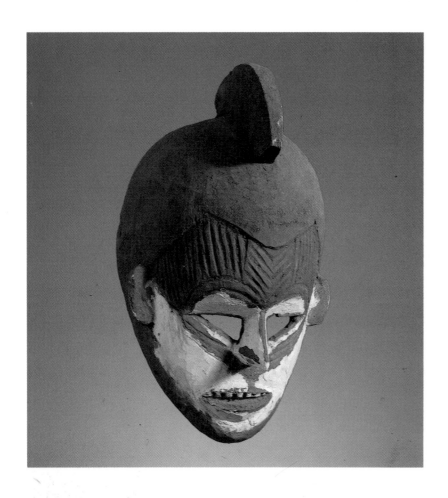

35 A face mask representing female beauty, made of painted wood. Ibo, Nigeria; now in Náprstek Museum, Prague. Height 33 cm.

36 A face mask of painted wood. Fang, Gabon; now in Náprstek Museum, Prague. Height 33.5 cm.

37 A helmet mask with a figure superstructure for the *epa* ceremony, made of painted wood. Ekiti-Yoruba, Nigeria; now in Náprstek 106.5 cm.

38 A face mask of
black-stained wood with
white clay pigment and
strings. Dan, Ivory Coast;
now in Náprstek Museum,
Prague. Height 24.5 cm.

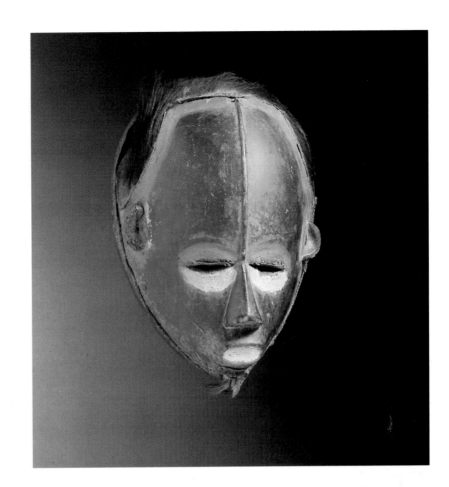

39   A face mask of painted
wood. Guro/Bete, Ivory
Coast; now in Náprstek
Museum, Prague. Height
29.5 cm.

40   *Mwana pwo* face mask
of painted wood with
a knitted extension of strings
and glass beads. Chokwe,
Zaire; now in Náprstek
Museum, Prague. Height
25 cm.

41 Initiation face mask of
painted wood, raffia cloth
and fringes. Pende, Zaire;
now in Náprstek Museum,
Prague. Height 46 cm.

42   A face mask of painted wood. Vuvi,
Gabon; now in Náprstek Museum, Prague.
Height 33.5 cm.

43 A face mask of painted wood. Aitape,
northern coast of New Guinea; now in
Náprstek Museum, Prague. Height 46 cm.

44 A helmet mask of painted wood. Bismarck Archipelago, Witu Island; now in Rautenstrauch-Joest Museum, Cologne.

through sheet of tortoise-shell makes a beard on the chin. The wooden frame is richly decorated with the white shells of sea lamellibranches or bunches of cassowary feathers at the sides.

Worth attention are the masks of the Baining who live in the interior of the Gazelle Peninsula in the north of New Britain in the Bismarck Archipelago. During the annual harvests, they organised celebrations connected with the boys' attainment of maturity. At these celebrations, sacred dances were performed with the purpose of drivilng away the *signal*, evil spirits dangerous to growing children. At the dance the *hareicha* masks, personifying mythical ancestors, were worn. These were helmet masks surmounted by a vertically placed cylindrical or a vertically placed cylindrical or rectangular superstructure or zoomorphic stylised figure. The mask was up to 20 m high. It was held up by strings and extremely large masks were supported by a whole group of men by means of wooden poles or

a simple scaffold. The masks were made of strong yellowish bark cloth attached to a bamboo framework. The ornamental details on the surface were either made of thin white or brown bark cloth or painted in yellow, white, black and red. There were also extant oval bark cloth masks (Plate 31), up to 1 m in height. Their eyes are suggested by a large concentric circles and the remaining area around them is decorated with geometric ornaments which are dark brown in colour. A broad mouth, reminiscent of a duck's beak, protrudes forward from the bottom edge of the mask.

The Tolai of the Gazelle Peninsula used masks called *lor* which were made by the members of the *iniet* secret religious society from the facial parts of skulls of former members of the society. The *lor* were an important feature at the rites, the purpose of which was to secure health, wealth, success in war, a rich harvest and the fertility of the Tolai women.

There are two types of *lor* masks. One

65

of them (Plate 32) is a human face modelled on the frontal part of the skull from black mastic made from nuts of the parinarium tree. The mask, and especially its lower part, is bordered with a flat and usually narrow protrusion, mostly decorated with shallow oblique grooves filled with white paint along its entire length. The remaining surface of the mask is smooth and often decorated with simple ornaments consisting of intersecting white, red and, occasionally, blue stripes. A tuft of human hair is attached with mas-tic to the upper edge of the mask above its forehead. The interior of the mask is covered with mastic only at the edge of the lower half. Here a horizontal piece of wood is fastened. This was gripped in the dancer's teeth to hold the mask in front of the face. The top of the dancer's head was covered by a wig made of coconut fibres and the entire body was hidden by a simple costume made of leaves.

In the masks of the second type, only the lower half of the face, with its wide-open mouth, is covered with mastic and

tufts of grass are attached to the cheeks. The upper part is not covered with mastic which does, however, fill the eyeholes and nostrils. In the interior of the mask, mastic is again only applied to the edge of the lower half, holding a couple of vertically positioned pieces of wood. In this case, the dancer holds the mask in front of his face by the hand, and is thus able to sing during the ceremony. The number of preserved *lor* masks of the first type suggests that they were far more common than the others.

The name *lor* was also given to the spirit masks of the eastern Tolai and the inhabitants of Duke of York Island. This is a helmet mask, attached at the sides to a basketwork frame covered with bark cloth (Fig. 21). The lower part of the forehead is defined by two areas meeting in the middle and passing on into a narrow, long nose. The face, mouth and chin are placed under the forehead. The eyes are narrow and set wide apart; the mouth is small and straight. The black and red colours of the nose, the forehead's edge, the eye area and the mouth contrast with the white surface of the face. The top of the head is sometimes decorated with a zoomorphic figure, probably a portrait of a clan ancestor.

The same population is known for the masks of the *duk-duk* secret society (Fig. 22), used at ceremonies and funerals. Both the smaller *tubuan* and the larger *duk-duk* masks take the form of a dark-coloured cone with expressive round eyes and a thick bunch of plant material fringes and feathers at the bottom edge. The *duk-duk* masks are decorated on top with geometric wood-carvings.

The Sulka, living in the eastern part of New Britain, used strips of tree bark to make their *sisu* masks (Plate 33). These are high cones which are pale brown in colour, with a large flat nose and conical protruding eyes under a bulging forehead. The forward-thrusting mouth is formed by a basketwork cylinder, the front of which is horizontally divided into two parts of approximately the same width. At the sides, on a level with the eyes, large triangular ears are placed, the tops being adorned with black cassowary feathers. A particular decoration is an S-shaped tail which protrudes from the side opposite to the mouth and is directed towards the top of the mask. The tail is adorned with geo-

46 *Nit* mask of painted wood and plant fibres. Northern New Ireland; now in Náprstek Museum, Prague. Height 105.5 cm.

Fig. 23
A cap-shaped mask made of palm leaves, a mark of membership of the *tamate* religious society. Banks Islands, dated from the beginning of the twentieth century. Now in the Museum of Mankind, London. Length 54.5 cm.

metric ornaments in dark colours. Fringes made of pandan leaves are attached to the bottom edge of the mask.

Similar to the *sisu* are masks the cones of which, made of basketwork, represent the upper part of a human body with the arms upraised in an arc towards the cylindrical head. This is carved from pale wood, as are the horizontally positioned flat palms of the long-fingered hands. These masks were used at festive ceremonies and their purpose was to secure health and success for the uninitiated members of the society.

In the Witu Islands west of New Britain, masks were used during initiation rites. These masks consist of basketwork frames and bark cloth and are cone-shaped. The oval eyes are made of wood, and the long, wide nose reaches to just above the wide, long, horizontal mouth which is filled with a row of vertical wooden sticks. Between the mouth and the nose there is a horizontally placed peg sharpened at both ends, representing a decoration inserted into the nose. The face is white and the forehead is adorned with a white oval motif of the sun with rays at the edges. The face is framed with narrow strips of brown, red and blue bark cloth of unequal length.

In the Witu Islands, wooden helmet masks with oblong faces (Plate 44) were worn at funerals. Their oval eyes have narrow horizontal slots and are placed near the top of a long and gradually enlarged nose. The mouth is narrow and almost imperceptible; long, low protrusions represent the ears. The top of the mask is rounded and is separated from the lower part by a flat, bow-shaped rib with scalloped edges, reminiscent of a European hat.

The northern coast of New Ireland and the adjacent small islands constitute the area of Melanesia which is richest of all in masks. The local inhabitant held the ceremonial *malanggan* cycle every year between the end of May and the beginning of July. This was a means of paying respect to actual as well as mythical ancestors. The cycle consisted of dances, feasts and a festive exhibition of carvings and masks. Both anthropomorphic and zoomorphic helmet masks were used, which may be divided into several groups.

The *tatanua* masks (Plate 55) represented an anthropomorphic mythical being and served as a dance mask in pantomimic dances. This type of mask usually has a complicated, carved, low face in many colours, with set-in eyes made of flat shells, and a bulky top formed by a bamboo frame covered with bark cloth, with a simulated head-dress. This area of the mask is usually divided into two parts, each of which is decorated in a different way. While twisted tufts of plant matter fibres are placed on one side, the other may be covered with a thick layer of white lime with narrow depressions following the line of the top, short fringes of fibre, or small, glued-on snail shells.

The *kulapteine* (Plate 45) is similar to the *tatanua* mask in shape and the execution of the bulky top, but the facial part is replaced by a horizontal panel, reaching far over the sides of the helmet-shaped top. The panel is decorated with simple open-work geometric ornaments. In the central part of the panel, covering the face, a much stylised face is placed, with emphasised eyes made of flat shells.

The *kepong* masks (Plate 54) were never used at dances. Men wearing them would only pass through the village, collecting gifts necessary to cover the expense of the preparation of the ritual. They are much more varied in shape than the two preceding types. Their facial part is relatively low and is carved from wood into a very realistic anthropomorphic appearance; in other cases, however, it is stylised to such an extent that the anthropomorphic traits disappear altogether. The top is flat and horizontal, decorated with bark cloth, feathers or tufts of fibre. Large, dropshaped ears are carved from wood or made of bark cloth stretched over a framework made of bent wood and attached to the sides of the mask. The nose is made of a separate piece of wood, carved in a complicated manner, and is of the same height as the entire facial part. In spite of a high degree of stylisation, these masks are always anthropomorphic in character.

The *matua*, although taking the form of masks, are heavy and unstable due to their large size and were therefore only exhibited in front of the ceremonial house. The top is always surmounted by the figure of a supernatural being and the eyes and nose, made from separate, richly carved pieces of wood, are set in.

The *nit* masks (Plate 46) are usually large but do not reach the size of the preceding type. The flat top is formed of twisted bunches of dark plant material fibres reminiscent of human hair. The ears are again carved from separate long and relatively narrow pieces of wood in the shape of inverted drops. Unlike the *matua* masks, however, they are not cut through, but decorated with complicated colourful geometric ornaments. The nose is also made from a separate piece of wood and extends beyond both the upper and the bottom edges of the mask.

The *dudul* masks are always zoomorphic. They consist of a wooden frame, to the front part of which a wooden face representing a mythical owl is attached. The rest of the mask is made of bark cloth and decorated with bird feathers or the soft pith of some undefined plant.

The *pi* have the form of much stylised birds' heads and are made from a frame covered with thick bark cloth. They usually have emphasised and relatively large, round eyes and are sometimes supplemented with a smaller carving of an entire bird's head or part of one. They probably represented the totems of the individual people.

The last type is a zoomorphic mask in the form of a pig's head. This personifies the mythical pig Lungalunga, which devoured people in legendary times. The pig was killed by the gnomes Davirvir and Damärmär, the latter being the first carver in the *malanggan* style, according to another myth. The shape of these masks is relatively uniform.

In Ambrym Island in the New Hebrides Archipelago, there occur wooden face masks which are oval in shape, with a strong, short nose placed high up and provided with a round hole in the middle. The eyes are horizontal and oval, the forehead is domed and the mouth, with its protruding lips, is narrow and long.

Famous for its masks is Malekula Island, in which the *nalawan* secret religious society existed. At the conclusion of a cere-

47 Mask made of stained wood and plant fibres. Northern New Caledonia; now in Náprstek Museum, Prague. Height 39 cm.

mony held for the members of the *nimbou timbarap* grade, the *napal* helmet mask was set on the head of a high-ranking member of the society. This mask consists of a frame made of bamboo splinters with an upper part made of the stem of a tree-fern, with four triangular faces decorated in black, red, white and blue. Carved boar-fangs are set into the corners of the half-open mouth.

The masks from the south-western part of Malekula were carved from the same sort of wood, but they were always face masks, attaining the height of about 75 cm (Plate 56). Their striking trait is a stout nose; the eyes are oval and the surface is decorated in many colours with blue prevailing, which is quite untraditional in Melanesia and shows the influence of Europeans.

The northern part of the New Hebrides and the neighbouring Banks Islands were the home of the *tamate* secret religious society. At its ceremonies, members wore caps made of palm leaves which functioned as masks (Fig. 23). Their shape was typical — a smal, narrow top similar to an upturned boat, placed on a low cylindrical base, one of the ends of the roof being strikingly shortened.

In New Caledonia we know of a single type of mask (Plate 47). The mask is oval and bulges crossways. The oval, horizontal eyes are always placed under wide, arched brows, and the dart-shaped nose often protrudes from the surface of the face at right angles. The mouth is narrow and half-open, often with suggested teeth.

The masks from the southern and central areas of the island are wide and the nose is relatively small. Those from the northern area are narrower and the sharp nose is formed by a protrusion curving in a semicircle towards the mouth and provided with massive earlobes. Tufts of twisted hair are attached to the upper edge of the mask, and a beard, made of the same material or of fibre fringes, is fixed to the lower one. The masks are inexpressive in colour, being black or greenish-black, only the eyes being light grey. An inevitable supplement was a costume made of feathers and attached to the basketwork.

In this survey we have paid attention only to the better-known extant Melanesian masks. There were many others, but their original purposes are not always known.

The American Continent

INUIT MASKS

The tradition of masks in the far north of America is mostly connected with shamanism or spirit possession and mediumship. The belief in the effectiveness of shamanistic rituals was brought by the ancestors of the present-day inhabitants from Asia (Figs. 24 and 25). Rituals performed in masks were most common in Alaska around the area of the Bering Strait. Shamanistic dance and clown masks are also known from this region.

The majority of the masks now kept in museums and private collections originated in the Bering Strait area (Plate 57). Side by side with face masks, there are objects in the shape and size of human faces but with unseeing eyes. These were used at the so-called whale dance, and were probably worn hanging from the neck.

Another kind of dance masks was the female finger mask (Fig. 26), made in pairs and worn on the third and fourth fingers of each hand. They have a rounded face, on to which the eyes and mouth are carved. Tlhe wide-toothed mouth suggests that the masks represent some animal spirit. However, there are also amusing variants of finger masks with a smiling face and toothless mouth. These are used in a sort of puppet show in which the masks converse with each other.

All wooden objects, including the masks, were made by the Inuit from tree stem trunks which drifted ashore. The size of the mask was thus, to some extent, dependent on the diameter of the trunk.

Some masks were made either by the shaman himself or according to his exact instructions. If the shaman was a woman, however, she never made the mask. We have no information as to who carved the other masks and do not know whether he was a specialist, or if every man was able to make them for his own personal use. The latter eventuality seems to be more probable, since there are reports of men who painted their own masks. These were the masks used at ceremonies connected with whaling. The owner of a boat decorated the top of his mask with a picture of the crew being attacked by a whale, and the members of the crew depicted men harpooning a seal or shooting an arrow at a caribou.

In some human-face masks we may find tattoo marks or other ornaments, either made of clay or carved in. Other masks are adorned with geometric motifs, most frequently on the forehead.

The masks preserved in the Museum of

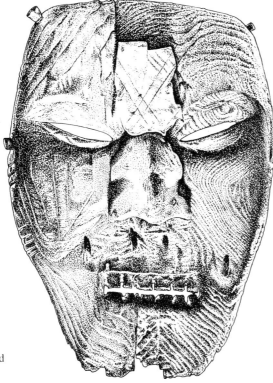

Fig. 24
A wooden mask found in Button Point, Bylot Island. Dorset culture, dated around 1000—500 BC.

Fig. 25
A mask made of walrus-tusks, inlaid with pieces of gagat, and perhaps originally supplemented with other materials. From the vicinity of Point Hope, northern Alaska. Ipiutak culture, dated AD 300—1000.

Fig. 26
Inuit female finger-mask, made in pairs for both hands and worn on the second and third fingers at a dance.

with 'animal' teeth and are, in terms of form, almost identical with the masks used at shamans' magic performances.

The masks were decorated in naturally available colours. For red, ochre was used, clay for white or yellow, graphite for black, and probably whortleberry for blue. In some cases, blood was applied and maybe also a mixture of powdered charcoal and fermented urine. Besides paints, other materials were used for decorating the masks, such as skin, hair, bone, feathers and basketwork, and there were several pendants, mostly made of wood. Various kinds of decoration were combined in a single mask. By contrast, other masks which have been found were very simple, consisting merely of an oval with the features of a human face.

In terms of geography, simpler masks are to be found in the northern area of the Bering Strait, around Point Hope and Point Barrow, whereas in the southern region of the Kuskokwim Bay, composite masks with many pendants and supplements were made. The Inuit used masks at religious ceremonies. All of them are expressions of the fundamental Inuit belief that a spirit forms the substance of everything in nature, be it a person, animal, wind, driftwood or a season of the year, and that this spirit may be seen in a certain form. The spirit is a being which thinks along the same lines as people do. These 'spiritual doubles' are contacted by the shaman at his rites and he talks to them in order to make them help his people whose lives are so dependent on the forces of nature in the tough conditions of the north.

The spiritual substance of all phenomena is called *inua* and mythological beings are derived from it, such as 'Man in the Moon', spirits which protect animals and assist the shaman, spirits of animals and so on. In the masks, the belief in the *inua* is expressed by a combination of human and other elements, mostly animal. This is why the exact significance of masks provided with many supplements is hard to define. Although in principle all masks were based on the same belief expressed by the same rituals, the individual attitude of the shaman was of decisive importance. Only the maker of the mask was able to explain what all the elements of his mask represented.

A mask portraying an animal or bird's

Sitka were found in the old cemetery of Point Hope, where they had been buried in separate graves. They are thought to have been masks of men who were not shamans. All of the masks are in the form of human faces, but some are provided

72

head with a human face or a skull placed on it is the mask of the animal *inua* at the moment when it is manifested in human form. In such a case it is not difficult to state the mask's significance. More complicated are the masks of the guardian spirits of animals, which some scholars identify with the mythological 'Man in the Moon'. The masks usually have a centrally placed human face, sometimes grinning in a grotesque way, with an open mouth and showing teeth. This represents danger and power. The face is encircled with one or two hoops made of rods with feathers attached to the edges. These hoops, provided with feathers or other materials, represent the sky and the stars. This basic scheme may be changed in various ways. In an actual case, it may be difficult to distinguish this type of mask from the previous one, since the 'human' face of the guardian spirit may be covered by a portrait of the animal whom the spirit protects. Only its supplements and pendants may help in identification, but these have not always been preserved. Even for the Inuit it is not easy nowadays to explain the significance of masks collected during the last century.

At hunting rituals, the shaman used a mask, in the open mouth of which the animal to be hunted (salmon, seal) or part of its body (seal's head, walrus's teeth, whale's tail) appeared at the end of the ceremony. These supplements were carved from wood, but sometimes they were replaced by blood rushing out of the mask's mouth.

Masks of this kind have now disappeared from the Inuit tradition. Their place has been taken by the masks of a 'good' and a 'bad' shaman, documented for the first time in Nome in 1914. They are only known from the Nome area, where they are used to entertain tourists. Present-day carvers often make replicas of masks which are preserved in museums, or create new pieces with traditional motifs.

THE NORTH-WESTERN COAST

For the inhabitants of the north-western coast of the American continent, masks were of great social importance. Practically every ritual object is decorated with the motif of the mask. The mask was one of the first artefacts to be seen by European explorers on the north-western coast.

Fig. 27
A painted wooden mask used at ceremonial dances. From the north-western coast of Canada. Dated from the end of the nineteenth century.

73

48 A mask of the False Face society, made of wood. Onondaga, USA; now in Deutsches Ledermuseum, Offenbach a.M. Height 32 cm.

Fig. 28
A dancer wearing a bird mask and carrying a rattle. The skull area of the head is covered with a feather hood. Used by tribes of the north-western coast of Canada. Dating from the end of the nineteenth century.

A report, written by a member of Cook's expedition of 1778, describes the dance performed by a man in one of the canoes which surrounded Cook's ships in Nootka Sound. The Indians were singing and pounding in rhythm on the sides of their canoes, while the dancer alternated two masks, each with a different aspect. Both are described as 'masks made of wood, well carved and painted in the same manner in which they usually paint their faces'. The dancer was clad in wolfskin with the hairy side out. The description does not mention the significance of the performed dance.

The use of masks was based on mythol-ogy among all the peoples living on the north-western coast. Masks and the dances connected with them which, according to Indian belief, were brought to the founders of the clans by various super-natural beings, played a similar role as coats-of-arms bestowed for some deed of valour by a rule in medieval Europe. The masks were reminiscent of meetings with supernatural beings and they se-cured a superior social position for their owners as descendants of a mythical hero. Dancing in a mask is a hereditary privilege of noble families. The annual repetition of these dances in the presence of the largest possible number of invited spectators en-

74

hances the family's prestige, and all the guests must be offered a feast and given gifts. By their presence, however, the guests acknowledge the host's claims to the respective rights substantiated by mythology. The larger the number of masks and dances belonging to the family, the greater its authority and nobility. In the old photographs of chieftains wearing ceremonial customs and surrounded by their families, we always see a large number of masks, the symbols of their power.

The best explanation of the origin of masks is offered by the Tlingit. According to one of their myths, masks originated at a remote time when all of the people were living in darkness in a village situated at the mouth of the Nass River. No heavenly bodies illuminated the earth then, because they had been imprisoned by the highest deity, the 'Raven from the Mouth of the Nass'. However, his sister's son, who was also a raven, set the sun at liberty and it flew up high into the sky with such a noise that some scared villagers hid in the woods and waters. Since they were wearing clothes made of animal skins, they were turned into furred animals. Those who stayed in the village accepted these animals into their emblems as a testimony to their original unity (Fig. 27).

Whereas the Tlingit, living in the northern area, enriched the common religious fund of myths on the origin of animal masks, the Kwakiutl, inhabiting the regions further south, contributed a complex of myths surrounding the winter dances which are dominated by the cannibal dancer, *hamatsa*. The family owning the *hamatsa* dances is the object of the greatest esteem and prestige, because its members rescue people from a cannibal monster and its attendants every year. According to the myth, four brave hunters went to the lair of the monster Bakhbakwalanoóksiwey where, after a fight, they seized masks and other ritual objects, bringing them back to their people. The central motif of this dance cycle, however, is the return of a novice who is to be admitted to the *hamatsa* society and is possessed by the cannibal spirit. The spirit has bewitched him, making him hanker after human flesh. The novice embodies the cannibal spirit and the assembly is obliged to turn him into a man again. This is done through a series of dances performed by the novice and his attendants. They first perform in masks personifying supernatural beings, the cannibal birds which accompany the cannibal spirit. Most frequent are the masks of a cannibal raven, thunderbird and the 'Crooked Beak of Heaven'.

All of the masks performing at a *hamatsa* dance (Plate 58) are made of red cedar wood and their bottom edges are decorated with fringes made of the bark of the same tree, covering the dancer's entire body. The fringes are reddish and serve to hide the dancer's hands. The dancer holds strings, by means of which he opens the beak of the cannibal bird. Although mechanical masks with an opening device also occur in other types of dances, their combination with red bast fringes is typical of the *hamatsa* dance.

Besides *hamatsa*, the Kwakiutl have yet another dance, which has also spread among neighbouring peoples. This is 'Winalagilis, Warrior of the World', whose hero is a giant travelling in a canoe which he never leaves. At this dance various effects are used, made possible by the use of masks and many illusions. Spirits bringing the dead to life also appear. One of the most outstanding characters performing in a mask is Toogwid, a successful fighter always represented as a woman. During

Fig. 29
A strikingly painted wooden mask of a monster, supplemented with a feather hood. Used by tribes of the north-western coast of Canada at the end of the nineteenth century.

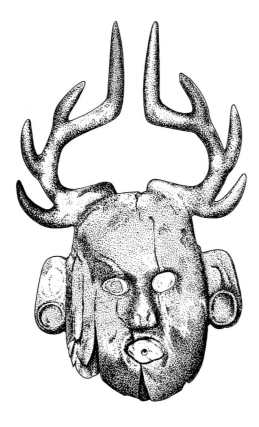

her dance, singers describe her deeds in war. Toogwid herself talks, urging the spectators to kill her; sometimes her attendant talks in her place. The killing occurs at a dramatic moment. A wedge is hewed into the top of the mask, blood spurts from hidden animal bladders, and seal's eyes simulate the eyes of the mask fallen out of the eyeholes. After the dancers have finished dancing around the entire house, however, the mask reappears, intact and without any traces of blood. In other dances, the Toogwid mask is beheaded. In this particular case, a mask is used, realistically reproducing a dead face with hair.

The Tsimshian perform a variant on this dance, at which a masked man representing the chieftain is beheaded. At a dramatic moment of the dance, the chieftain's uncle rushes upon him and cuts his head off. The head then dances around the fire in the dim light in which the strings controlling it from a roof cannot be seen.

A dance with a cut-off head is also known among the Nootka. Female masks of 'dead' faces are among the oldest masks of the north-western coast, and many are preserved in world collections. Some were brought back by Cook following his expedition of 1778. These masks lack any painting. Most of them have closed eyes suggested by narrow slots. The mouth is half-open and long hair is inserted into holes drilled into the upper part of the mask.

The *tsalulá* dances are also common in this area. These represent family myths. One of the parts of this dance cycle is the *gyídakhania* dance. Here the Kwakiutl use a mask, the forehead of which is provided with a rounded hole which holds a bunch of feathers. The mask bears a human face painted white; the eyes, moustache and eyebrows are black; the lips and nostrils red. All the masks have moustaches and some have beards. Among the Tsimshian, the *gyídakhania* dance is performed by a dancer personifying a mythical being and a group representing the chieftain and the members of his family, but more frequently the chieftain is accompanied by slaves. They use a series of seven masks, that of the chieftain being the largest in size. The chieftain does not dance; he only walks around the dancers. Besides the mask, he also wears a

49 'Suffering Moor' mask for the scenes *Moros y Cristianos*. Nahua, Mexico; now in Náprstek Museum, Prague. Height 29 cm.

blanket. The dancers are not wrapped up in this way; their costume originally imitated the traditional dress of the Tlingit, but nowadays they wear a dance apron over their normal clothes.

In the *tsalulá* dance cycle, we find a mask of a personified earthquake and the 'Echo' mask, with half-human and half-animal features. The dancer performs in a mask and a blanket, under which he hides various mask parts. Turning away from the fire, he covers his face with the blanket and alters the respective part of the mask under it. This part slots through the body of the mask and is held

in position inside by the dancer's teeth. The masks represent different kinds of animals, the beaks various birds and the muzzles animals. Even a stylised human figure or the body of a fish may appear. The dancer's attendants mimic or echo the voices of various animals.

Gamblers' masks are also used at the *tsalulá* dances. Here guests are invited to play against the masked hosts in the Hand Game or Bone Game. They are rewarded well if they win.

Among the masks worn at a *tsalulá* dance mention must be made of a combined mask of the sun and the killer

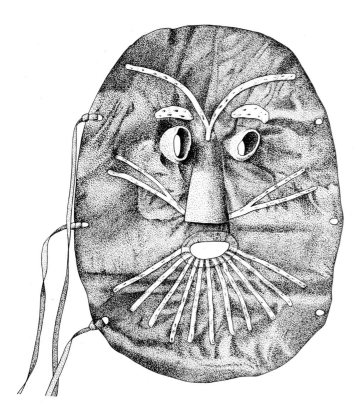

Fig. 32
A leather veil with marked face features used at healing rituals. Inuit from Blacklead Island.

Fig. 33
Participant in a bison dance, wearing a mask made of a bison head. According to a drawing by Ch. Bodmer. Mandan, nineteenth century.

whale. A human face with animal features is placed in the centre of the mask, with a dorsal fin, symbolising a killer whale, placed above the forehead. The dancer wearing this mask moves slowly round the fire, its glow illuminating the mask from below. Another element of these dances is the mythological being Dzoonokwa, a fearsome female creature of gigantic size. The lips of this mask are distinctly O-shaped to suggest cannibalism. Some of the Dzoonokwa masks are realistic, others being provided with disfigured features, but zoomorphic elements are missing. Besides the lips, inflated cheeks are also emphasised. The traditional colours of the mask are black and red. Flat areas are painted with powdered graphite, the lips, nostrils and cheeks being red. Their effectiveness is enhanced by the eyebrows, moustache and beard made of black fur, although the mask is female in principle.

Similar to the preceding mask, both in appearance and the character of the personified being, is the *bukwoos* mask representing the 'Wild Man of the Woods'. This is characterised by a strongly hooked, beak-shaped nose placed under an expressive forehead. Teeth are often shown. The eyebrows may be emphasised and supplemented with hair. The wearer of the mask is clad in a tight dress and he must express vigilance and hidden strength.

Tséyka (or *tsetseka*) is the dance of sacred cedar bark. As in other dance cycles, a large number of mask types appear in it, especially in the *atlákem* (animal) dance in which as many as 40 masked dancers participate. Their leader is usually a grouse, but in some variants a wolf or a raven take his place (Fig. 28). Not all of the masks used are animal in character. Some personify natural formations such as rocks, trees or shrubs.

Quite different is another mask used at this dance, that of a midwife. She appears either alone or accompanied by a lot of children whom she has helped to be born. The 'children' are represented by real children, but their masks portray standardised faces of adults. Such a mask was made for a child in order to keep it healthy, and participation in the dance was part of the child's protection and a prevention of illness.

Many complicated masks may be seen at this particular dance. For instance, bird masks have a beak consisting of two parts which may be opened sideways, thus forming wings between which a human face is placed. Masks of woodland animals are provided with movable jaws. In the human masks we sometimes find movable eyes or a movable lower jaw.

50 Mask of Pedro de
Alvarado for the dance *La
Conquista*, made of painted
wood. Chichicastenango,
Guatemala; now in
a private collection in
Prague. Height 19 cm.

These masks were originally thrown into a fire after they had been used, but nevertheless a considerable number of them have reached museum collections (Fig. 29).

Among the best-defined masks to be seen in collections are those of the shamans. This is because a large number of them were buried in shamans' graves. A magician was usually buried along with his equipment, or at least its most precious parts, i.e. masks, drums, rattles, etc. Part of the gear would be given by the shaman to his successor during his lifetime, especially when the latter was one of his relatives whom the shaman had personally trained to succeed him.

We have no information on who made shamans' masks, but it was probably the same established craftsmen who were the makers of dance masks, since there are no apparent differences between the two types in terms of technique. A mask carved into a certain likeness had to be painted or have some of its features emphasised, or sometimes its surface was decorated with abstract paintings. Before the Hudson Bay Company started to supply the north-western coast with synthetic paints, the Indians mixed their own pigments with good results. Black was made of a mixture of charcoal and graphite (Plate 59), red of hematite (later on replaced by cinnabar imported from China) and green and blue-green were obtained from copper. Various decoctions or juices of bark, moss, mushrooms and forest fruits were also used. Before being applied, the pigments were mixed with chewed salmon spawn.

The masks of the inhabitants of the north-western coast combine animal elements with human ones, although it is sometimes difficult to determine which of the two predominates. This is because in some animal masks only certain characteristic traits (ears, beak, etc.) are maintained, while the size of the face and other features are human. Animal masks, especially those with heavy beaks or muzzles, were not worn on the face, but on the top of the head and the nape of the neck, the beak being slanted obliquely upwards. The edges of the mask rested on the shoulders. Fringes made of cedar bark or animal skin, covering the entire dancer's body, were attached to the lower part of the beak or the bottom edge of the mask. At some dances, the dancers were covered with blankets, making further effects possible, such as creating the illusion of a 'headless' trunk or the impression of bird wings. The masks were also supplemented with animal skins which flowed down at the back.

Further supplements of the masks are hair and beards, either genuine or made of fur, and eyebrows made of animal hair or strips of copper. Copper sheets were also used to emphasise the mouth of the mask. Female masks of the Haida are given a labret inlaid with shells. In other cases a shelled head decoration was used (e.g. among the Tsimshian).

From the middle of the nineteenth century onwards, masks were often made to be sold. With the exception of the eyes, through which one cannot see, they uphold traditional forms. They were made especially by the Haida, who quickly adapted their style to the buyers' demands and who even started making masks of Europeans or supplementing the Indian-faced masks with earrings, nose-rings, etc. Some of these masks have the features individualised to such an extent that they are undoubtedly portraits of actual persons. The tradition of carving has remained alive along the north-western coast, flourishing in the individual works of known artists.

Fig. 34
Irokeze masks of the False Face society are carved from a living tree and cut off only after they are finished in rough outline.

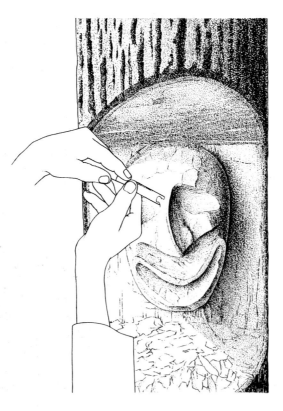

51   A face mask of painted
wood. Sepik, northern New
Guinea; now in Náprstek
Museum, Prague. Height
53 cm.

52 A *kani* mask of painted wood. Tami Island, northern New Guinea; now in Náprstek Museum, Prague. Height 44.5 cm.

53 Painted *eharo* mask of
bark cloth on a wicker
construction. Elema, Papuan
Gulf, southern New Guinea;
now in Náprstek Museum,
Prague. Height (without
fringes) 58 cm.

54 *Kepong* mask of painted wood.
Northern New Ireland; now in Náprstek
Museum, Prague. Height (without fringes)
62 cm.

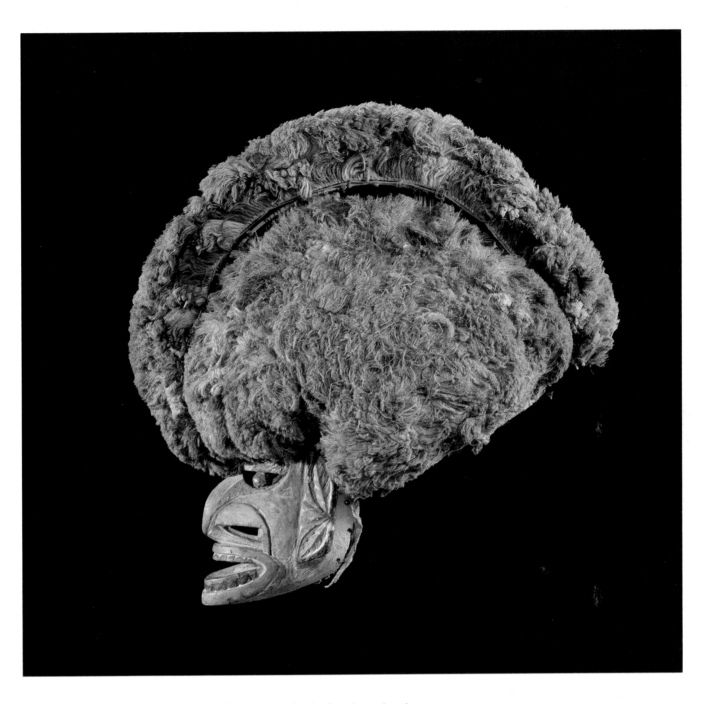

55   *Tatanua* mask of painted wood and
bark cloth on a bamboo frame. Northern
New Ireland; now in Náprstek Museum,
Prague. Height 32 cm.

56 Painted mask of the
quat secret society, made
from the wood of
a fern-tree and clay. New
Hebrides; now in Náprstek
Museum, Prague. Height
65 cm.

57   A painted face mask made of
driftwood. Nunivak, Alaska; now in St
Museum für Völkerkunde, Munich.
Perimeter 55 cm.

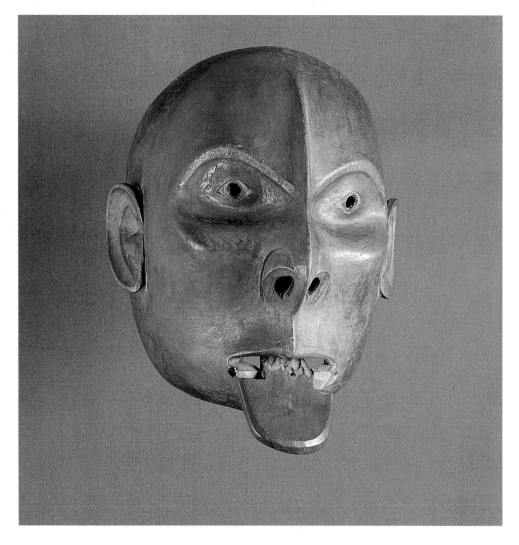

58   A dance mask of
a wolf made of painted
wood. Kwakiutl, British
Columbia, Canada; now in
Náprstek Museum, Prague.
Length 63 cm.

59   A dance mask made of
wood coloured with
graphite. Kwakiutl, British
Columbia, Canada; now in
a private collection in
Prague. Height 27 cm.

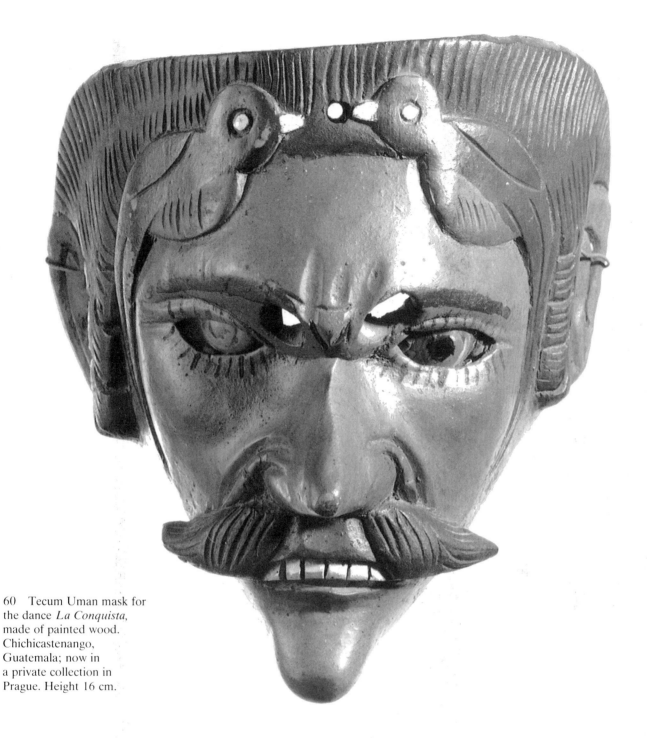

60 Tecum Uman mask for the dance *La Conquista*, made of painted wood. Chichicastenango, Guatemala; now in a private collection in Prague. Height 16 cm.

One such is Mungo Martin. From the beginning of the present century he made both exact copies of old carvings and his own personal artefacts, presenting new ideas in traditional forms.

THE EASTERN FORESTS, GREAT LAKES AND PRAIRIES

Whereas on the north-western coast of America the tradition of masks is still liv-ing, even flourishing in its own way, it has been maintained by only a few peoples in the regions to the east. However, archaeo-logical finds testify to the use of masks in a much wider area. A bone mask was found in archaeological diggings of the Hopewell culture, dated to the period be-tween 400 BC and AD 500, and another find was reported from the Mississippi ba-sin, assigned to the years AD 700—1200 (Fig. 30). The collection of masks dis-covered in Key Marco in Florida reveals

striking affinities with later masks. These masks used by the Kalusa are carved in the form of a simple human face and painted in many colours. Among the objects found in Key Marco, there is a wooden mask of a man-stag and an alligator's head with movable jaws, which may have been used in a similar way to the masks of the north-western coast.

Hunting, ceremonial and shamans' masks of the ancient peoples are preserved in drawings by Karl Bodmer, George Catlin, Théodore de Bry and Jacques Le Moyne, and a shaman's mask was immortalised in literature by James Fenimore Cooper in his novel, *The Last of the Mohicans.*

Hunting masks, either complete or partial covers made of skin with animal heads, were recorded by Catlin among the Indians of the prairies in the nineteenth century. He depicted them wearing the masks of white wolves while hunting bison. A similar drawing of the Florida Indians, from the sixteenth century, in this particular case wearing stag-masks, may be found among the drawings of Le Moyne. Hunting masks were also mentioned as existing among the Cherokee.

Similar in form to the hunting masks are skin covers for the faces, provided with stag's antlers (Fig. 31), the clown mask, which was used over a large area from the eastern coast up to the Great Lakes at a dance connected with barter, or healing masks bearing no antlers (Fig. 32).

Also documented by drawings are the masks and costumes of the shamans who performed their rituals cloaked in bear skin, such as the shaman of the Mandan depicted by Catlin, or the shaman of the Huron mentioned by Cooper. In the category of ceremonial masks the dance masks from the prairies can be seen in other drawings by Catlin or Bodmer. They portray men at a bison dance, with masks made of bison heads (Fig. 33).

90

The oldest masks are reported to have been found among the Delaware, where a man wearing a mask performed dances in the ceremonial house called the Big House. The masked dancer personified a spirit protecting all wild animals. The same human face, executed in simple features, was repeated on the main column of the ceremonial house and on the columns standing along the walls. Altogehter 12 faces were shown here, the right half of each painted red and the left half black. The same type of masks, with the two halves of the face differing in colour, may also be met with among the neighbouring Irokeze, of whose masks we are best informed. However, the faces on the columns also suggest a possible connection with an extant drawing from the sixteenth century, depicting a dance of the Virginia Indians, performed within a circle which is formed by columns decorated with human heads.

Two kinds of masks are known among the Irokeze, one made of wood and the other of corn husks. The wooden mask, called the False Face (Plate 48), was used by the healing fraternity bearing the same name, and is still used today. The ceremonies at which masks are worn are not taboo, so more information concerning them is available than is usually the case. The mask personifies an evil spirit who fought against the Creator for the domination of the world. During the fight the Creator threw a rock at him, which hit the spirit's face and broke his nose. This is why the spirit is portrayed as disfigured, with a broken nose and an expression of pain on his face. The 'Old Broken Nose'

61   Mask of a young bull for the dance *La Conquista*, made of painted wood. The mask is used along with those in Nos. 50 and 60. Chichicastenango, Guatemala; now in a private collection in Prague. Height 16 cm.

or else the 'Great World Rim Being', by its very disfiguration is known as a symbol of evil, illness and imperfection, and may be worn at a dance in order to help cure an illness. This is done at a ritual performed by the False Face fraternity in the house of the sick person, with all the members of the family present. The mask endows its wearer with the power to cure by means of hot ashes which the masked dancer blows on to the patient through the mouth of the mask. The ritual takes a couple of minutes and during its performance one of the masks, called the 'Doorkeeper', guards the door, lest anyone should enter during the course of the ceremony, which would destroy the cure. The Doorkeeper's mask has a mouth shaped like two spoons. The guardian of the door is also equipped with rattles made of tortoise-shell.

The cured person becomes a member of the society and must procure a mask for himself. He either carves it in the form of a being or spirit which he has seen in a dream, or commissions a carver to make it. The mask must be carved from the trunk of a living tree, so that all the tree's forces of life will be concentrated in it (Fig. 34). During carving the tree is deco-

rated with offerings such as tobacco, and the mask is cut from the trunk only after it is finished. In theory the mask should be painted red or black, or half-red and half-black. If the carver starts his work in the morning, the mask is painted red, but should be blackened if he begins to work on it in the afternoon. In actual fact, however, masks of other colours also occur, such as brown and orange, or yellow and brown, and even unpainted masks may be found. Black masks are often provided with red lips and tongue and sometimes even a red nose. The hair is made of black or white horsehair and the eyes are often emphasised with copper or bone rings. All False Face masks represent human faces, albeit deformed in various ways, such as by wrinkles or bulging eyes.

An exception among the anthropomorphic False Face masks is the mask of a pig appearing in a procession along with the others. In the sphere of ritual, the pig replaced the bear as a symbol of supernatural forces. The change was probably brought about through European influence.

The second important healing society of the Irokeze is the Corn Husk society, also called Husk Faces or Husky Heads. The mask of this society serve agricultur-

Fig. 36
The initiation ceremonies among the Pueblo are performed in the masks of mountain spirits called *kachina*. According to a drawing by J. More. Hopi culture, from the beginning of the twentieth century.

92

Fig. 37
A wooden mosaic mask representing a jaguar. Aztec, from the thirteenth to the fifteenth centuries.

62   A dance mask of sheep skin and horsehair, with horns made of wood covered with leather. Mapuche, Chile; now in Náprstek Museum, Prague. Height 46 cm.

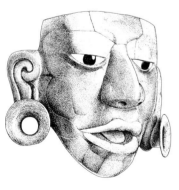

Fig. 38
A Maya funeral mask made of green stone, with a mouth of red stone and eyes of tortoise-shell. From the classic period, AD 300—600.

al cults, being used particularly at winter festivities. The masked dancers embody people from another world, or the inhabitants of the opposite ends of the world. These aliens are the messengers of three sisters, Corn, Squash and Beans, who endow them with healing abilities.

The masks of the Corn Husk society are made of corn husks. Long, strong braids are first plaited and then wound up into a spiral and sewn together to form the oval shape of the face, with holes for the eyes and the mouth; the nose is modelled separately. The masks are made in pairs, both male and female, and may occasionally be painted red. All around the oval face, fringes are attached, forming a kind of mane or halo (Fig. 35).

The Corn Husk society has healing rituals of its own, based on principles similar to those of the False Face fraternity. The masks of both of them sometimes perform together, the Corn Husk dancers announcing the arrival of the False Face dancer on occasions.

From the past wooden masks are known among the Cherokee, too. They performed at the Booger dance, thus protecting the wearers against the evil influences of the white men, especially European illnesses. This may suggest that the Booger masks may be as old as the first contacts with Europeans. These masks are provided with human and animal features, sometimes painted and in some cases supplemented with fur. They represent white and black men, but also Indian neighbours. Masks representing the Cherokee as hunters are also known, bearing human faces with buffalo features. Another Cherokee mask is surmounted by a coiled snake.

93

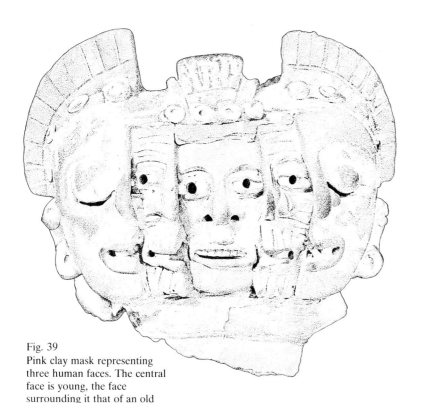

Fig. 39
Pink clay mask representing three human faces. The central face is young, the face surrounding it that of an old man, and the outer face that of a dead man. From central Veracruz, dated from the post-classic period, AD 1000—1500.

Fig. 40
Ceramic figures clad in a complicated costume and carrying a mask, perhaps representing a priest disguised as a deity. From central Veracruz, dated as the classic period, AD 600—900.

THE SOUTH-WESTERN PART OF THE USA

The tradition of masks in the south-western area of the United States has two-fold roots. The Navajo and Apache brought the tradition from their original homes in the north, from where they came south to the area of present-day New Mexico, Arizona and Sonora three centuries ago. This tradition was based on the hunting tribes' belief in wood spirits, who must be made favourably inclined. However, the local south-western tradition was agricultural in character. Its adherents were, and still are, the Pueblo, especially the Zuñi, considered to be heirs to the traditions of the Casas Grandes culture. This agricultural culture included both local elements and some features of the classical cultures of central Mexico. For this reason, spirits bringing rain for crops occupy an important place in it.

The *Gans* wood-spirits of the Apache are a reminder of the original inhabitants of what is today Apache territory. The Apache conceive of them as teachers and guardians inhabiting mountain caves. They especially guard sacred lakes and heal illnesses. The masked dancers personifying them perform at healing ceremonies, the rituals taking place when girls reach puberty. The dancers prevent the activities of the evil spirits who bring epidemic diseases.

Navajo mythology describes the adventures of heroes or heroines who have to experience a series of mishaps, both merited and unmerited, due to the intervention of supernatural beings. In some stories, the heroes fall ill and have to be cured, on this occasion acquiring the knowledge of some healing ritual, which they then give to their people.

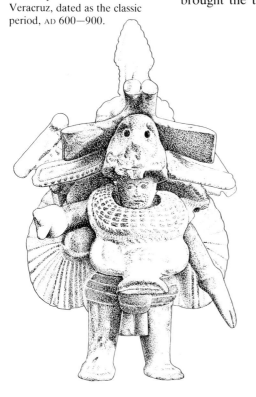

63 A dance mask of sheep skin with horns made of wood covered with leather. Mapuche, Chile; now in Náprstek Museum, Prague. Height 41 cm.

The Pueblo masks also represent mythological beings who at one time helped the Pueblo to summon rain. Before leaving for the forests, the spirits gave the Pueblo their images in the form of masks which are now preserved in the ceremonial houses called *kiva*. The spirits' masks, *kachina*, perform at the rituals connected with the agricultural cycle; these ceremonies take place in the period between the beginning of the year and the harvest of the first fruits. These masks are very numerous among the Hopi and Zuñi tribes.

By contrast, the performance of Apache masks is not bound to any definite date. The suitable time is decided by the shaman following a vision which he has had while taking part in a dance of masked spirits. His narrative forms the basis of the dances, at which the dancers represent masked spirits and not spirits in their 'natural' likeness.

The masks of the Navajo and Pueblo do, however, represent spirits in what is conceived of as their 'actual' appearance, portraying the 'natural' faces of supernatural beings. The old masks of spirits, sometimes preserved in ceremonial houses for several generations, were even believed to be real portraits of the spirits, who had given them to the ancestors of the present-day Indians in order to make it possible for them to take upon themselves their ancient form, along with the power owned by this or that other spirit.

Only two of the Apache spirits taking part in the ceremonies survive today. These are the 'Black Gans' and the 'Grey Gans'. The Black Gans is a sacred dreaded mask, only performing at seri-

64   A bat mask for an animal dance, made of painted wood. Nahua, Mexico; now in Náprstek Museum, Prague. Height 67 cm.

It is usually men who perform in the Navajo masks, but this rule is not observed so strictly as among the Apache and Pueblo. In some groups, women may replace men or have masks of their own. Two ceremonies are of the utmost importance among the Pueblo — the *powamu*, the ceremony of planting fruits, and the *niman*, which is the departure of the *kachina* spirits with harvested fruits. The organisers also wear *kachina* masks at the ceremony; they are called Side Dancers and their masks, for example that of a wolf, bear, 'uncle', etc., are connected with particular dances.

The most important masks of the Hopi take part in both main ceremonies. Side by side with the dance *kachina*, there are also clown *kachina*, equally sacred among the Pueblo. They perform during the intervals between the dances, entertaining the spectators with funny scenes. There is also a particular mask of a clown-messenger among the Hopi, bringing information about the ceremonies to the other ceremonial houses.

In terms of form, the basic part of a mask of the south-western area is a leather or skin cover for the entire head of the wearer, i.e. a hood or helmet mask, but in some more recent Pueblo masks only the face type is extant. In the Apache tribe, this is a soft skin hood, now often replaced by cloth, under which a framework holds the superstructure of the mask. This is constructed of light laths formerly made of yuka wood, but now mostly of plywood. The superstructure has the shape of rays, a cross, a kind of antlers or upraised arms bent at the elbows. The superstructures are painted yellow, green, blue or black and decorated with various pendants made of light materials, such as feathers, twigs, grass and small pieces of wood representing rain. These headpieces are a differentiating mark between the products of the western Apache, being more massive and more compact, and those of the Chiricahua and Mescalero Apache, who make superstructures of a more complicated and subtle construction. The dark (either black or dark blue) hoods are sometimes decorated with yellow paint and holes are cut for the eyes and the mouth. The mask is complemented with a costume consisting of a skin skirt. Rattles are attached to the feet of the dancer; the hands hold

ous ceremonies. The Grey Gans appears in other roles, for instance representing the herald of the Black Gans, playing the part of a clown in ceremonies, or frightening children.

The Navajo masks are known in several types, personifying heroes of the myths. Up to 24 masks may appear at a single ceremony, their purpose being to secure stability in the community and especially to cure the sick. The ceremony consists of several parts, but is based on two subjects, the Blessing Way and the Enemy or Evil Way. Both ceremonies have different variants, based on a few original myths.

96

65 A butterfly mask for an animal dance, made of painted wood. Nahua, Mexico; now in Náprstek Museum, Prague. Height 63 cm.

sword-shaped sticks for the fight against evil spirits. Another component of the mask is a symbolic painting on the body.

The Navajo masks have the same basic form, i.e. a soft leather hood sewn from two pieces, the join passing over the top of the head from one ear to the other. The masks are light in colour and painted in a symbolic pattern, or the face part is painted in one of the symbolic colours, i.e. yellow, red, green, blue or white. In some spirit masks, small holes for the eyes and the mouth are supplemented with gourds, feathers, little shells, in the case of female masks wooden 'earrings', etc. To the top of these hoods either a dense mane of horsehair or a single feather may be attached, depending on which spirit is to be represented. Some masks are also

bearded, their bottom edge being formed by a sort of collar made of twigs of needle-leafed trees or of fur. Further equipment consists of a skin skirt; ordinary clothes are worn when the ceremony takes place in winter.

The Pueblo masks from the oldest period are shaped from heavy fur-tubes made of untanned skin, the entire weight resting on the dancer's shoulders. Later on, pot or helmet masks started to appear. The Pueblo also have masks shaped from soft hoods of the type known among the Apache and Navajo.

The masks of the Pueblo are painted and appear in many variants, but in principle they may be divided into a few groups. The first group consists of symbolical masks lacking a real face. An

Fig. 41
A helmet mask made of papier-mâché, used at a 'devil dance' in the town of Yare in Venezuela. Dated 1970s.

Fig. 42
A master of ceremonies clad in a skin of a leopard whom he embodied at the ceremony. Aztec culture, dated AD 1300—1500.

masks is different. The women usually wear female dresses, sometimes with a hairstyle typical of girls of marriageable age. Face masks also appear.

The masks are kept in the *kiva*, along with other ceremonial objects. The highest esteem is enjoyed by those which have been the property of the clan for several generations. Those are kept with particular care in ceramic vessels, may be put on and off exclusively with the left hand, are 'fed' and even the paint, which is rubbed off from their surface before they are painted anew, is credited with supernatural powers. The old masks are worn only by the dignitaries of the clan who do not dance but who are partners of the maskless *kachina* priests at the ceremonies. The latter talk to the masks on behalf of the inhabitants of the village during the ceremony.

MEXICO AND CENTRAL AMERICA

The tradition of masks is very old in this region, masks appearing along with the earliest archaeological finds (Fig. 37). Most of the masks so far discovered during archaeological excavations are of a funeral character, such as the stone masks from Teotihuacan, the Maya masks (Fig. 38), those of the Olmec, or metal and ceramic masks from Ecuador and Peru. The ceramic figures from Mexico, wearing richly decorated masks, suggest yet another purpose of the masks, which was probably their ceremonial use (Figs. 39, 40).

The first written information on masks in this area originated as late as the sixteenth century and was recorded by Spanish chroniclers. They mention animal-head masks, notably decorated with feathers and precious stones, wooden masks the faces of which were covered with various gems and strips of gold, etc. Aztec poetry also mentions masks in the context of rituals (Fig. 42).

Centuries-long co-existence with the culture of Europe brought about many changes in America. Wooden masks were no longer decorated with mosaics made of gold and precious stones, the decoration being replaced by mere painting. In accordance with the Christian creed, funeral masks ceased to be made, but the new religion did not refute masks at festive cel-

example of this kind is the Hopi *kachina hemis (niman)*, decorated with painted symbols of budding corn, maize, sun, rain-clouds and a rainbow. In the 'Crow Mother' mask, the face is formed by one triangle or two placed one above the other. There is also the mask of the sun, rainbow, etc. (Fig. 36).

The *kachina* may also be in the likeness of human faces, but these are used as accompanying masks, for instance those of hunters, Navajo girls, girl-warriors or Hopi grandmothers. Most common are animal masks, the most powerful among them belonging to a bear, with healing abilities. Others represent quadrupeds and birds, every animal being personified by a different mask.

A significant role in the symbolism of the Pueblo masks is played by eagle feathers, particularly effective when entreaties are to be made to the spirits. On the other hand, sheep horns, stag antlers and a fox tail signify wisdom. Colours are also of symbolic significance; the same types of *kachina* exist in several colours corresponding to the painting of the body. A wrap-round ceremonial skirt and sometimes also a cloak are further parts of the mask. Almost every mask is supplemented with a rattle held in the hand and others are often fastened to the feet.

The costume belonging to female

66 'Fariseo' mask for Easter plays, helmet-shaped and made of untanned skin. Yaki, Mexico; now in Náprstek Museum, Prague. Height 27 cm.

ebrations, making them part of religious festivities, just as they were used to some extent in Europe too. For this reason it is very difficult, and in most cases impossible, to draw a dividing line between the original American culture and the beginning of European influences.

Nevertheless, the masks worn at the *venado* (stag) dance by the Mayo and Yaki peoples of northern Mexico, or those used at the *chokela* dance or ceremony in Bolivia's uplands are considered to be of American provenance. Both of these dances or ceremonies are participated in by men wearing animal masks (the stag in northern Mexico, and the vicuña in Bolivia) as well as by one or more masked clowns. The dancers use small face masks, mostly black in colour, portraying human or goat faces. The stag mask only appears in the second part of the dance. This is a dried stag-head attached to the dancer's head which is covered with a scarf up to the eyes. The chests of all the dancers are naked and they hold rattles in their hands. A characteristic supplement of the costume is rattles made of dry butterfly cocoons which are sewn on to laces wound around the calves. When the dance is serious in mood, clowns called Paskolas dance with the stag-mask on, but as soon as it changes to a clown scene, every dancer pushes the mask back from his face.

Similar in form is a dance of the Bolivian Ayamara, at which a dancer personifying a vicuña dances carrying a stuffed animal and the masked clowns pretend to hunt it. Their masks are made of fur, with

99

holes for the eyes, and the top of the head and the nape of the neck covered with fur hoods. The ordinary clothes of the clowns are decorated with tufts of dyed llama hair.

The agricultural populations of Central and South America worshipped the masks of spirits and local deities in order to secure sufficient rain for their fields. The Spanish conquistadores knew of rain rituals from their home country, which is why they so easily found patrons for the Indian rituals among the Christian saints. The masks of the spirits were provided with horns, thus being turned into the masks of devils who had a place in the Christian tradition, for example at the processions taking place on Corpus Christi Day. Complicated masks of devils with many animal attributes are to be found among the Nahua in central Mexico (Plate 73), and further devil masks in Guatemala and Panama, the Caribbean Islands, the town of Yare in Venezuela (Fig. 42) or Oruro in Bolivia.

67　A dance mask of wood, with glass eyes and painted. Mexico; now in Náprstek Museum, Prague. Height 19 cm.

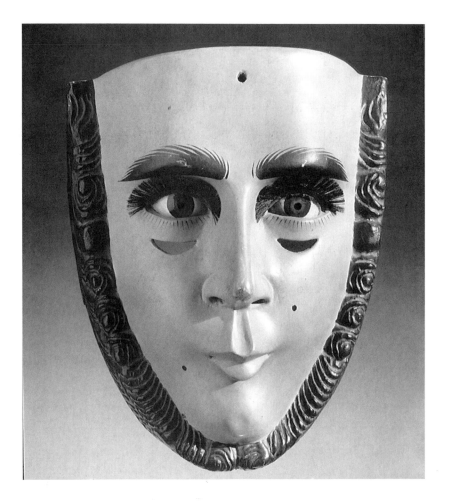

The animal masks used at rain ceremonies mostly represented animals which are in some way connected with water. Dances of alligators, fish, serpents and other animals are particularly well known in Mexico. Some of the masks used at these dances were made in pairs, for instance those of armadillos. For the individual dances new types of masks were even created, such as those of water nymphs, portraying the entire figure, or face masks bearing the features of different faces. Heavy helmet masks with headpieces were also used, up to 2 m in height, but only at the beginning of the ceremonies. Afterwards the mask was placed in the centre and the dancers danced around it. At a serpent dance in Michoacán, a snake head-mask may be found, attached in an unusual way at the back over the dancer's waist. Masks are also sometimes supplemented with wooden animal figures which are attached to the dancer's waist.

The largest number of masks were used in Mexico at Christmas, at the so-called animal or bat dances, when animals came to venerate the Infant Jesus. The dance was led by a dancer wearing the mask of a bat, who is considered here to be the lord of the animals, due both to its relationship with the supernatural forces of the night and because it lives in caves which are the seat of waters — Mexican farmers are very dependent on water. However, not only animal masks are used at rain rituals. The most beautiful of all the masks worn at these ceremonies are those portraying bearded faces of a European type with a pink complexion and blue eyes, and perfect in craftsmanship. These are symbols of water.

Masks are also used at dance plays which relate a story. One of them in Mexico is a dramatic scene representing a cougar hunt. The play has many variants and titles (*Tlacololero, Tecuani, El Tigre, El Doctor*) and its characters differ according to local custom. Only the roles played by the hunter, the cougar (called El Tigre) and the hunter's dog are unchanging, whose representatives almost always wear masks (Plate 72). Masks of forest animals, particularly stags, and villagers also often occur.

The 'Old Men' dance (*Viejitos, Huehuenches*) is also considered to be Mexican in origin. This dance originated in Mi-

68　A helmet-shaped dance mask of painted wood with leather ears, hart antlers and a hart's hooves. Nahua, Mexico; now in Náprstek Museum, Prague. Height 85 cm.

choacán and is the only one at which all participants are masked. The masks represent old men's wrinkled faces with toothless mouths and are supplemented with a stick topped by a little carved human head.

After the Spanish conquest, some dramatic Spanish scenes were brought to America, especialy *The Christians and the Moors*, a performance celebrating the final victory of the Spanish over the Moors. It is usually the main characters who wear masks at these dances, namely St James, Pilate and Cain, besides the anonymous leaders of both parties. In the area of the Nahua masks such as the red 'Moro Chino' mask and that of the 'Suffering Moor', provided with a large hooked nose (Plate 49), are used.

At *Dances of the Conquista*, masked

69 The mask of a spirit, made of tree bark painted with white clay. Yaghan, Argentine; now in Museum of the American Indians, Heye Foundation. Height 61 cm.

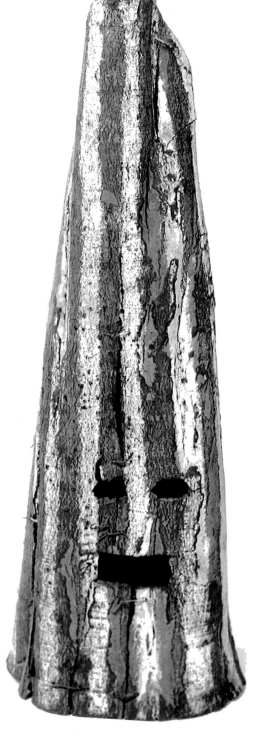

Fig. 43
A mask or masking costume from Jamaica, called in English 'Jack in Green', one of the main characters of the New Year carnival. Dated from the eighteenth century.

dancers usually represent Cortés and his Indian lady-love Malinche (in Mexico), or Pedro de Alvarado (in Guatemala, Plates 50 and 75), and their Indian adversaries Montezuma and Tecum Uman (Plates 60 and 61), or other Indian chieftains not defined in a more exact way. The representatives of these characters are

usually masked, which is always the case with the dancer representing Malinche, maybe because the role of a woman is played here by a man. In the Nahua region two-faced masks, representing both Cortés and Malinche, may also be found.

Dances, or rather dramatic scenes, about Cortés and Malinche were originally performed on horseback. This kind of performance is now rather exceptional (e.g. among the Zogie in Chiapas). However, the use of small wooden or papier-mâché horses is frequent, with either the riders 'mounted', or the horse's head and the neck attached in front of the dancer's dress, the point where it is fastened being covered with a poncho. A variant of this dance is also known from the northern and central Chile where small wooden horses are used (Plates 62 and 63).

In terms of form, the *Dances of the Conquista* may also be classed with scenes enacted in the Puebla state, depicting the victorious battle of the Mexicans against the French army of the Emperor Maximilian. Used in these are face masks of Mexican generals and soldiers as well as those of simple villagers; on the opposing side masks of colonial soldiers, the *zouaves*, are favoured.

In Latin America masks are connected with celebrations of Christian holidays. The largest number are used at Christmas plays called *Pastorelas*, which begin on 23 December with the adoration (Plates 64 and 65), but are mainly concentrated around Epiphany. Many masked figures, differing in individual regions, perform at these. The central characters are the Three Wise Men from the East, whose face masks are carved together with crowns. Further characters appearing in masks are Angels, Shepherds, Devil, Hermit, Gardener, Death, Lucifer, and others. In the state of Guerrero, the *Dance of Three Forces* (*Danza de las Tres Potencias*) is performed, at which dancers wearing the masks of the Death, Devil, Belief, Christ and the Virgin, Sin and Soul appear. The subject of these dances is the battle of good and evil powers for the soul.

The dance cycle is also participated in by people of African descent; in actual fact, they are part of the Black King's (Melchior's) train, but their dances have become completely independent and are also performed on other festive occasions

70 A dance mask of fired clay. Mexico; now in a private collection in Prague. Height 13 cm.

during the year. They are danced either in masks or merely with blackened faces.

Carnival processions form another opportunity for the use of masks. The most frequently occurring carnival masks are the face masks of Death at various executions, the Devil and animal masks.

Easter plays usually include representations of Calvary and Christ's crucifixion. In most of the places where these plays are performed, either no masks are used or they are only worn by the centurions who arrest Christ. Some of the oldest extant masks of Mexico belong to this type. Among the Mayo and Yaki in northern Mexico, it is masked men called 'Fariseos' or 'Judas' who pursue and capture Christ. Their masks are usually white and provided with horns, ears and long noses. A more recent wooden pig's snout is added to untanned skin (Plate 66) or the

bald area of the mask is decorated with painted ornaments.

In the 1930s, the custom of 'burning Judas' took root in Mexico. Judas is represented by a figurine of above life-size, made of inflammable materials. The face of the figurine is covered with a mask which may represent not only Judas, but also the Devil, death, a well-known politician or a film-actor. Men wearing masks of devils and various monsters walk around on Maundy Thursday, after which they 'hang' Judas in a place where he can be burned on Holy Saturday.

In late spring, festivals of the May Cross and Corpus Christi are celebrated with processions, again participated in by masked dancers, especially devils whose tradition goes back to medieval Spain (Plates 74 and 76). In some places, such as the small town of Yare in Venezuela,

103

Corpus Christi is among the most important festive days of the year. Then devils clad in red costumes and wearing helmet masks made of papier-mâché appear (Fig. 41). In Chiapas in Mexico the mountain spirit Kalalá, wearing a stag mask, dances at this festival. His company consists of 'tigers' in yellow spotted masking costumes, with masks attached to the top of the head.

Throughout the year the holy days of local saints and patrons of the church are celebrated. To honour the saints, dances are organised, characterised as 'Dances before the Saint', many of which are performed in masks (*La Ofrenda, La Palma, El Parachico*, etc.). Dances of this type, typical of which is their simple choreo-

graphy, are found all over Latin America. The masks used are often made of wax or papier-mâché, representing faces of European men, and sometimes provided with glass eyes (Plate 67). There are also old masks made of leather. The best-executed masks are covered with the so-called Spanish white paint (blanco de España), under a coloured surface (Plate 68). Some masks are first pasted with a thinly woven cloth of a natural colour, over which a layer of the Spanish white paint is applied. Only then are they painted.

Other materials may also be used for making the masks (Fig. 43). For instance, in Mochitlan in Mexico masks were made from the pelvic bone of a large animal. Exceptional are stone or clay masks (Plate 70), serving rather as matrices for moulding masks made of leather (Plate 77), wax or papier-mâché. The use of masks made of metal or wire-netting is also rare.

Helmet or face masks made of fur are known to be extant among some peoples, such as the Mapuche of southern Chile. Masks were also to be found made from gourds (Plate 78) and cloth.

SOUTH AMERICA

Masks were, or still are, common in some areas of South America. These are ritual masks, but some intended for hunting purposes may also be found. The ritual masks of spirits were mentioned in the early reports of missionaries. These masks are among the oldest exhibits of museums, e.g. in Coimbra, Portugal, where masks from the eighteenth century are kept.

The main area in which masks are made and used is south of the Amazon in central Ecuador and north of the Amazon basin in north-western Brazil and eastern Colombia. We shall also group with them masks from the southernmost region of South America, those of the peoples inhabiting Tierra del Fuego.

Masks are used at ceremonies connected with the initiation of boys and girls, those held in honour of ancestors, rites of fertility, and funeral rites. They mostly represent ancestors, often in animal form, since, according to myths, certain animals are considered to be the forefathers of some peoples. Various monsters are also

71 The mask of a giant, made of calabashes and bark cloth. Kobéua, Brazil; now in Museum für Völkerkunde, Berlin. Height 33 cm.

104

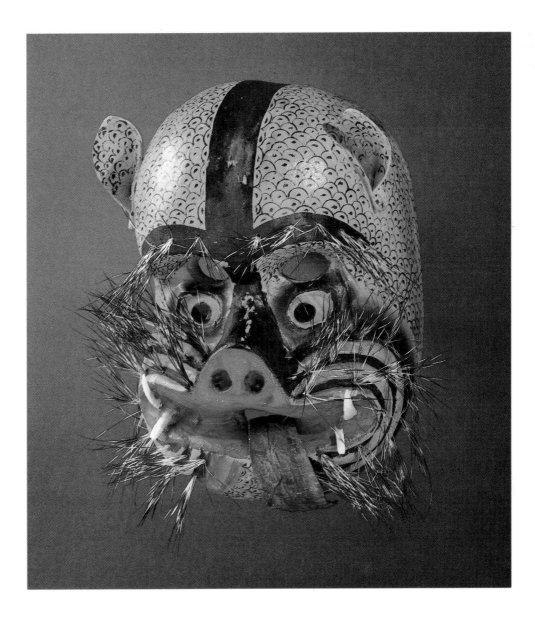

72   Mask worn in tiger plays, made of
painted wood. Oaxaca, Mexico; now in
Náprstek Museum, Prague. Height 26 cm.

73 Mask used at the
'Diablo Macho' dance, made
of painted wood. Nahua,
Mexico; now in Náprstek
Museum, Prague. Height
71 cm.

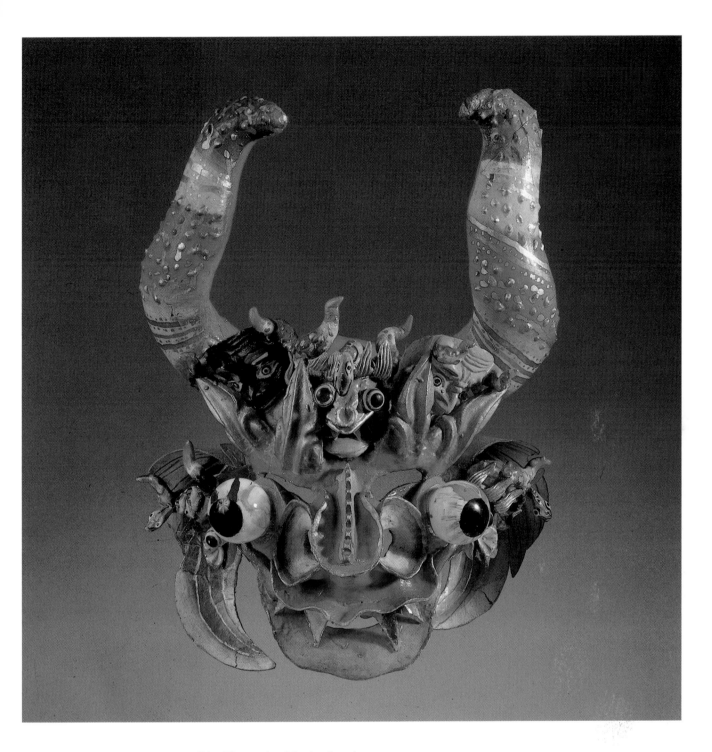

74   The mask of the leading dancer at
a devils' dance, made of textile, plaster
and paste-board and painted. Bolivia; now
in Náprstek Museum, Prague. Height 57 cm.

75 Mask of a Spaniard for the dance *La
Conquista*, made of painted wood.
Guatemala; now in Náprstek Museum,
Prague. Height 19 cm.

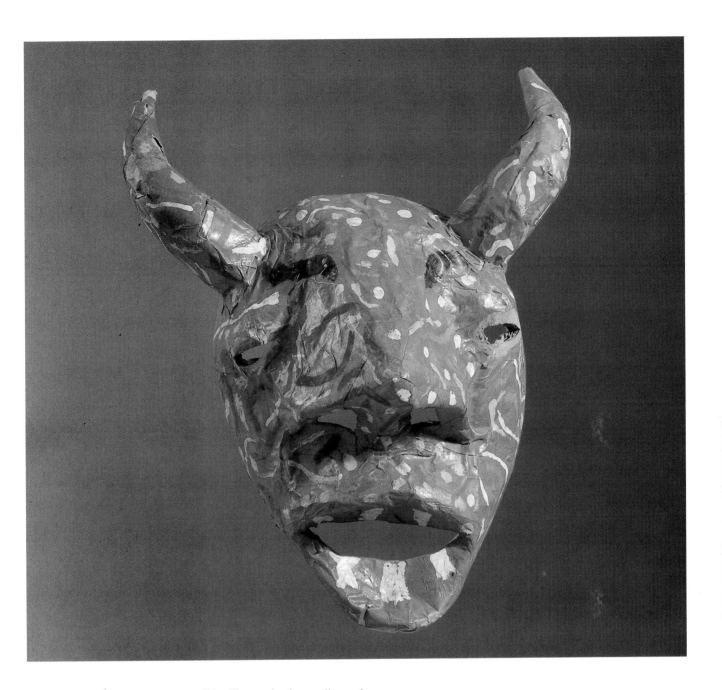

76 The mask of an ordinary dancer at
a devils' dance, made of painted
papier-mâché. Bolivia; now in Náprstek
Museum, Prague. Height 26 cm.

77   A dance mask of painted leather.
Mexico; now in Náprstek Museum, Prague.
Height 23 cm.

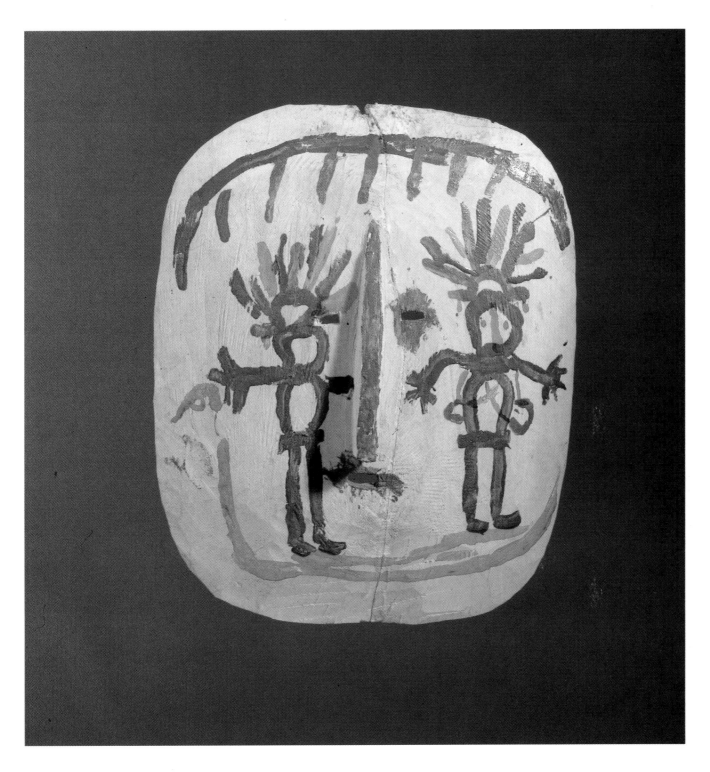

78   A wooden mask with decoration
derived from the painting of the face.
Huichol, Mexico; now in Náprstek Museum,
Prague. Height 25 cm.

111

79　A bark cloth mask, covered with a layer of resin with yellow and white decoration. Central Brazil; now in Náprstek Museum, Prague. Height 33 cm.

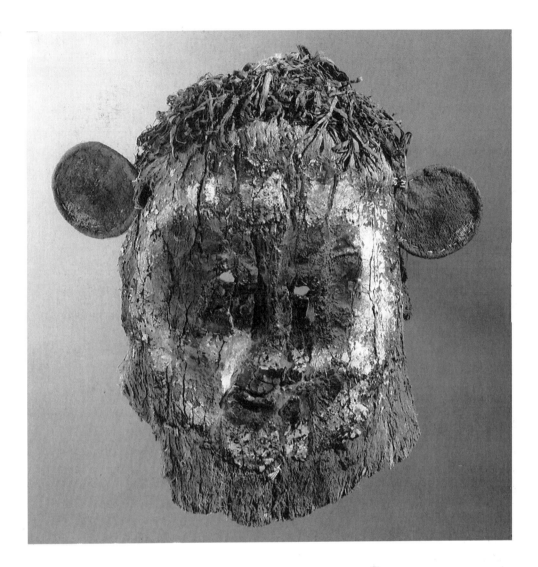

Fig. 44
Masked dancers wearing
apparel made of bark cloth,
which also covers the head,
with a painted wooden
superstructure. Worn by the
Opaina of eastern Colombia at
the end of the nineteenth
century.

personified, their likeness depending on
the imagination of their makers (e.g.
masks for rituals at girls' puberty among
the Tucuna), or being exactly defined by
tradition. Masks of the spirits of nature
are used, too, for example that of the
spirit of storm (Tucuna), demons, wood
giants (Plate 71) and goblins (Kobéua).

Masked dancers personifying the ancestors' spirits also control the proper
execution of funeral rites. This is because
the spirits of the dead are powerful and
feared and they might harm people if all
the components of the funeral were not
performed in the right way. One of the
functions of the masked men among the
Tucuna was to regulate the activities of
a dead man's spirit and to make him leave
his house. By taking part in a funeral, the
spirits of the ancestors, mythical beings,
animals and wood monsters proclaim
their kinship with the dead man and thus

also with the other members of the community. Among some peoples the masks
were burned after the funeral rites were
over.

Spirits also appear at a ritual the purpose
of which is to secure plentiful crops and
game and the fertility of women. These
spirits are venerated at ceremonies aimed
at winning their favour and help for the
sake of the prosperity of the entire group.
The times of these ceremonies and rituals
differ from tribe to tribe, but the types of
dances and masks are generally the same
everywhere. Although the masked dances
are performed almost exclusively by men,
girls and young women also wear masks at
a ritual celebrating girls' puberty among
the Tucuna. The masks, only a small number of which consist of female ones, personify fantastic animals and demons as
created individually by their wearers.
They are sometimes as many as 50 in

113

81 Mask of the sun demon, made of wood painted black. Kágaba, Colombia; now in Museum für Völkerkunde, Berlin. Height 17 cm.

number and are marshalled in a sacred corner of the forest. From there they come in groups to the host's house, where they dance, afterwards being offered a feast. Because of the individual manner of portraying the supernatural beings, these masks may sometimes be classified according to their songs rather than their forms. After the ritual, the dancers take their masks off (they are not sacred), piling them around the initiated girl, along with their apparel. At this moment both the masks and the costumes are the property of the host, but they are not preserved, being thrown away after the ceremony is finished.

Masks may also appear on other festive occasions. For instance, all peoples celebrate the completion of the roof construction of a new house, this celebration being connected with a performance of masks among the Wittoto. The harvest of

some kinds of fruit offers an opportunity to celebrate and to hold masked dances, as is the case among the Bora and Muenane, where the festivities are performed by men.

Some masks, especially those of the ancestors, are preserved for further use. In the Xingú River basin, special houses are built for them, called 'flute houses'; in other areas, masks of the entire community are kept hanging in the central part of a large dwelling house.

By their dances in masks, the Indians of Tierra del Fuego personify spirits who are expected to frighten women so that they might obey men and remain subordinate to them. There is a legend that, formerly, the women were the rulers and wore masks to frighten men and keep them in bondage. The manly dances performed in masks, at which the dancers frighten and beat the women, make sure that the situation will never again be turned in favour of the women.

In all of these areas, the use of masks and masking costumes alternates with applying paints to the face and the entire body. Both of these customs are combined by the tribes of Tierra del Fuego, among whom cone-shaped masks made of bark or skin are worn on the head, whereas the body is painted with stripes directly mimicking the mask's decoration.

Masks are ordered to be made by the village shaman or chieftain. The men used to make the masks for themselves, either in the ceremonial houses or in such places where women could not observe them. Besides masks and costumes, among some peoples (such as the Kana) supplements in the form of animals were used, made of the same material as the costume. These supplements were held in the hands during the dance, or attached to the heads as headpieces. Individual masks are connected with certain melodies, or else accompanying instruments are prescribed.

There are wooden masks of two types: headpieces and face masks. Headpieces were worn by the male members of the Opaina in eastern Colombia, at the beginning of the present century. This is a hollow cylinder set on the upper part of the head, the dancer's face and the remaining part of the head being covered with bark cloth. The ears are replaced by thin, flat plates. The entire mask is painted. There is a hole at the back of the upper

82 Mask of the sun demon, made of wood painted brown with feathers. Chiriguano, Bolivia; now in Museum für Völkerkunde, Berlin. Height 21 cm.

part of the mask, through which the end of the bark cloth covering the dancer's face is passed. Bark cloth forms a sort of straight robe falling to the knees. The decoration on the headpiece consists of simple painted geometric ornaments, except for the 'face' which is placed in a circle on the headpiece (Fig. 44).

Wooden face masks are used by the peoples inhabiting the central area of Brazil (the Auetö, Kamayura, Menihakú and Bakairi). Their masks are more or less square, with a massive forehead, as well as a nose protruding strikingly from the remaining surface of the face. Some masks, for instance those worn at the fish dance among the Kamayura, have 'faces' which are only suggested by a design with the motif of a net, without any eyes or mouth. In other masks, the mouth is replaced by a glued-on piece of piranha jaw or shell. A fringed hood made of palm leaves is

attached to the mask, and further fringes attached to the bottom edge of the mask hide the dancer from the front.

In central Brazil basketwork masks have been documented (Plate 79). These are made for the fish dance by the Kamayura. The basketwork is stretched over a framework and the surface of the mask is decorated in the same way as a wooden mask. Basketwork and cylindrical head-pieces decorated with feathers are known among the Karajá. A flat semicircular basketwork mask covered with a feather mosaic and representing a face originated among the Tapirapé. This is the 'Cara Grande', personifying a spirit.

In north-eastern Brazil and eastern Colombia, among the Kobéua, Yuri, Kana, Tucuna and some other peoples, bark cloth is used for making masks (Plate 80). There are two basic types of bark cloth masks — painted ones and modelled ones. The Kobéua make their masks as a whole, together with a costume in the form of a conical case, the wide bottom border of which is provided with a skirt made of bark fringes. The top of the head is usually surmounted by a headpiece made of bark cloth and feathers, and the arms of the dancer are clothed in long sleeves made separately of bark cloth. The sleeves are not painted, but are decorated with fringes. In the masks of anthropomorphic demons a human face is suggested, the animal masks being faceless and painted in patterns which are symbols of certain animals (e.g. rings of the jaguar). The mask of a caterpillar, however, is provided with a small human face placed on the headpiece, the body being decorated with oblique stripes.

The members of the Tucuna modelled their animal masks in clay spread on bark cloth stretched over a framework of rods. These are animal heads, the eyes of which are sometimes painted and sometimes made of metal sheets or mirror shreds, the open muzzle being fitted with animal or tin teeth.

To some masks made of bark cloth, a face carved from a gourd is attached, as is the case with the masks representing giants of the Kobéua people.

On the eastern slopes of the Andes (Plates 81 and 82), wooden face masks are made, the features of which show a human character and reveal European influence.

115

India

The significance of masks in the ancient cultures of the Indian sub-continent have received little attention to date. The archaeological find of a mask in Kalibangan in Rajasthan, one of the sites of the Harappa culture, bears testimony to the fact that their history goes back to the third millennium BC and is as old as this great civilisation itself. The sum of scattered information on the development of mask-making justifies the assumption that masks were a distinctive and varied creation in India. Even nowadays, when the traditional domestic culture is increasingly being pushed into the background by modern civilisation, this creation is maintained all over the Indian sub-continent, upholding old conventions, developing the local people's craftsmanship and artistry, and utilising domestic materials in a witty and ingenious way.

The variety seen in mask-making was considerably enhanced by the varied ethnic structure of the sub-continent's inhabitants, consisting of Indo-European and Dravidian peoples as well as numerous aboriginal tribes, all with different religio-social systems. Hinduism and the religious beliefs of the individual tribes seem to have been of the utmost importance in the creation of masks, as was the ritual practice of Tantric Buddhism, followed in the northern high mountain area. Islam has never been favourably disposed to this art, since, according to the Koran, the orthodox Muslim was never allowed to change the form given to him by Allah in any way.

In terms of typology, the masks made before the present day are predominantly dance or theatre masks of the face type. Helmet masks, helmets and other dance head-dresses, as well as figurines (Plate 90), are much less widespread, their use rather depending on local cus-

tom. Some masks have retained their original cult or ritual character, but others have lost this, becoming a tool of general entertainment. Archaic forms of performances in masks have survived, for example in the exorcist and cult dances connected with the worship of local guardian deities, spirits of nature, ancestors' spirits and demons, and also in the ritual dance dramas held at large temples, pilgrim centres or local village shrines.

More frequent, however, is the use of masks in both classical and folk dance dramas, performed on the occasion of numerous religious festivals. The main purpose of these plays is to entertain the spectators, and during these humorous and satirical scenes or masquerades are performed in masks. Their subjects, mostly taken from mythology, are generally known. Their main source is the classical epics of India, *Mahabharata* and *Ramayana*, especially the episedes depicting fights and battles, for example the struggle of the hero Rama to liberate his wife Sita who was abducted by the demon king Ravana, and various legends to be found in the mythological collections called *puranas*. Among the latter legends about the miraculous deeds of Krishna are much favoured, as are the fights of the goddess Kali against demons, and the fourth incarnation of the god Vishnu as Narasinha in a form of half-man and half-lion. Also among the main subjects must be ranked the myths of many village guardian deities, both Hindu and tribal, connected with the age-old cults of fertility and animism.

The majority of the dances and dance dramas are performed once a year in the open spaces in front of temples and shrines, sometimes even within the temples, and are connected with the festivals of the annual cycle. The performances are staged before work begins in the fields, in

116

83 The god Ganesha's ceremonial dance mask, made of layered painted paper covered with transparent varnish. Orissa, India; now in Náprstek Museum, Prague. Height 39.5 cm.

the dry season preceding the monsoon, and after the harvest. They usually start around nine o'clock in the evening, lasting until dawn, and may be continued over several successive nights. Some of them are also performed in the streets at important village markets and fairs. Every performance is accompanied by music, the main and sometimes the only instrument of which is the drum. Besides the dancers, a significant part is played by the narrator and the chorus, who introduce the individual pantomimic scenes with the recital of the respective myths.

Both the makers and the wearers of masks are bound by several taboos as far as performances of a ritual character are concerned. Usually they are not allowed to eat certain foods, drink spirits, have sexual intercourse, etc. In some places, the masks are believed to be endowed with a spirit of their own, which might harm people, and therefore they are offered sacrifices. The masks are preserved at a sacred place near the temple or shrine, or are destroyed immediately after the performance.

The making of masks is exacting seasonal work demanding the efforts of a considerable number of qualified and gifted individuals. These people mostly belong to craftsmen's groups and castes, such as carpenters, potters, painters and producers of votive objects and traditional ornaments. These craftsmen have inherited their profession from their ancestors. The masks are often excellent, being modelled along the lines of long-

84 Rakshasa, a demon of the *Ramayana.* Mask of the dance drama *Ramlila*, made of cloth on a stiff paper base, silver tinsel, textile appliqué, sewn-on glass beads, bullions and pailletes, by the so-called *zari* technique; beard made of strings and cotton yarn. Varanasi, Uttarpradesh, India; now in Náprstek Museum, Prague. Height 36 cm.

established schemes and painted in various colours according to appropriate iconographic rules. In terms of the schemes common to a family or workshop, or even to an entire area, the masks may be divided into independent groups characterised not only by uniform workmanship but also by uniform principles of style.

The masks incorporate archaic forms which evolved centuries ago with the predecessors of the present-day makers and testify to the history of local culture and art, sometimes in a more eloquent way than an individual piece would. They are made for sale, but the radius of their demand does not usually pass beyond the area of a few neighbouring villages. An independent group of mask producers may be seen in the village priests of south India, who are generally also the performers of rites and ritual dancers. They usually make masks and other dance requisites only for themselves and their attendants. Their work is also subject to established local practices and iconographic traditions.

As a form of an individual or free artistic creativity masks are found in the Indian sub-continent, but only among the aboriginal peoples. These include masks used for general entertainment, or ritual masks without a strict formal appearance, the artistic execution of which depends on the talent and skill of the tribal artist. The result is, of course, a sum of products diverse in style, varied in form and of different levels of workmanship.

To make all of these masks, various natural or easily accessible materials are used. The fundamental material is wood. Preference is given to a wood which is light in weight and easy to carve. The carver traditionally uses an axe and a knife, holding the piece of wood in place with his feet. In recent times various kinds of chisels have also been used. Another common procedure is the modelling of masks from paper which is laid in layers upon a clay-mould and glued together. Before it is painted, the surface of the mask must be hardened and carefully finished. This is done by means of a piece of thin, well-washed cloth which is laid upon the mask and covered with a layer of fine potter's clay mixed with water. The clay is carefully spread over the surface in order to smooth out tiny defects and the mask is painted after the clay has dried. Both wooden and paper masks are usually painted in vivid colours. The colours are chosen in accordance with their traditional symbolic significance. Natural pigments were originally used, both mineral and vegetable, but these are now frequently replaced by powdered pigments or even synthetic paints. The design is usually executed in rich, bright and intentionally contrasting colours and then covered with transparent varnish, which protects the paint and makes it more vivid. Other materials such as textiles, metal, wicker, gourds and other natural raw substances are not as popular as wood and paper. They occur locally and their employment in making dance masks is interesting and sometimes entirely original.

Irrespective of the materials used, the representation of masks in the individual performances varies. Their number is between a single mask, for instance at some cult dances, and several dozens of masks performing in showy dramas or masquer-ades. Fully masked performances are un-doubtedly fewer in number than those in which masked actors alternate with others wearing only make-up. The make-up may be either quite simple and entirely unlike the masks, the dancer's face being covered with ochre clay or chalk paste, or it may closely resemble a mask. In an in-teresting and choreographically attractive way, this combination is used in some south Indian dance dramas. A complicat-ed and exacting make-up is worn here which resembles the painted design of the masks, and, equally with the masks, acts as an identification of the iconographic significance of the respective character.

This is not the common rule, however, since the same significance may also be borne by the dance costume and especial-

85   Mask of Ganesha with a Shivaist trident carved in relief on the forehead and the sacred syllable 'om' at the top of the trunk, made of wood stained dark brown and oiled, decorated with white dots. Nepal; now in a private collection in Prague. Height 65 cm.

119

ly by various head decorations such as diadems and crowns, as well as by objects held in the actor's hand. This conception of masking is current in various regions of India, but nowhere has it such a fanciful form as in south India.

Local tradition determines which characters are to wear a mask and which are to remain unmasked. Masks are usually worn by the actors representing the local guardian deities and standard Hindu gods of theriomorphic forms, the terrible aspects of which are expected to arouse awe in people and fear in the evil forces. Their group includes various village gods and godesses, spirits of nature, ancestors' spirits and deified heroes. Among the Hindu gods, these are the black goddess Kali, Narasinha, and the five-headed creator Brahma, besides the ape Hanuman, who was a devoted helper of the hero Rama, and the elephant-headed and dwarf-bodied god Ganesha who is believed to be able to remove all obstacles in life.

Ganesha's mask is perhaps most frequent, because a dancer wearing it begins every theatrical performance all over In-

dia. His introductory dance, combined with an offering to Ganesha (Plates 83 and 85), is expected to ensure the success of every performance.

A number of demons also appear among the characters performing in masks. They are sometimes reminiscent of the masks of fearsome guardian deities and are therefore occasionally mistaken for them, although entirely different in function.

In the northern plains of India, masks are used especially in the religious plays inspired by the Bhakti movement, whose idea of devoted love *(bhakti)* as the only right way to God gave considerable emotional support to the local Hindu inhabitants facing the expansion of Islam in the Middle Ages, and later also during British colonial rule. The plays, called *lila*, deal with the life and miraculous deeds of the main deities of this movement. These are Krishna and the deified hero Rama who was declared to be an incarnation of the god Vishnu; the plays are still enacted today during autumn festivals in villages and cities (Plates 84, 87, 88, 89, 92, 97,

Fig. 45
A *beta* spirit, guardian against death as a mask of the Mahakali Pyakhan dance ceremony in Nepal. Height *c.* 35 cm.

120

86 Mahakala, king of the kingdom of the dead. Note the third eye on the forehead. Nepal; now in a private collection in Prague. Height 37 cm.

102 and 105). Their village form is more modest, but in the cities of Ayodhya, Chitrakut, Vrindavan, Allahabad (Plates 87 and 88), Mathura or Varanasi (formerly Benares), they have developed into an elaborate show performed in front of thousands of spectators in the streets.

Particularly remarkable, in terms of their use of masks, are the *Ramlila* dramas organised in the sacred pilgrim centre of Varanasi and nearby Ramnagar. They are conceived as a series of individual scenes accompanied by music, rather than real dance dramas. The *Ramlila* lasts for 31 nights, is staged in a different place every night, and culminates with Rama's victory over Ravana and his army. Side by

side with made-up characters, those wearing two interesting types of face masks appear. These are metal masks and masks made of textiles. This differentiation of the masks serves not only to identify the represented beings, but also their outer characterisation.

The 'good' characters such as the goddess Durga, who is Rama's patron, and his friends, the ape Hanuman and his army of monkeys, wear masks which are chiselled from sheets of brass. Each of these masks consists of a facial part and a crown richly decorated with engraved and embossed ornaments. They are relatively wide and shallow, their faces being modelled in an economical way, except

121

that in some places certain details are emphasised with white, red or black paint. The masks of the 'evil' characters, i.e. the demons headed by Ravana and his retinue, are usually made of cloth stretched over a solid base. The masks have eye-holes cut through, and the other parts of the face and the ornamental elements are embroidered with gold and silver tinsel and metal threads combined with paillettes (decorative spangles) in the *zari* technique of embroidery (Plate 84). There is no hole for the mouth, and the actor must therefore lift the mask with his hand to uncover his mouth while talking.

In the mountainous areas of northern India and neighbouring Nepal and Bhutan, masks occur in large numbers (Plates 85, 86, 91, 100 and 101). Hinduism is dominated here by the ancient Tantric Buddhism and a strong influence is also exerted by the cults of the local Tibeto-Burmese peoples as well as Tibetan Lamaism.

The traditional material used by the local mask-makers was wood from the mountain forests. Carving has thus developed to a high level here. The masks are usually carved in high relief from a single piece of wood and their style and features are defined, on the one hand, by the ethnic origin of the majority of the people of the Tibeto-Burmese group, and, on the other, by outside contacts, especially with the Tibetans and Chinese. Thanks to the favourable climate of the high mountains, masks made in the sixteenth century, if not earlier, have been preserved. They are characterised by differing styles of painting, in some cases complemented with gilding; they may also be stained with plant juices and saturated with oil (Plate 85). The painted decoration of the masks made at later times is usually expressive, more recent and contemporary products being painted with rich pigments or even synthetic paints. Another material used frequently in recent times is papier-mâché, and occasionally also felt and textiles.

The most frequently reproduced masks of this area are those used at lamas' dances (Plate 91), performed annually at religious festivals in the courts of Lamaistic

87 Jatayu. A bird mask of the dance drama *Ramlila*, made of painted lacquered paper. Allahabad, Uttarpradesh, India; now in a private collection in Prague. Height 30 cm.

122

88 Animal masks of the dance drama *Ramlila* (from left to right): Sugriva, tiger, bear, Jatayu, and Hanuman; made of painted lacquered paper. Allahabad, Uttarpradesh, India; now in a private collection in Prague. Height c. 30—40 cm.

monasteries. On these occasions, as well as at the majority of dances and dance dramas of other types, masks of the 'protective-horror' type are used. Their purpose is to secure happiness and material prosperity for the inhabitants and to protect them against evil forces and illnesses. Dances are performed in masks which take the form of stylised skulls. These skeleton dances effectively represent the world of the dead (Plate 86).

Much favoured are dances honouring animals, especially among the Buddhist peoples of the Monpa, Sherdukpen and Khamba communities, who live in the northern part of Assam. Here there are yak and peacock dances, a cow dance, a horse dance and a stag dance. In accordance with the compassionate attitude of the Buddhists towards animals, these dances contain a moralistic and didactic message, and conclude with a lesson on the necessity of protecting animals.

The Monpa and the Sherdukpen are

excellent carvers and their masks are mostly made of wood. The Sherdukpen also use felt for some of their masks, decorating the felt with applications of colourful materials and cowrie shells and framing them with the hair of mountain goats. In the tribal culture of the Khamba, there are interesting masks which consist of yellow fabric stretched over a reed framework. These masks personify the demons who try to disturb Buddha's meditations.

The masks of the Nepalese dances, which worship goddesses and are called *Mahakali Pyakhan*, are a by-product of Hinduism. This dance is performed during the eight-day autumn festival which takes place in Kathmandu, the capital of Nepal. Its organisers are the Nepalese Newar. The Newar live mostly as farmers and the dance drama is meant to celebrate their patron, the goddess Durga, who is invoked in nine different aspects. Only three of these, however, are represented at the dance — Mahakali (Plate 101), Mahalakshmi and Kumari — all of them masked, as are the other characters, the lion and the tiger who are the mounts of the goddess, the demons Shumbha and Nishumbha against whom the goddess fights, spirits (*bhuta*) waiting upon Durga, etc.

The masks are made of layered paper, their bright paint being covered with transparent varnish or egg-white. These are face masks, with 'deer' eyes placed close to each other, which endow them with a naive, wondering expression (Fig. 45). The masks are attached to the head with a metal ring bearing a massive crown, up to 10 kg in weight, and made of metal with many-coloured paper ornaments and pendants. A striking decorative element of the crown is the flag-shaped fans hanging from rods inserted into the ring. The nape of the dancer's neck is covered with a veil in the fashion of Lamaistic masks, with a picture of the goddess attached to this. The masks are made by a few families belonging to the *chitrakar* caste of traditional painters. They live in Timi village in the vicinity of Bhaktapur.

Masks are also frequently used in the eastern Indian states of Bihar, Bengal, Orissa and Assam. This is obviously partly due to a considerable concentration of tribal peoples in this particular area (for instance of Dravidian, Munda and Tibeto-Burmese origins), and the influence exerted by these peoples upon the Indo-Arian culture of their neighbours. The main inspiration for the dances and dance dramas using masks were battles of gods and demons, mythical heroes and demons, and various groups of demons fighting against one another, as depicted in the local versions of classical Indian epics, mythological collections and local folk and tribe myths.

One of the oldest Bengali dance-dramatic genres performed in masks is thought to be the folk drama called *gambhira*, which, in a degenerated form, is preserved in the Maldah district of West Bengal. This drama consists of a series of solo dances about mythological subjects, the central figure being the goddess Kali who symbolises the vital energy (*shakti*) of her godly partner Shiva. The drama also contains a comic scene performed by two dancers wearing the masks of an old man and an old woman.

Accompanied by a single drum *(dhol)*

massive, heavy masks carved from wood and decorated in many colours are worn in all of the scenes. The masks of the gods are provided with strikingly emphasised features and their carving and painting concentrates on representing the main iconographic symbols; for example, Kali is characterised by her black colour, a long thrust-out tongue and a high ray-shaped crown decorated with a tuft; Shiva by a white face provided with a third eye on the forehead, and a knot of hair wound-up with snakes on the head. Typical of the demon masks are large pointed ears and a cock-crest-shaped ridge on their heads.

A peculiarity of all these masks is their painted decoration. This consists of tiny plant elements such as geometrical stylised rosettes, spirals and tendrils, symmetrically spread over the cheeks, forehead, temples and chin of the mask; in contrast with the massive size of the mask, they produce an unusually gentle effect.

Formerly the *gambhira* was performed at the spring solstice festival and was considered to be an effective offering, able to secure substantial rain and a good harvest for the villagers. Nowadays it is only danced in remote villages and its artistic level has declined. The dancers wear old battered masks, do not make new ones and are even said not to know how to make them any more.

An unusual natural material, called *sola* and taken from the *Aeschynomene indica* tree, is sometimes used at dances celebrating the goddess Kali. This material is worked by the members of the *malakar* caste, who carve it, using a special knife called a *kath*, into traditional decorations and jewels for the clay sculptures of Hindu deities, and wedding crowns for Bengali brides and bridegrooms. *Sola* is very fragile and can only be used once (Plate 93).

A similar purpose, as in *gambhira*, is served by the masks of the dance performance called *asura-vadha*, organised annually at the spring solstice. Its dramatic plot is the fight of the goddess Kali with demons *(asura)* and their destruction *(vadha)*. Wooden masks are used, the faces of which, in contrast with the static *gambhira* masks, are carved into a dramatic grimace, reminding one of the masks of late Buddhist and Lamaistic dances performed by some local tribes.

Fig. 46
A demon mask of the *gambhira* ritual dance drama. Maldah district, West Bengal, India. Height *c*. 60 cm.

124

89 Rakshasa. The mask of a demon of the dance drama *Ramlila*, made of painted layered paper. Jaynagar, West Bengal, India; now in Náprstek Museum, Prague. Height 28 cm.

Assam is the home of masks used at a dance called *Yuddhar nach*. In this 'war-dance', the pastoral god Krishna appears as a suppressor of demons. Here the masks are reserved for demons, including the bird-demon Bakasura with a huge beak, and the mythological bird Garuda who attends the god Vishnu. The masks are made by the members of the local *khanikar* caste, traditional producers of votive sculpture made of clay.

Village dance dramas called *mukha-khel*, which means 'play of faces', are performed today in northern Bengal. These mostly borrow their subjects from the Bengali version of the Ramayana. They are also performed by local Hinduised peoples, nowadays classed among the scheduled castes. Other members of this caste are the Deshi-Polia farming community, who originally belonged to two tribes, the Deshi and the Polia. They perform episodes of the *Ramayana* in many-coloured masks which they carve themselves. These masks are stylised in a simple but expressive way, with the eyes placed close to each other, with narrow, slot-shaped or rounded holes placed below them for seeing out, and decorative painting of the details of the face, somewhat reminiscent of the painting of the *gambhira* masks (Plate 92). For example, the chin is decorated with a three-petalled flower on a stalk, the cheeks with a geometric stylised rosette, etc. Masks are also worn here by the main characters of the story, i.e. Rama, his brother Lakshmana and Princess Sita, and numerous animals who helped Rama to fight the demons. The play has maintained a ritual character, with both Hindu and local cult elements. An offering is brought by a priest not only to the god Ganesha, but also to the masks. All the makers and wearers of the masks are placed under various taboos during the entire preparation and performance of the play.

The face masks of Orissa may also

125

Fig. 47
Moonmaid, a *chau* mask of the love drama *Chandrabhaga*, from Seraikela, Bihar, India. Height *c.* 26 cm.

be classed with eastern India's wooden masks because of their very high level of craftsmanship. They are carved from local wood by *chitrakars*, the traditional painters and producers of votive objects, who live scattered all over Orissa. However, large masks are made in two particular places, the village of Karadagadi in the Puri district and the village of Parlakhemundi in the Ganjam district. The majority of the large masks, about 45 in number, are made for the Orissa Rama plays performed in spring, which is, in legend, the time of Rama's birth. The main characters, both male and female, perform in masks (Plate 97). For the dramas about Krishna and his fights against the demons, around 20 masks are made. The carvers of Parlakhemundi also specialise in a mask which is above life-size, and is used to represent Narasinha in the dramas of Prahlad, particularly favoured in the Ganjam district. The same carvers also make a number of other masks of large processions which take place at various religious festivities (Rathayatra, Dolayatra, Shahiyatra). Among them we may see, for example, a mask of the goddess Kali, the mythical animal Navagunjara, the black

horse dance masks, those of demons, a half-figure of the goddess Sarasvati, and the mask of Nagaraj (Plate 103).

The axe still remains the traditional instrument for making these masks, but knives and natural pigments have been replaced by chisels and purchased paints. In other respects, however, the *chitrakars* still uphold some interesting traditional customs, both men and women taking part in the work. The men work the wood into basic forms with an axe and chisel, except for the nose which, for economic reasons, is carved from a small wooden prism and is attached to the mask later. For modelling the details of the facial part, a special paste called *putuni* is used, which is mixed from potter's clay, water, sawdust, and tamarind mastic. This must be allowed to dry thoroughly. A further procedure is carried out by the women. They sand down the mask with a rough-surfaced stone, and then glue on tiny rectangular cuttings of old cotton fabric using tamarind mastic. Then the men take over again, covering the mask with two layers of chalk paste. After the paste dries, they polish the surface with a smooth stone, and then the painting, using powdered

126

pigments mixed with water, may start. Deep, bright colours are used, the paint being applied by brushes of various sizes or with the little finger; the established iconography is decisive in the selection of colours for the individual characters. The work is concluded by covering the mask's surface with a layer of shellac and cutting narrow slots under the eyes.

A special group of Orissa wooden masks consists of those which are not painted in several colours, but only tinted with natural oil. These masks are usually large, heavy and carved from a single piece of wood, including the nose. They show deep and perfectly executed carv-ing, the style of which reveals the links between the Orissa folk sculpture and the classical one (Plate 102). The masks are usually decorated with crowns and diadems made of natural *sola* carved into lace-like ornaments, their ivory colour contrasting impressively with the dark brown surface of the mask.

Instead of wooden masks, the *chitrakars* have recently begun to make more masks of layered paper, which is more easily accessible due to the growing scarcity of wood. Even these paper masks are executed in the traditional way (Plates 83 and 104). Paper masks are now made, for example, in Jayapur in the Koraput dis-

90   A horse mask of dance dramas dealing with the legends of Rajput aristocracy, made of textile with bamboo frame, sewn-on bullions, fringes, ribbons etc. Rajasthan, India; now in Náprstek Museum, Prague. Height (including the skirt) 190 cm.

trict, where local peoples are the main customers of the *chitrakars*. The Jayapur masks are less decorative in appearance than those from the other two Orissa centres and some facial features are apparently adapted to the ethnic origins of the local communities. They are provided with a somewhat asymmetrical face, eyes placed far apart, a low forehead, a short stubby nose and a large mouth with fleshy lips.

The type of eastern Indian masks which is probably best known are the dance-drama masks called *chau, cho* or *cha*. These plays are performed in connection with the Shivaganjan, a Shivaistic festival, in the Purulia and Midnapore districts of West Bengal and the Seraikela district of Bihar. The subjects of the Purulia and Midnapore dramas are, as usual, the fights and battles narrated in the Hindu epics and mythology (Plate 106). They are almost exclusively performed by the members of local tribes, wearing masks and clad in colourful costumes. According to local tradition, the plays have developed

from tribal war dances, the forms of which, endowed with a new, i.e. Hindu, content, were utilised by the Hinduised tribal rulers in order to spread Hinduism among their subjects.

The dance masks are made of layered paper, cloth and potter's clay and are modelled in a clay mould. The main centres of production are the village of Charida near the town of Bhagmundi in Purulia, which is the oldest centre of these dances, and the town of Seraikela in Bihar. Both these places have gradually created a style of their own, which distinguishes them from each other.

The Charida masks may be divided into two groups, in terms of physiology. The masks of godly beings have an oval, symmetric face painted in white, pink, yellow or other colours corresponding to the iconographic rules (Plate 98). Their eyes are drop-shaped, emphasised by slightly arched eyebrows; the nose is slim; the small, closed mouth is full-lipped and provided with a slight double chin, being thus in accordance with the Hindu, i.e. Indo-Aryan, ideal of beauty. By contrast, the demon masks are broad-faced, with bulging eyes, massive and high-arched eyebrows and a large, grinning mouth showing large teeth with protruding canines. They often bear a huge moustache and a beard as well as dishevelled hair. The colour of their faces is always dark, i.e. deep-red, deep-blue, etc., according to the character of the demon in question.

With few exceptions, the masks are made by the descendants of the former *sutradhars*, the caste of carpenters and producers of traditional objects, who moved to Charida from Bankura, in the Midnapore district, at the invitation of the Bhagmunda rulers around the beginning of the eighteenth century and started making various votive and ceremonial objects, including masks, for them. Their caste indication, i.e. the caste of carpenters, suggests that masks were originally carved from wood, but no wooden masks have been preserved. Even the oldest extant pieces are made of paper, differing from the present-day masks more or less only in the degree of their ornamentation. Altogether around 40 families now work on the production of masks in Charida.

Due to the long experience of their makers, the Charida masks have reached a high level of craftsmanship, but they are

Fig. 48
A mask for the comic scenes of the Muria, made of wood, bear skin and metal. From Bastar, Madhyapradesh, India. Height 32.7 cm.

128

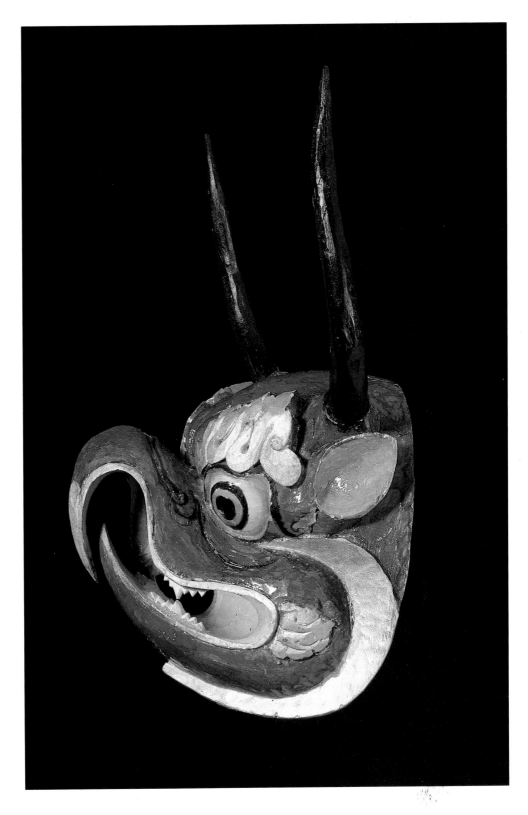

91   The mask of a mythical bird from
a lamas' dance, made of painted and
lacquered wood. Bhutan; now in Náprstek
Museum, Prague. Height (without horns)
22.5 cm.

92 Dushana, a general of Ravana's army.
A wooden, painted and lacquered mask for
a dance drama of the Deshi-Polia, inspired
by the *Ramayana*. Dinajpur, West Bengal,
India; now in the Indian Museum, Calcutta.
Height 32 cm.

93   The black goddess Kali. A mask of
a ritual *gambhira* drama, made of painted
sola (*Aeschynomene indica*). Maldah district,
West Bengal, India; photo from field
research. Height *c.* 40 cm.

94 The mask of a wife of a British colonial official, used in a comic scene filling up an interval of a puppet theatre performance; made of painted and lacquered wood. Jodhpur district, Rajasthan, India; now in Rupayan Sansthan (Institute of Folklore), Borunda, Rajasthan. Height 40 cm.

95 A mask of Shiva for the *chau* dance drama, executed in the Dumurdi style, made of painted and lacquered paper covered with a layer of clay and fabric. Purulia district, West Bengal, India; now in the Indian Museum, Calcutta. Height 35 cm.

96   Kariraya, an attendant deity of local
willage goddesses, made of painted and
lacquered wood. Mandya district, Karnataka,
India; photo from field research. Height
40 cm.

97 A hero of noble origin with a shivaistic mark on his forehead, made of wood carved with paste called *putuni* and a layer of textile, decorated with paint. Orissa, India; now in Náprstek Museum, Prague. Height 36 cm.

▷

98 The goddess Durga. A mask for the *chau* dance dramas, executed in the Charida style, made of layered paper covered with a layer of clay and textile and decorated with coloured varnish. Ornaments are made of synthetic materials, glass beads, gold-foil, wool tassels, etc. Purulia district, West Bengal, India; now in a private collection in Prague. Height 91 cm.

99　The tribal deity Buriya. A mask for
a dance drama of the Bhil tribe, named
Gauri; made of wood lacquered in orange
with many-coloured tinsel. The hair and
moustache are made of black fibres and the
teeth of peacock quills. Udaipur district,
Rajasthan, India; now in a private collection
in Prague. Height 32.5 cm.

100 Masks of a man and a woman of comic interludes of religious dance dramas, made of dark brown stained wood. Borderland of India and Nepal; now in a private collection in Prague. Height 35 and 32 cm.

much more decorative now than they were in the past. The mask was formerly adorned with a relatively low diadem or crown, made of paper and modelled together with the facial part and a ring, by means of which the mask was set firmly on the dancer's head. Now the diadem is covered with a high network construction, to which various glittering and deep-coloured decorative elements of industrial origin are attached, such as chains made of silvery fringes, braids of silver glass beads, little wire spirals, artificial flowers, many-coloured feathers, and numerous pendants in the form of little tufts and woollen balls, etc. This new type of decoration, made by the women, creates a powerful effect at the dance.

Somewhat different were the types of masks produced by a small workshop in the village of Dumurdi near Shrirampur until the end of the 1970s. Thanks to the field research of S. R. Sarkar from the Indian Museum in Calcutta, we know that the workshop was founded by Madhu

Roy, one of the Charida Bhatta Brahmins, who moved from Charida to Dumurdi in 1937. His conception of the masks differs from the Charida ones by assimilating into the facial features of all masks the physiognomy of the local peoples who wear them at their dance performances. The masks are characterised by a wide and bulging forehead, strikingly rounded eyes, a broad and short nose, fleshy lips and the corners of the mouth being pulled upwards as if in a smile. Typical also is the asymmetry of the eyes, one of which is placed higher than the other, the stuck-out ears and an original low crown, all of which endow the mask with a lively but also naive expression (Plate 95). It is a pity that this particular type vanished at the death of the workshop's founder. The masks produced in Dumurdi nowadays are made in the Charida style.

The *chau* masks from Seraikela in Bihar are only used locally, unlike those of Charida, and have long been made under the supervision and with the direct participation of the members of the former ruling family. The refined taste of this family, expressed by the romantic conception of the dances and a preference for erotic lyrical subjects, has naturally influenced the conception of the masks, too. They are heart-shaped, reminding one of the shape of betel leaves, and are provided with oblique half-closed eyes and a tiny mouth. Along with the painted decoration, executed in fine pastel colours, these traits turn them into an unusually sophisticated type which strikes us as incongruous among the other earthy, dynamic and sometimes even bizarre Indian masks. In actual fact, this type is unparalleled in India, but is remotely reminiscent of the type of masks which originated in the Indonesian island of Bali, which has had many commercial and cultural contacts with Bihar from the early Middle Ages. The prototype of this style is, among others, the mask of the moonmaid in the love drama *Chandrabhaga* (Fig. 47).

Interesting performances in masks are to be witnessed in Rajasthan. One of them is in a surprising way connected with the traditional Rajasthani puppet-show called *kathputli*, staged until recently by a group of itinerant puppeteers in the

Fig. 49
Archaic type of a dance costume with a head-dress decorated with serpent symbols. From the Parava community of southern Karnataka, *c.* 1909.

Jodhpur district. There are two masks here, one of a European lady and the other of her husband, an officer in the British colonial army. These masks obviously served the purpose of creating a direct contact with the spectators, otherwise impossible in a traditionally conceived puppet-show. The mask of the officer was worn by an actor (Plate 94), while talking with some of the spectators, the mask of the lady only looked on, hanging on the wooden framework of the theatre tent. This scene was a kind of satire about the insensitivity of the administration in the colonial period, when the episode was introduced into the play. The masks were made by the puppeteers themselves, being carved from wood in the same way as their puppets.

Another remarkable function is served by the masks in the Jodhpur district at a traditional wedding ceremony, the 'second wedding', when the bride is taken by the bridegroom from the house of her parents to his own home. On this occasion, women from the bride's house entertain the bridegroom by enacting a comic scene in masks. According to the information of a witness, the masks represent a Muslim couple taking part in a dialogue concerning matrimonial duties and the intimate conjugal life, especially on the wedding-night. The women are said to make the masks for this scene themselves, from materials which are at hand — a mixture of clay, water and cow-dung. The masks are, in principle, formed from rounded and slightly convex discs with oval holes for the eyes and the mouth. After the discs are dry the women paint them with chalk clay, emphasising the eyes with blue colour and the mouth with red. The masks are attached to the head with strings threaded through holes drilled in the edges (Plate 107).

Like the tribal masks of the other parts of India, the masks of the communities of Rajasthan are still little known and one would undoubtedly find among them pieces worth attention not only from the ethnographic point of view but also that of art. An eloquent testimony to this fact is the mask used by the Bhil people in the Udaipur district in a ritual dance drama called *Gauri*. Although 26 people take part in the play, only one of them wears a mask — the main character, called Buria by the Bhils. He is also the leader of the

138

101 Mahakali. A mask of religious dances performed during the Mahakali Pyakhan festival, made of papier-mâché, covered with polychrome and transparent lacquer. Kathmandu, Nepal; now in Náprstek Museum, Prague. Height 65 cm.

entire group and, to use a modern term, the director of the performance, ordering its course by his instructions. Buria is obviously an original tribal deity, now identified with the Hindu god Shankara, or Shiva. His counterpart is the tribal goddess Rai, considered to be a form of Shiva's godly spouse Gauri. The performance is done in her honour, lasting for 40 days, and is one of the few dramas performed in daylight.

The Bhil artist traditionally shapes the mask as a large wooden disc with sharp and geometric stylised facial features, covers it with orange paint and decorates it in a distinctive and very effective way with variously coloured strips of paper, and symbols of the sun and moon, which he spreads all over the mask's surface

(Plate 99). Above the oblong mouth, filled with porcupine's spines, he glues a long, drooping moustache made of black horsehair, using the same material, cut short, to frame the whole mask. Some of the Bhil groups are reported to use clay masks at their Gauri dances, the artistic conception of which is little different from that of the wooden masks.

Thanks to Verrier Elwin, we possess more detailed information on the tribal masks to be found in the territory formerly called central India, which is present-day Madhyapradesh and it borders with Orissa and Bihar. Invaluable information, collected by Elwin among the Muria, Gond, Pardhan, Baiga, Agaria, Bhuiya, Kond and other peoples, is of immense historical value now, because half a century has passed since he recorded it and many masks seen by Elwin in the field are now only unique museum exhibits in the National Museum in New Delhi.

The masks of this area serve two entirely different purposes, that of cult and of pure entertainment. The masks used as a means of arousing gaiety and humour are much more numerous than the cult masks, due to a characteristic trait of these peoples, i.e. their spontaneous enjoyment of life and an inborn sense of humour. The masks are used, for example, to amuse children at a popular children's festival called Cherta, or at masquerades organised annually by the young people of Muria when they visit their contemporaries in a neighbouring village (Fig. 48). Hilarious merriment accompanies a scene in which one of the members of the tribe, wearing the mask of a Hindu ascetic, presents a caricature of these holy men at tribal festivities, the pretended ab-

stinence with which he refuses the offered meat and liquors becoming the target of rough ridicule by the spectators.

In terms of typology, all of the masks of these tribes are face masks. They are either carved from wood or made from gourds *(Lagenaria vulgaris).* Their makers always concentrate on emphasising the most significant traits, supplementing the details with many-coloured painting or other materials. For example, they replace the teeth with grains of rice, gourd seeds or pieces of wood and glass. The hair and beard are simulated by using the hair of horses, goats, bears and cows, or by hemp fibres, glued to the mask with beeswax. Sometimes paints are added. In the masks made from gourds, the features are depicted by means of parallel lines burned into the surface of the mask with a red hot poker. The eyes are usually cut through as rounded holes and the mouth into a four-sided hole. The nose is huge,

102   The monkey god Hanuman, attendant of the hero Rama, with the mark of Vishnu on his forehead. Wood with a dark brown stained surface. Puri, Orissa, India; now in a private collection in Prague. Height 41 cm.

140

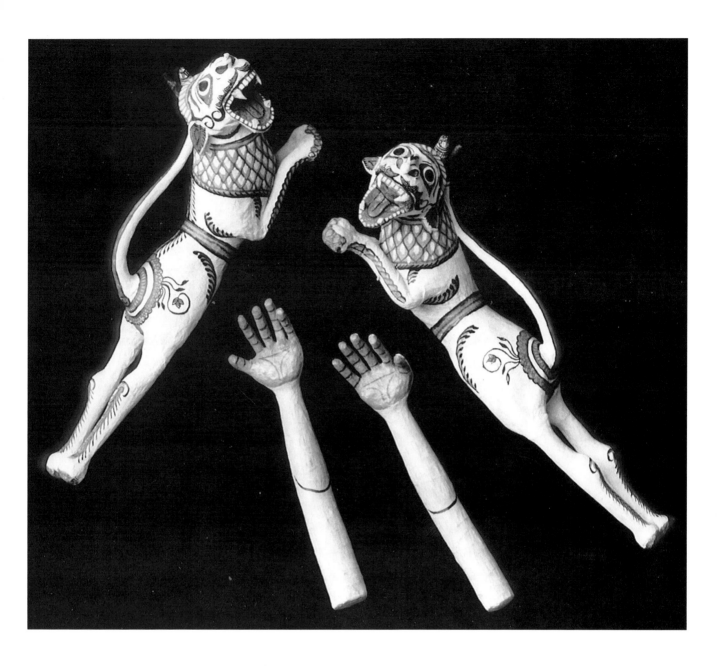

103　A mask of the Nagaraj mythical being which performed at masquerades. It has a pair of arms and two lion figures with a lion-tail handle. The arms are made of painted layered paper; lions made of painted layered paper are glued to the layer of clay covering the straw core. Raghurajpur, Puri district, Orissa, India; now in Náprstek Museum, Prague. Length of the arms 62 and 61 cm, length of the lions 91 and 89 cm.

with no vents, and made of wood or bees-wax. The basic colour of the paint is white, made from white clay, with red and black pigments. The masks made from gourds are unpainted.

The stylistic diversity of these masks documents the free character of the tribal creation. Side by side with simply, or even primitively, executed face masks, such as the now rare examples from the Bizon-horn Maria people in Madhyapradesh, we may find masks characterised by a strict and almost mysterious carving serving the hunting rituals of the Bhuiya people in Orissa (Fig. 52). Their very op-posite are the dynamic masks, provided

with caricature-like features, representing the Hindu ascetics. One telling represen-tation of such an ascetic was made by a Gond carver. His mask is a portrait of a man with long dishevelled hair made of hemp and a wide-open hungry mouth showing a few large teeth. The repulsive-ness of his appearance is emphasised by three-coloured decorative painting (red and black on white) forming a restless geometric ornamentation on the flat sur-face of the mask.

Helmet masks were also recorded among the Gond. They personify demons (rakshasa) appearing at tribal festivals which are influenced by Hinduism, and are connected with an interesting myth about the origin of Gond masks. They are said to be the heads of demons, cut off by Lord Krishna after they had tried to disturb his games of love with girls guarding cattle. The latter were sorry for the demons and they begged Krishna to put their heads back. Krishna refused, but he promised that their heads, in the form of masks, would serve the purpose of entertaining people. The Krishna element of the myth is undoubtedly Hindu, but the witty plot concerning the heads is certainly Gond in origin.

In the artefacts produced by the Gond as well as the Baiga, a special category consists of the masks which Verrier Elwin saw in the Mandla district, describing them as pictographic. The masks are made of wood and all of their surface is covered with pictures of human and animal figures and plant motifs, stylised into fundamental geometric forms in the same way as they are sometimes painted by the local peoples on the walls of their houses. Even that specific tendency to asymmetry is maintained, which renders the tribal pictographs so effective. The painting of the masks is confined to three characteristic colours, i.e. white on the background and red and black in the painting itself.

Masks made from gourds are typical of the Muria. They take advantage of the gourd's natural form, reminiscent of a human head, and turn them into masks used in comic and satirical scenes at the children's festivals as well as the masquerades, in which the young people perform funny scenes from the community's life (Plate 109). Older masks have eyeholes which are rounded and provided with brass rings, repeated again in the earlobes as earrings. In later masks, however, this combination with metals is rather exceptional.

Very rich and still fully alive is the tradition of masks in south India. In this part of the sub-continent, considered to be a treasury of Indian arts and culture, a large number of dance scenes and dramas have been preserved, in which we may find remarkable archaic forms of, and invaluable information about, types of masking known not only in the south of India, but in the entire sub-continent and even in Sri Lanka. This is easy to explain. The development of the south, including south Indian Hinduism, the establishment of which participated in by both Indo-Aryans and the Dravidians, was different from that of the northern regions. Within the framework of Hinduism, the Dravidians have retained many of their concepts of a settled community with a well-developed agriculture, which was exactly how they lived in the middle of the third millennium BC, when they were pushed by the nomadic Indo-Aryans from the northern plains to the south of the Dakkhin upland.

The south Indian form of Hinduism was spared the ideological and social impact of Islam which influenced the development of Hinduism in the north to some extent. This is why, in the south, dances and masks are connected with both classical Hindu gods and goddesses and Dravidian guardian deities and supernatural beings of local or wider significance. An important role is played by masks, for instance, in some local exorcist dances connected with driving away evil forces, or in magic dance performances, the purpose of which is to expel an illness or to summon rain. This is also the case with ritual dance-dramatic performances connected with the festivals of the annual cycle, and

Fig. 50
A metal mask of Jumadi *bhuta*.

142

104 The demon Taraka. A mask for a masquerade at the spring festival, made of layered painted paper, silver tinsel (jewels) and sola (teeth). Radasahi, Bhuvaneshvar district, Orissa, India; now in Náprstek Museum, Prague. Height 30 cm.

in showy dance plays organised at temples and pilgrim centres. It was especially the village performances, with their large numbers of Dravidian tribal communities or scheduled castes, which upheld interesting local peculiarities in masking.

In this respect our attention is attracted first of all to two south Indian states, Kerala and southern Karnataka. The masking in this region indulges in fanciful, if not bizarre, costumes and unusually huge head-decorations, optically enlarging the figures of the dancers, especially their height, to as much as a couple of metres. An archaic type of this way of masking, with a headpiece decorated with serpent symbols, has been preserved in a photograph from 1909 (Fig. 49). Another element is sometimes a complicated and time-consuming make-up, applied on the face in thick layers and reminding one of actual masks to such an extent that it is difficult to differentiate it from a mask at the performance.

The masks themselves are usually worn on the dancers' faces, but they may also hang from the waist or around the neck or be attached to the diadem of crown. Half-masks and partial masks are also used, such as knob-shaped noses, decorative covers for the eyes and the so-called chutti, supplements made of chalk-paste which frame the two clavicles, including the chin, within a narrow strip.

The masks mostly portray the theriomorphic or purely zoomorphic look of supernatural beings. The usual masks of Ganesha, Narasinha, Kali and the demons are joined by masks of local deities, including tribal gods whose names differ from one village to another and who have often taken over the names and attributes of the gods of the orthodox Hindu pantheon. These are the masks of deified heroes (viran), serpents (naga) connected with the fertility cult, and guardian spirits (bhuta), who, according to local belief, do not dwell far away in the sky as the classical gods do, but on the earth among the people.

For the making of masks, various easily accessible materials are offered by the tropical vegetation. Apart from the wood, sap, oil, and leaves of trees, there are various kinds of grass, bamboo, rice stalks and many natural fibres. A local speciality is the coconut tree (Cocos nucifera). Its leaves serve for making the bases of monumental diadems and fan-shaped dance head-dresses, fringes and tufts for decorating the costumes and masks, broad fringed skirts, etc. A raw material probably unparalleled anywhere for making masks are the leaf-sheaths of the areca palm (Areca catechu), much used in Kerala. Young sheaths are very elastic and may be unfolded into an area approximately 70 by 35 cm. They are easy to work with a knife, absorb paint quickly, may be sewn together to make larger areas and can be used, by adding extra materials, for decorating headpieces and diadems, and for making unusual supplements for costumes as well as imitations of jewels (Plate 110). However, they do not offer many possibilities in modelling. This is why the masks made of this material are entirely flat, slightly convex, or curved a little on the vertical axis. The facial part of some of them is edged with a narrow decorative border with fringes, others being topped by a vast fan-shaped or slightly

105　A tiger with a Vishnuist mark on his forehead. A mask for local dance dramas, inspired by the epic *Ramayana*. Vishnupur, West Bengal, India; now in Náprstek Museum, Prague. Height 25 cm.

Fig. 51
A mask of a member of the army of demons. From Melattur, Tamilnadu, India.

Leaf-sheath masks and other dance requisites, such as gigantic dance head-dresses, are made by local priests. The dancers wearing them are turned into fearsome monsters representing local gods, goddesses and spirits. Neither the masks nor the head-dresses and voluminous costumes burden the dancer as much as might seem at first sight, since they are very light in weight. Local tradition orders them to be used once and then destroyed. A telling example of this kind of masking is the Kerala ritual drama called *Pataiya-ni*. The play praises the gods, supernatural beings and all living things for saving the world and preserving the balance and order of the universe against the devastating activities of the goddess Kali. The drama is staged between March and June in an open space in front of some of the goddess's temples and may last up to ten nights. The traditional illumination is provided by torches.

Other examples are the Kerala ritual dramas of the *teyyam* type. These serve the ritual celebration of deities (*teyyam* means a deity in Malayalam) and are performed in front of their shrines. The plays consist of a series of solo pantomime scenes called *kolam*, preceded by the recital of the respective myth. The recital is presented by a narrator accompanied by a chorus, as in other south Indian dramas as well as the famous mask performances of Sri Lanka, also known under the name *kolam*. Masks made of leaf-sheaths are worn by the representatives of spirits (*bhuta*) at a Mudiyetu cult dance honouring the goddess Bhadrakali and connected with magic practices, and at the *kolam tullal* (meaning 'dance in disguise') exorcist dance scene, in which the *bhutas*, in the role of attendants of Kali, drive evil forces from the temple complex consecrated to this goddess. Unlike the *bhutas*, the dancer embodying kali does not cover his face with a mask, but only makes it up, the mask of the goddess being placed in the centre of a huge head-dress, up to 3 m in width and shaped like a semi-circular fan, which rises over the head of the dancer like a colourful aureola.

Interesting and probably also very old is the Kerala tradition of masks cast in metal. This tradition is documented, for example, by a photograph of the Jumadi *bhuta* mask, published in 1909 (Fig. 50), as well as a description from 1872, pre-

tipped diadem made of the same material and combined with coconut leaves. The facial part is usually painted with fancifully stylized details, among which the most prominent are the eyes, simulated by large, concentric circles or ovals which cover almost the entire area of the face. A face stylised in a similar way is sometimes repeated in the painted decoration of the diadem and supplemented with plant motifs. Among the latter are large rosettes set into circular medallions which are placed on a level with the upper or lower end of the ears. They also occur in the masks of other parts of south India, as well as in Sri Lanka, where they probably spread under the influence of Indian dances.

144

106 Mask of the god Shiva, made of painted layered paper. Midnapore district, West Bengal, India; now in Náprstek Museum, Prague. Height 21 cm.

serpent masks are used, pointing to an obvious connection of these dramas with the local cult of fertility.

It is the same cult, as well as that of the *bhutas*, to which an interesting type of wooden painted mask in the neighbouring Karnataka is connected. Their characteristic feature is a high and comparatively slim diadem carved together with the facial part and decorated with plant material ornaments, richly carved and stylised, covering the entire area. When these masks are not being used at a dance, they are preserved, along with further iconographic symbols of the *bhutas,* such as swords and shields, under a shelter situated near the village shrine and called *bhutasthan.* The mask is worn by the priest of the shrine or his assistant at a dance, and a magic formula is uttered during the dance by the same person, who falls into a trance at the moment when the dance reaches its climax.

The stylistic variety is also contributed to by southern Karnataka, with another type of mask remarkable for its quality of carving. These masks originated in the Mandya district, where they are still carved by the members of the local caste of carpenters, called *acharya.* The masks personify demonic-looking beings who are called *rayas* by the local people. A legend narrates that these *rayas* attend the village goddesses, helping them to drive away evil forces. Their masks are worn by dancers who are chosen from among local farmers, who dance in a procession on the occasion of religious festivals, for example the festival of ritual chariots (Rathayatra) or another festival worshipping the village deities. The festivals are held annually between mid-March and mid-June, when there is no work in the fields; their purpose is to protect the inhabitants against infectious diseases, often prevalent in the hot weather before the monsoon and afflicting both men and animals. The masks thus have a ritual function. Their wearers must perform a purifying ritual before the dance, must carry the masks out of the temple in a ceremonial way, under the supervision of the priest, and, after the festival is over, must deposit them again in the temple's vestibule where they remain until the next festival.

The *acharyas* make the masks from light wood. They carve deep and massive

sented by A. C. Burney in his monograph *Devil Worship of Tuluvas.* The author took part in a festival connected with the *bhuta* cult in Mangalore, recording that on the occasion of summoning the *bhutas* at a cult dance, the dancer of the *pombad* caste, representing Jarandaya *bhuta,* covered his face, already overlayed with ochre clay, with a mask of this *bhuta* to show that he was embodying it. His attendant, a member of the same caste, playing the role of a servant of the *bhuta,* was holding a similar mask in his hand and both of them, clad in costumes made of coconut fringes, danced with these masks.

In the other dances and dance dramas of south India, as elsewhere in India, wooden masks, or those made of layered paper are mostly worn. Their shape, style and content depend on the locality of their origin and their purpose. For example, in the Kerala dance drama of the *tira* type, performed in the Calicut district, masks of the face type, flat on top, to which a decorative crown and a huge wig are bound. The face of the mask is given large bulging eyes, a massive nose with widely flaring nostrils and wide fleshy lips, out of which long tusks protrude. Semi-circled slots are made under the eyes. Compared to the masks made of leaf-sheaths, their painting is less striking and synthetic powdered paints and purchased mastic are used, mixed with water by the *acharyas*.

The pigments prepared in this way are laid with a brush on the wood which has been covered with a layer of white zinc paint, the iconography deciding upon the choice of colours: red for Kencharaya, yellow for Bhutaraya and black for Kariraya. The surface of the mask is covered with copal varnish (Plate 96).

In Madras and Andhrapradesh, masks are connected, among other occasions, with the religious festival named Bhaga-vatmela, at which the *Parahladacharitam*, a drama about Prahlad and Vishnu, incarnated in Narasinha, is performed. Masks are particularly worn by Narasinha and the demon-king Hiranyakashipu who is Prahlad's father and an enemy of the gods, especially Vishnu. In some places, such as Kuchipudi in Andhrapradesh, the mask of Narasinha, larger than the others used at the performance, is modelled from layered paper. Its size is approxi-

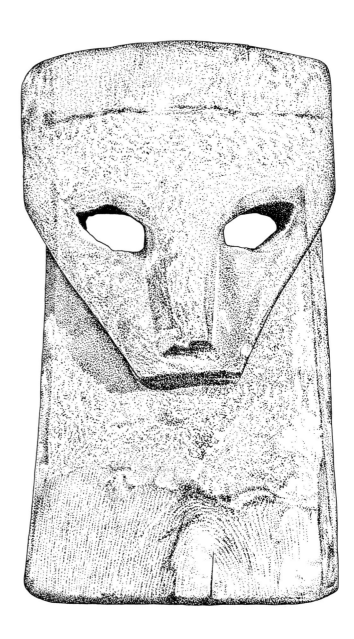

Fig. 52
A mask of a ritual dance connected with a divination and performed during a festive lion-hunt of the Bhuiya tribe, made of wood saturated with oil. From the border between Orissa and Madhyapradesh, India; now in National Museum, New Delhi. Height 27.5 cm.

146

Fig. 53
A mask of the Mura demon, used in the dance drama *Krishnanattam*. Made of wood with painted decoration reminiscent of the 'pop art' style. From Guruvayur, Kerala, India. Height *c.* 60 cm.

mately 60 by 60 cm and it is provided with a huge red mane and a large decorated crown. The dancer personifying the enraged Narasinha usually falls into a trance and must be bound with a rope in order to prevent him from attacking spectators.

Among many other variants, best known are the masks made for the performance given in the Melattur pilgrim centre in Madras. This performance is a kind of replacement of an offering to the god Narasinha, the main deity of the local temple, and has therefore the character of an ancient majestic ceremony, the participants of which are the members of the local Brahmin families. The dancer representing Narasinha wears a sacred mask made of hammered gold, alleged to have been preserved at the local temple for two centuries. The other masks, e.g. those of the members of a demon army, are made of layered paper and painted in many dark colours. They are not tied to the head, but held in front of the dancer's face by hand (Fig. 51). The neck of the mask serves as a handle here. It is modelled from paper together with the facial part.

One of the most significant performances is the *Krishnanattam*, a classical ritual drama of Kerala. Its subject is the childhood and youth of the god Krishna. The entire performance lasts for eight consecutive nights and takes place in the Guruvayur pilgrim centre in October and November as an offering to Krishna. The drama was written by Manvedra, a king of the Zamorin dynasty, in the second half of the seventeenth century. A few characters such as the god Brahma, the god of death, Yama, the king of hell, Narakasura, and the demoness Putana are prescribed to wear masks.

These are carved from wood in an established style, especially observable in demonic beings, e.g. the demon Mura. They have large and seemingly bloodshot bulging eyes (Fig. 53), simulated by con-

107 The demon king Hiranyakashipu. A mask for the dance drama *Prahladacharitam*, made of lacquered papier-mâché and painted. Jodhpur district, Rajasthan, India; now in a private collection in Prague. Height 23 cm.

centric red circles drawn around the pupils, a half-open mouth with strong protruding canines, and a large moustache with the ends twisted into spirals under the nose. The holes enabling the wearer to see out are round and placed in the centre of the pupils. A characteristic mark is the painted decoration forming a geometric ornament all over the face area, consisting of parallel stripes and stripes in contrasting colours. The masks are provided with stepped crowns with a large circular disc at the back. The crowns are gilded and decorated with horizontal stripes of plant material inlaid with colourful pieces of glass and mirrors.

The privilege of wearing a mask and thus turning one's identity into that of another being, often one from the world of the supernatural, is reserved for men, with few exceptions. In a tribe, for example,

every male member of the community may wear a mask, except for the ritual masks usualy worn only by the tribal priest. Members of the higher castes generally do not take part in these activities, in Hindu society, since these are incompatible with their status according to the caste precepts. Exceptions to this rule are some of the ritual dramas performed under the auspices of temples and forming a kind of offering to the temple deity. In such cases some masked characters, mostly representing godly beings, are played by young boys around the age of 13 or 14, selected from the local Brahmin families, or else the representation of certain characters has been hereditary in Brahmin families, from father to son, for several centuries. Such is the case with the traditional play about the Narasinha incarnation of the god Vishnu, performed in the

148

Madras Melattur from the sixteenth century onwards.

It is, however, mostly the members of the lower social strata and castes who wear masks in public. This is true both among the tribes upholding their aboriginal traditions, and the castes in the Hindu social structure. The main wearers of the masks are professional dancers. Their art is a hereditary profession, the fundamental skill of which has long since been an ability to fall into a trance during the ritual and cult dance. Many of them only pretend this ability nowadays, for instance those who roam through towns and villages and whose performances are an entertainment for which they receive meagre remuneration in money or food from the onlookers. However, there are also persons among them who perform cult and ritual dances connected with the summoning of deities and exorcising of illnesses and evil spirits. They take this very seriously and really do have the ability to fall into a trance. They are believed to identify themselves with the supernatural being into which they have been turned by means of masking, to be able to control it and to negotiate a direct contact between it and the onlookers.

The group of sculptures modelled in the form of masks belong to the wider

108 An icon of Shiva-Khandoba in the form of a metal face mask, made of brass. Bangalore district, Karnataka, India; now in Náprstek Museum, Prague. Height 18.5 cm.

area of masks. These are mostly cultic in purpose and are often made of bronze and brass.

Shaped like masks, with serene face details, and stylised in a simplified way, are the icons of some south Indian deities who are still worshipped on altars installed in the streets during religious festivals. They are the property of low-caste priests, and passers-by place small gifts of money in front of them. The masks are usually cast of brass and are the same size as a face mask (Plate 108). As a rule only a single mask is placed on the street altar, which may be merely an ordinary box garnished with flowers and wreaths.

Miniature masks are also typical of the south Indian tradition. About 15—20 cm in height, they represent fearsome guardian deities with their facial features executed in detail. This type of mask is part of the ritual apparel of the so-called *jangam*, priests of the Lingayat sect of south India (worshippers of the god Shiva incarnated in the form of *linga*, i.e. the phallus), who carry the masks hanging from their waists. A metal mask may also be used to emphasise some natural material, for example a stone worshipped as a deity. Such is the case with the archaically stylised mask of the goddess Sambaleshvari in Sambalpur, Orissa. This is simulated by a bird's beak in the mask, following the lines of local iconography.

Entirely different in character are the cult masks of the Kuttiya-Kond of Orissa. These masks are made of gourds and are used instead of the human heads which used to be placed in front of the tribal goddess at a human sacrifice called *meri-ah.* After this sacrifice was prohibited by the Government in the first half of the nineteenth century, the tribal priests had the idea of replacing human heads with gourds. A local legend says that the priests were ordered to do this by the goddess herself, and also to make offerings of cockerels to the gourd masks, since otherwise they would weap and cry for a human head on nights with a full moon. The masks are characterised by an unusual white and red glass-bead decoration, used to simulate or emphasise the facial area. A row of glass beads borders the rounded eyeholes and the oblong or circular mouth, emphasises the ridge and nostrils of the nose and forms a continuous line from the eyebrows up to the ears which are stylised in the form of a circle and again framed with a row of glass beads.

Among other types of cult masks is the mask of the Dravidian goddess Mariamma, to be found in the Bangalore district of Karnataka. This mask is made of many-coloured layered paper and is worn by itinerant exorcists who beg for alms. They carry the mask along with a large bunch of bracelets, iconographic symbols of this goddess, which are placed in a large semicircular basket. Accompanied by a small drum, they recite magic formulas *(mantra)* to drive away evil forces and illnesses. The local people reward them with small gifts.

Sri Lanka

By its geographical situation and the ethnic origin of its inhabitants, the Indo-Aryan Sinhalese and the Dravidian minority of the Tamils, the island of Sri Lanka has belonged to an area the cultural development of which was dominated by the culture of India. Thus Hinayana Buddhism became the official ideology of Sri Lanka, contributing much to the specific character of the island and its people. Nor did Sri Lanka withstand the influence of south Indian Hinduism, encouraged by frequent commercial and cultural contacts with the states of south India, on the one hand, and its own Tamil minority, on the other.

In the study of official classic culture, the contribution of the local Sinhalese element is rather easy to distinguish from the Indian import, but a similar differentiation is very difficult in the sphere of folk culture, due to a lack of historical documentation. The folk art, as a component of the unofficial culture, has not been studied in the past, its products vanishing over centuries. Thus it was only at the

Fig. 54
An asymmetrically conceived mask of a Sanni demon with a 'joker's' expression. Made of painted wood. From Sri Lanka. Height 18 cm.

151

particular stage of development at which this creation was first recorded in the nineteenth century (Callaway, 1829; Grünwedel, 1893) that the foundations of its study could be set. The first scholarly treatise on the ritual dances and dance dramas performed in masks was not published until the 1930s (Pertold, 1930). An ethnographically well-founded analysis of Sinhalese folk plays appeared as late as the 1950s (Sarathchandra, 1953), presenting much unexpected information and revealing the links connecting these plays with south Indian folk culture. This important book was followed by a significant attempt at a systematic identification of masks (Lucas, 1958).

The results of contemporary research testify to the existence of two types of performance in masks in Sri Lanka: a ritual dance connected with the exorcism of evil spirits, and a dance drama, at one time significant, but now degenerated into a form of popular amusement.

The first group of masks is derived from the exorcist dances called *tovil* and *sanni.* They are connected with the old belief of the Sinhalese in demons or evil spirits as the originators of illnesses. Tradition has it that there are 18 of these demons, their leader being Maha-kola Sanniya. The purpose of the dances is to exorcise 'the devil with a devil', by which, according to Sinhalese custom, the exorcists must correctly identify the spirit who has caused the illness and drive him out of the patient's body by means of magic formulas, and using disguises and alternations of the masks representing the 18 demons. The dancer must fall into a trance, in which he identifies himself with the demon, being then able to control him fully. People also believe that the demon can only be summoned if the mask is his 'true' portrait. This is why the masks are of primary significance in the ritual and their preparation is subject to iconographic rules which are handed down from one generation to the next in the carvers' families and are still carefully maintained today.

The masks are carved from local, light wood, painted in many colours and always given the shape of face masks or at least half-masks adapted in such a way that the dancers wearing them may easily imitate the symptoms of the illness represented by the mask. The mask is usually not very large, and has slot-like holes under the lower edge of the eyes and a hole for the mouth. The masks are attached to the head by means of tapes or leather bands.

According to local tradition, the demons of the exorcist dances both strike terror and arouse disgust in the onlookers. The artistic conception of the masks is subordinate to this purpose, their entire faces (Fig. 54) or individual parts being disfigured, although masks with a playful rather than terrible aspect may be found. Their supplements are various diadems, mostly carved into the form of upraised cobra heads, and other decorations such as flat, rounded discs with rosettes, inserted into holes drilled along the edges of the mask on both sides of the face.

Entirely different from this type is the Maha-kola Sanniya mask (Plate 111). This is large and heavy, in the shape of a panel carved in relief, around 110 by 75 cm in size. Besides being a theriomorphic figure of Maha-kola Sanniya, it also represents the faces of all his 18 attendants. The form and the size of the mask justify the assumption that it only looked on at the dance, leaning against the wall of a simple ritual stall.

In terms of their number and artistic execution, the masks used at the dance dramas called *kolam* are most important. This word is Dravidian in origin (as is the name of the ritual dances, *tovil*), meaning 'performance in disguise, in an actor's costume'. Masks may also be part of this disguise, and it is in this sense that the Sinhalese use the word for their dance dramas. The term obviously penetrated into Sri Lanka along with a direct influence of ancient south Indian dance-dramatic forms, also called *kolam* in Kerala and Karnataka and sharing certain common traits with the Sinhalese form.

The *kolam* dramas underwent many changes during their development, from an original pantomime performed under the patronage of local rulers, up to the present-day well-developed dramatic form with music, dances, songs and diversion of a village audience, with no ritual subtext. However, the combination of this form with masks seams to be of a recent date, probably connected with the very beginning of this type of drama in Sri Lanka. Now it is traditionally performed in the southern part of the island only, by

109 The mask of an ascetic for a satirical
dance scene of the Muria tribe, made from
a gourd (*Lagenaria vulgaris*) with details
burned in with a red-hot poker. The nose is
carved from wood. Jagdalpur district,
Madhyapradesh, India; now in Náprstek
Museum, Prague. Height 34.5 cm.

110 The mask of a *bhuta,* made of painted
leaf-sheaths of the areca palm (*Areca
catechu*), coconut leaves and plant fibres.
Kerala, India; photo from field research.
Height *c.* 45 cm.

▷
111 Maha-kola Sanniya,
leader of the Sanni-demons.
Eighteen spirits of illnesses
stand at both sides of the
main figure. A mask made
of painted wood. Sri Lanka;
now in Náprstek Museum,
Prague. Size 110 × 78 cm.

154

155

112 Rukdeviya, a tree-deity identified by
O. Pertold, which, according to
E. R. Sarathchandra, appears in a *kolam*
drama entitled *Gothayimbara Katava*; made
of painted wood. Sri Lanka; now in Náprstek
Museum, Prague. Height 23.8 cm.

113 Sandakinduru. A mask of one of the
main *kolam* dramas entitled *Sandakinduru
Katava*. Identified by Gamini Wijesuriya.
Colombo, Sri Lanka; now in Náprstek
Museum, Prague. Height 22.5 cm.

114   The mask of a king of the *kolam*
dramas, made of painted wood. It is
helmet-shaped, and consists of three
individual parts. Sri Lanka; now in Náprstek
Museum, Prague. Height 115 cm.

115 The mask of Totsakan (Ravana) of the *khon* plays, made of painted and gilded papier-mâché, leather, mother of pearl, wood and mirrors. Thailand; now in Museum für Völkerkunde, Berlin. Height 70.5 cm.

116 The mask of the demon Bilua, made of
painted papier-mâché. Mandalay, Burma;
now in Náprstek Museum, Prague. Height
29 cm.

117 The second queen or princess mask of a *kolam* drama, made of painted wood, with the basic colour being yellow. Sri Lanka; now in Náprstek Museum, Prague. Height 34.5 cm.

local professionals. The performance is organised once a year, lasting for six or seven nights, each part beginning at nine in the evening. The performance takes place on an improvised stage under the open sky, usually in the courtyard of some village house.

Most features of the original form have apparently been maintained by that part of the performance which is now considered to form only a prelude to the drama proper and in which the largest number of masks participate. The prelude consists of a series of independent pantomimic dance scenes also called *kolam*. Each scene is introduced by the narrator with a short verse description of its contents and the dancing characters, before the actors appear in front of the audience. They are mostly characters taken from life, making fun of human foibles by means of masks,

disguises and exaggerated dance gestures (Plate 118). The king and queen, the prince royal and the chief minister all appear on the stage (Plates 114 and 117). Their scene is obviously reminiscent of the time when the *kolam* drama was one of the forms of entertainment at court. There is a parade of demons, in the form of a dynamic masquerade. Only two animal masks may be seen, that of a bull and a leopard (Plate 119). They usually perform in a scene immediately following the prelude.

The main dramas increase the repertory of the masks with further types. The masks of the characters called Kinduras (Plate 113), half-man and half-bird, belong to a ballad story with a happy ending, dealing with the tender love of these two mythological beings, and the mask of Prince Maname belongs to a play ending

161

119 A lion with its mane stylised into a ridge. A mask of a *kolam* drama, made of painted wood, with the basic colour being yellow. Sri Lanka; now in Náprstek Museum, Prague. Height 42 cm.

◁
118 Hevaya, a soldier disfigured by wounds suffered in fierce battles. A mask introducing a *kolam* drama, made of painted wood with a basic colour of yellowish-brown. Sri Lanka; now in Náprstek Museum, Prague. Height 27 cm.

in a moralistic lesson. All of the main dramas are based on the *jatakas*, ancient narratives about Buddha's previous births.

The traditional arrangement of the entire performance, in the form of a series of entirely independent scenes, offered the artists an opportunity to alter its course whenever necessary, to leave out antiquated scenes and to replace them with new and actual ones, without disturbing the traditional composition of the performance. This development of the *kolam* drama is also recorded by a few documents detailing its history. These are, among others, the manuscripts of the plays, in various editions and translations, especially a translation by John Callaway, dated 1829, and the treatise by Otakar Pertold, also containing a description of a *kolam* performance witnessed by the author around 1925. He stated that the masked actors talked and sang on the stage, whereas according to Callaway's translation they only performed their scenes in a pantomimic way, and the text relating to them was given in the third

163

person by the narrator. The same fact is obvious from the masks themselves, their mouths are mostly closed, with no apertures for speaking through.

Along with a change in the repertory, masks began to disappear from the stage. Those which did not 'play' any more were often intentionally destroyed, so that their spirits might not harm people at night. The masks which survived attracted the attention of Europeans and are now mostly preserved in European museums. The first reached Europe during the second half of the nineteenth century, their route into the collections sometimes being very strange indeed. Thus a few masks kept in the Asian Collection of the Náprstek Museum in Prague were purchased, in 1900, from the owner of the John Hagenbeck Circus, who had presented Sinhalese wearing the masks as one of the exotic items of his circus programme.

Two types of masks are represented in the *kolam* dramas — a face mask and a helmet mask. The majority are face masks, the helmet masks only occurring as those of the kings and queens, whose high diadems were meant to emphasise their high social status (Fig. 55).

All of the older masks showed carving of high quality, every detail being carefully worked in a three-dimensional way. Only the ears are treated schematically.

They are mostly shaped as flat, projecting ovals, the profile of the inner lobes being suggested only by drawn lines. For such drawing of facial parts, black and red pigments were usually used. The black emphasised the line of the eyebrows, the shape of the moustache, beard and the hairstyle, the side whiskers on the cheeks of men and a tress of hair falling on to the face and twisted into a spiral at the ears of women. Red was used particularly to render the eyes, mouth and chin more expressive.

A separate group is formed by the *kolam* masks of demons (Plate 120). In their disfigured features, they are reminiscent of the masks of the *sanni* demons, but are larger and heavier, their diadems and decorations being richer, too. The crowns, diadems and various head-covers in the human masks, and the snake-shaped decorations and crowns of flames in the demon masks are usually carved from a single piece of wood together with the facial part and they are always ingeniously executed. Plant motifs such as variously stylised rosettes, buds and leaves intertwined in a complicated way are supplemented in a harmonious manner with geometric elements of darts, wavy lines, crosses, tetragons, spirals and circles, carved in horizontal and vertical bands. In some masks, figures of men, demons, ani-

Fig. 55
First queen, a mask of the helmet type, made of painted wood. The hair is richly ornamented with flowers and leaves. From Sri Lanka; now in the Museum für Völkerkunde, Berlin. Height 44 cm.

120 A serpent-demon mask of the *kolam* dramas, made of painted wood, with a base colour of green. Sri Lanka; now in Náprstek Museum, Prague. Height 49 cm.

mals and birds are combined with them, as required by the iconography of the respective character. The kings' and queens' crowns are sometimes provided with head-dresses, or even two or three of them in the case of a king (Plate 114). These masks are heavy and unstable and have always been rather static decorative aids of the performance, as any movement is very difficult when wearing them. At present-day performances, dancers wearing these masks simply walk around the stage a few times, assisted by other actors, and then sit down and look on. A photograph from the beginning of the 1920s shows a dancer wearing the king's mask, the high crown of which he is supporting with the tip of his sword.

Older masks were carved with a knife. Before being painted, their surface was covered with a layer of fine, sifted clay mixed with water, similar in quality to pipe-makers' clay or kaolin and called *al-liyadu* in Sinhalese. Natural pigments, of both plant and mineral origin, were used for colours. Important for the finish of the mask's surface was the *dorana tel* or *bal-samum gurjunal* of the *Dipterocarpus* tree, which was used as a varnish after adding pigments. This was spread on the surface of the mask with a finger. Natural pigments and the traditional finish rendered the masks more resistant to external influences and made their paint shine.

The masks produced more recently are not carved in such an ingenious way, their details being indicated only by painting in some cases. Natural pigments are replaced by artificial paints made in factories and synthetic varnishes. The decline of mask production is obviously connected with the degeneration of the *kolam* dramas from a significant type of moral and religious enlightenment supported by the rulers and the rich into mere amusement for the masses.

The increased interest in the *kolam* and *sanni* masks, observed among collectors and tourists during the last decades, has inspired local carvers to produce masks of a souvenir type. These include more or less successful reproductions of old models, especially the masks of various demons, which have thus become an exotic symbol of Sri Lanka for tourists. When the carvers make the masks in the form of traditional models, they maintain the established iconography, also selecting the colours corresponding to their traditional symbolic significance. Light colours, from white, flesh, pink and various shades of yellow up to gold-brown, may be stated in general to symbolise beauty, majesty, a higher social status and wealth. They are usually applied to the masks of a royal family, gods and goddesses, representatives of the rich and some other unique types. Brown and brownish-red are colours typical of the characters of a lower social rank such as villagers and some serpent demons and *sanni* demons. Red is mostly the colour symbolising anger and aggression and occurs in the masks of men, gods in their terrible forms and demons. Green and dark blue are the colours of the *sanni* demons, black being reserved for some *sanni* and *gara* demons as well as the representatives of the lower social strata. However, the iconographic rules concerning the symbolic significance of colours seem to have been dependent on local custom and were to some degree either mutually different or overlapping, especially in minor characters. These masks are difficult to identify, which is even more true of the older types which are no longer used nowadays and have no documentary records.

South-East Asia

There is little doubt that, in the past, masks played a more important role in South-East Asia than appears to be the case nowadays.

The masks of most of the countries of South-East Asia are inspired by Indian influences, although this does not mean that masks had been unknown before contact with India or that local masks lack any stylistic peculiarities of their own. Only the masks of Laos deviate from the general cultural framework of South-East Asia. Here European travellers of the nineteenth century recorded mask performances at various festivals. These rare

Fig. 56
An actor wearing a Totsakan (Ravana) mask in the *Ramakien*, the Thai version of the *Ramayana*.

masks now included in collections bear traces of a Chinese artistic influence.

India exerted a strong influence on most of the countries of South-East Asia during the past two centuries. Along with Buddhism and Hinduism, Indian narrative literature also penetrated into this area, in a popular form intended to propagate religious principles. In the Buddhist literature, it was the so-called *jatakas*, stories of Buddha's previous lives, and in the Hindu literature the great Indian epics, particularly the *Ramayana*. Both of these literary monuments of ancient India became the fundamental sources of inspiration for the arts of South-East Asia, especially the fine arts, but also dramas.

THAILAND

It is interesting to note that Thailand, an entirely Buddhist country, chose the Hindu *Ramayana* (here called *Ramakien*) for the permanent main subject of its drama, performed both by living actors and marionettes or flat shadow-puppets. This fact may be connected with the ruling dynasty which derived its origin from the hero of the epic, Rama. In the Thai version, the religious aspect was gradually pushed in to the background, romantically inclined fairy-tale elements predominating.

The epic contents of the *Ramayana* express, in a symbolic way, the struggle of the good forces, particularly personified by the main hero, Prince Rama, called Phra Ram in the Thai version, who is an incarnation of the god Vishnu, and his faithful consort Sita, or Nang Sida in the *Ramakien*. The evil forces fighting against the celestial gods are personified by demons. These are led by the ten-headed Ravana, called Totsakan in Thai, i.e. 'a ten-faced one' (Plate 115). The main plot

167

121 *Topeng* mask personifying a dead only son, made of wood. Toba-Batak, Sumatra, Indonesia; now in Rijkmuseum voor Volkenkunde, Leiden. Height 31 cm.

is Sita's abduction by Ravana, her temptation and Rama's fight for her liberation with the help of an army of monkeys headed by the clever and devoted monkey Hanuman. This fundamental story, in which many other heroes appear on both sides, is infolded in numerous episodes.

The Thai dance drama, performed by living actors and based on the *Ramakien*, is called *khon*. All the roles except those of the main female characters are played by men. Whereas the women representing the heroines perform with made-up faces, the men appear wearing masks (Fig. 56).

These Thai masks are the most outstanding among the masks of South-East Asia. They are made of papier-mâché, only their supplements, such as the decorations on the top of the head and the ears, being carved from wood. The masks are often gilded and inlaid with mirrors, colourful glass or mother of pearl. The fundamental colour of the masks differs according to the traditional iconographic conception of the individual heroes. They are red, white, golden, green etc., the three-dimensional features of the face being emphasised by linear painting. Two holes for the eyes en-

168

able the dancers to see, but there are no holes for the mouth, since the dance performances are pantomimic in character.

Only one man dances at a time, while the others remain still on the simple stage. A singer recites the explanatory text, accompanied by an orchestra. The iconographic form of the masks is established in such a way that the spectator is able to identify the individual characters at once. In their decorativeness and predilection for pointed tower-like forms and protrusions reminiscent of flames, they correspond to the decadent Bangkok style of Thai art from the time when Bangkok was the royal seat and the *khon* plays were in high favour.

BURMA

The Thai version of the *Ramayana* in its dramatic form, along with the characteristic masks, penetrated into neighbouring Burma in the second half of the eighteenth century. In 1767, the Burmese captured the then royal seat of Thailand, Ajuthia, and brought back Thai courtiers, actors, dancers and musicians to the capital of their own kingdom, Ava. The Thai de-Hinduised *Ramakien* became very popular at the Burmese court and later began to be staged by professional Burmese actors.

The theatre is among the most popular forms of folk entertainment in Burma. Masks were known here even before the

122 A fanciful dance mask of wood, bone, tortoise-shell and glass beads. Leti Island, Indonesia; now in Koninklijk Instituut voor de Tropen, Amsterdam. Height 14 cm.

123 A half-mask, probably used in the *kuda kepang* plays, made of painted wood. Madura, Indonesia; now in Náprstek Museum, Prague. Height 13.7 cm.

Thai impetus. They were worn mainly by persons representing supernatural beings, such as the giant Bhilu, the dragon Naga and the bird Galoum, the Burmese version of the Indian mythical bird Garuda. Masks must have existed in Burma before the advent of Buddhism, in connection with the cult of fertility. Dancers wearing animal masks imitate the movements of animals as in other countries and other continents. Until modern times, villages were visited by processions of masks at the festivals of the annual cycle, and even at Buddhist festivals, in accordance with the Burmese ability to absorb pre-Buddhist religious elements in a syncretic way.

INDONESIA

Indonesia possesses a much richer repertory of masks. This has resulted from the varied ethnic composition of the local inhabitants, on the one hand, and the

cultural impulses received by Indonesia during various periods, on the other. The present-day inhabitants came to the islands from the Asian continent in several waves. The arrival of the first wave is dated to between the fourth and third millenniums BC. These were the Old Malays or Proto-Indonesians, who were later pushed back, by further immigrants, from the coastal plains into the inaccessible mountainous inland or to the small islands. Prominent among them are the Batak living in the interior of the northern part of Sumatra, the inhabitants of the small Nias Island near the western coast of Sumatra, the Toraja from the interior of Sulawesi (formerly Celebes) and numerous peoples of Kalimantan (Borneo), usually summed up under the common denomination of the Dayak. In spite of great geographic distances dividing these peoples one from another and the large time gap between the present and the time when they left their original home, they have maintained common cultural traits, which are also preserved among some mountainous peoples in the south-eastern part of Asia. Masks which may be seen among almost all the ethnic groups of Indonesia may be included in this common cultural heritage.

The most ancient type is obviously represented by the funeral masks, recorded as still in use by European travellers among the eastern Toraja peoples living in the Poko Lake area, at the beginning of the present century. The Toraja call these masks *pemia*. They are oval, almost flat human faces made of pale wood, with a narrow, long nose thrusting forward, horizontal eyes carved into an almond shape and eyebrows with double-arches.

The eyes are black as are the tops of these masks. The ears stand out at the sides and the chin is cut horizontally. The top of some of these masks is surmounted by a spiral-shaped bronze-coloured jewel of socio-hierarchic significance. A sort of handle is attached to the bottom edge under the chin.

The Toraja celebrate the second funeral of their dead. At the first funeral, the remains of the deceased person are buried in the earth. After a few years, the bones are unearthed, bound in a bundle made of *fuya* cloth, which is hammered from bark, and placed for some time in the village shrine. After a memorial ceremony, the remains are again laid to rest in peace. According to mutually contradictory information, the *pemia* funeral mask is

124 *Wayang topeng* face mask, made of painted wood. Madura, Indonesia; now in Náprstek Museum, Prague. Height 20 cm.

either tied to the bundle containing the bones during the corpse's deposition in the shrine, or attached to the bones by means of the above-mentioned handle. This practice is strongly reminiscent of the purpose of reliquary figures in Gabon, in Africa, but whereas the Gabon reliquaries were kept in a dwelling hut, along with the fugures, forever, the Toraja funeral masks were taken off the bundle before the second burial and then preserved in rice granaries. These masks are primitive 'portraits' of the dead, meant to offer a shelter for their souls. Although the appearance of the masks seems stereotyped to us, the Toraja say that they do discern individual features.

The Batak of northern Sumatra wear masks (Plate 121), which are also connected with the cult of the dead and funeral rites. Best known are those from the Toba-Batak group living in the vicinity of Toba Lake and on Samosir Island, situated in this lake. The masks take the form of an elongated human face, equally wide from the upper edge down to the mouth. Some of the applied stylistic procedures are reminiscent of the Toraja *pemia* masks. Those of the Toba-Batak are made of wood, coloured black and slightly convex on the vertical axis. The horizontally placed almond-shaped eyes are cut through, thus making possible good visibility, and the nose is long and narrow. The mouth is wide, arch-shaped, open and provided with two rows of carved teeth; the corners are uplifted in such a manner that the mask gives the impression of smiling. The arched peripheral line of the chin follows the line of the mouth. Protruding ears are carved at the sides and human hair is attached to the upper edge of the mask and the chin. Dancers wearing this mask also used a pair of wooden arms. The mask was used to commemorate a deceased only son, which it represented. When entering the village, the son's mother welcomed and kissed it.

125 *Wayang topeng* face mask, made of painted wood. Java, Indonesia; now in Náprstek Museum, Prague.

126 *Wayang topeng* face mask, made of painted wood. Java, Indonesia; now in Náprstek Museum, Prague.

The purpose of all of this was to win over the son's soul so that it might bless the mother in order that she would soon bear another son.

Masks in the form of human faces, embodying the spirits of the dead, were also used among other Batak groups until as late as the first decades of the present century. These masks, however, are most realistic and are stylistically divergent. They are more or less oval in shape, the hair, beard and eyebrows being simulated by means of human hair, pieces of furred animal skin or strings, and an effort at portraying the features of the person in question is obvious in them. When a Raja died, all his vassals attended the funeral, each accompanied by one or two dancers wearing these masks, which were made to order for this single use. The dancers danced during the funeral ceremony, accompanied by music, and then followed the coffin to the grave. After the coffin was covered with earth, the masks were taken off and left lying on the grave, since their repeated use was believed to cause another death in the ruler's family.

Besides these face masks, called *topeng* (the same name being used for the Javanese and Balinese theatre masks and the Dayak masks from Kalimantan), the Batak made animal masks for the same purpose, consisting of a horn-bill's head attached to a wooden construction with rotang. White or red cotton cloth was stretched over the construction, thus hiding the dancer. The head of the horn-bill was decorated with magic symbols, especially crosses made of thread. The mask was called *hoda-hoda*, literally meaning 'a horse mask'. Instead of masks with a horn-bill's head, similar ones with a horse-head were used in Samosir.

Information on the use of masks in Nias Island, near the western coast of Sumatra, is very incomplete. According to F. M. Schnitger (1939), masks were used in the south of the island at a special ritual, the purpose of which was to secure offspring for a childless chieftain. A wooden mask illustrated by that author takes the form of a relatively large oval shield with holes for the eyes, a big nose, a huge moustache and a beard on the chin. The top of the dancer's head is hidden in a large cap made of plant fibres and feathers, and a horn-bill's head is again attached above the forehead of the mask. Local folk tradition says that one of the female ancestors of the local inhabitants was impregnated by a horn-bill's feather which fell into her lap, and this is why it is forbidden to kill this bird here.

In the Nias Collection of the Náprstek Museum in Prague, one of the oldest in the world, dating from the beginning of the 1880s, there are four masks from Nias, but without any exact information on their provenance (Plate 127). These are schematic human faces made from bark cloth, with cut-through square holes for the eyes and mouth and a tied on wooden nose. The hair and the beard are made of palm fibres. Bands made of palm-leaf-sheaths, stretching over the top of the head and nape of the neck, held these masks in position over the face. The purpose of these masks is uncertain. According to some collectors, they were warriors' masks, meant to strike terror into the enemy in a battle, in a similar way as the *menpo* masks of the Japanese Samurai, but they may also have been simply men's masks, since all the male inhabitants of Nias were naturally warriors.

In terms of subjects, masks of some Dayak groups in Kalimantan are among the most varied and artistically outstanding masks of the Old Malay peoples (Plate 129). In the north-eastern part of the island, in the group of the Land-Dayak, and in the Ot-Danum and Ngaju peoples in the south-western interior, masks were worn at funeral rites. Among the Land-Dayaks, all young men, except the members of the aristocracy, appeared in masks called *topeng*, which represented ancestors, at funeral ceremonies. We even hear that when rice was distributed, they used their masks in order to obtain more than one portion.

The use of masks was most common, however, in the Ot-Danum and Ngaju tribal groups at the *tiwah* funeral ceremony. Men wearing anthropomorphic as well as zoomorphic masks danced around the corpse every evening. The funeral ceremony was concluded in the presence of the entire community, including its dead members, who were personified by masks. Guests came to the village, where the ceremony took place, in decorated boats along with their 'ancestors'. In the vicinity of the village, they were met by masked dancers who embodied the ancestors of the hosts. A simulated ritualistic fight was performed by the two groups, after which the local dancers withdrew to their village. It was only after this fight that the guests' boat was allowed to land.

Masking also existed in a developed form among the tribal groups of the south-eastern inland, but masks were used here on different ritual occasions. With the Kenya people, dances with masks were directly prohibited at a time of mourning. Among the Kayan and Bahau, living in the same area, dances in masks were connected with the agricultural cult of fertility. They were performed at the time of planting and harvesting rice. Different masks were worn by men and women on these two occasions. The masks represented evil spirits. Among the Kayan, a special boar mask performed a pantomimic dance at the time of sowing the rice, which was a choreographic representation of a wild-pig hunt.

The Dayak masks, carved from light wood, are fully subordinate to the Dayak carving style also to be seen in figure carving, carved sword-hilts or funeral catafalques as well as on painted shields or in the patterning of the famous textiles dyed and woven in the so-called *ikat* technique. Most striking are their large disc-shaped eyes, at first usually inlaid with metal and later with mirrors. Another characteristic mask has large, curved canines, often protruding like boar's tusks from both jaws. The Dayak style generally prefers curved and pointed forms. This predilection is

174

manifested by an overall abstract tendency for elegant curves and protrusions in the form of open, unfinished spirals. The Dayak masks are either many-coloured or their painted decoration is based on a striking contrast of black and white areas. The masks are provided with a beard made of goat hair and decorated on the top with horn-bill's feathers, in a similar way to the basketwork caps of the Dayak warriors. The great variety of form of the Dayak masks, at the same time maintaining an apparent stylistic unity, may be perhaps explained by the fact that their production was not confined to a few specialised carvers, but that every young man carved his own mask according to his abilities and concepts, at the same time fully respecting the traditional stylistic principles. It is not surprising to find that every man was able to give an artistic form to his mask, just as every Dayak woman was able to weave an originally conceived *ikat*.

The masks occurring among the later Muslim peoples inhabiting the coasts of some of the islands, about which we know little, may perhaps be considered a product of the influence of the Old Malay peoples. The Malays living in the west of Kalimantan wore large *topeng buta* masks at circumcision, ear-perforation and wedding ceremonies. At the very beginning of the present century, the scholars P. and F. Sarasin (1905) also saw masks among the Bugi in southern Sulawesi; these were large wooden masks provided with hair and beards made of animal fur, and teeth made of porcelain shreds. However, they did not succeed in finding out what purpose was served by these masks. Wooden masks, with human hair instead of beards, were found in Flores, and in Timor the priests are reported to have used masks at a war-dance performed on their return from a warring expedition. The small island of Leti in eastern Indonesia is the home of a fantastic theriomorphic mask made of wood, tortoise-shell, boar's tusks and glass beads (Plate 122). This list, albeit undoubtedly incomplete, shows that ritual masks were probably far more common than we know before the Indonesian islands became Muslim.

JAVA, MADURA AND BALI

In Java, Madura and Bali, the original Malay tradition of masking is lost under the layers of foreign cultural influences which affected these areas for almost two centuries. This does not mean to say, of course, that they disappeared altogether. They only changed their significance and their original magic-ritual function. Some functions were degraded to the level of folk entertainment, others combined with the imported cultural traditions of India and thus attained a new and higher quality as part of the dance drama, also becoming a component of a refined court culture.

Among the various folk-dance performances in masks which took place in Javanese cities and villages, the hobby-horse-dance' at least should be mentioned. Its original magic-ritual form was upheld among the Batak in Sumatra until the present century, when the Batak accepted baptism. As in Lombok, this dance has survived in Java in a secularised form. Until recently it was performed in the streets of Javanese cities and towns by groups of itinerant actors. The central figure is a dancer who holds a stick between his

Fig. 57
An actor wearing the mask of the Javanese *wayang topeng* theatre.

knees, with a flat basketwork horse-head made of bamboo attached to the end of the stick. In this form the play is called *kuda kepang*. In western Java, where the head is cut from leather, the name of the play is *kuda lumping*. This name changes again in other parts of the island. The dancer, accompanied by a couple of musicians, imitates the movements of a horse. Along with the dancer-rider, another man performs, masked and holding a whip in his hand. This is the simplest form of the horse-dance. Sometimes, however, a whole group of such 'riders' appear, four, six or eight in number, besides a further four masked men. Their masks, or half-masks, which may cover only the upper part of the face, bear four colours, black (Plate 123), white, yellow and red, which symbolise the four cardinal points of the compass. The riders move in a circle and are sometimes divided into two groups which pretend to fight with each other.

Although this horse-dance has been maintained as a popular folk entertain-

Fig. 58
An actor of the Balinese *topeng pajegan* theatre, wearing a mask.

ment, its original magic ritual base may still by recognised. The dance performance culminated in a trance into which one of the 'riders' fell, to the ever-increasing tempo of the musical accompaniment, and only the spiritual leader of the group was able to arouse him. Traces of the original ritual function of this dance may also perhaps be found in the performances seen at a circumcision or in wedding processions.

In artistic importance, these folk masks are overshadowed by the masks of the dance drama called *wayang topeng* which is to be found in central and eastern Java and Bali. It was obviously once in existence in Madura, too (Plate 124), but literature concerning this island is extremely scarce and collections from there rare. All the information on this particular branch of theatre is therefore from Java and Bali.

The exact time of the rise of *wayang topeng* is not known. Javanese tradition dates it to the sixteenth century, linking it with one of the Javanese apostles of Islam, Sunan Kalidjaga. It must have arisen earlier, however, a later legend trying to reconcile the favoured 'pagan' spectacle with iconoclastic Islam. The early origin of the *wayang topeng* is attested to by both the contents of, and the characters appearing in, these dramas, based on the Indian epics and Javanese pre-Islamic historical traditions; some other dance elements were also taken over from Indian classical dances. After Java became Islamic in the sixteenth century, dances in masks were only temporarily maintained among the lower strata. In the eighteenth century, however, the *wayang topeng* again became fashionable at the courts in Kartasura and Surakarta. The interest of the royal courts in this theatrical form was pushed into the background later on by the dance drama *wayang wong,* drawing from the two Indian epics. In this most dancers, except the representatives of monsters and animals, perform unmasked.

The masks of the *wayang topeng* cover only the dancer's face. The play is a pantomime, the texts being recited by the principal called *dalang,* as in the Javanese puppet-theatre. This fact indicates that the *wayang topeng* of Java has developed from puppet performances. The dancer held the mask in position by gripping with his teeth a short leather band or a flat

127 A warrior's mask made of
palm-leaf-sheath, coconut fibres, wood and
red cotton strips. Nias, Indonesia; now in
Náprstek Museum, Prague. Height *c.* 50 cm.

128 *Hodo-apah* dance mask made of
painted wood and mirrors. Kajan or Bahau,
Kalimantan, Indonesia; now in Koninklijk
Instituut voor de Tropen, Amsterdam.
Height 30 cm.

178

129 *Wayang topeng* face mask made of
painted wood. Java, Indonesia; now in
Náprstek Museum, Prague. Height 20 cm.

130 *Wayang wong* mask of a monkey,
made of painted wood. Bali, Indonesia; now
in Náprstek Museum, Prague. Height 19 cm.

131 *Wayang topeng* masks of a prince and
a princess, made of painted wood, mother of
pearl and animal hair. Bali, Indonesia; now
in Náprstek Museum, Prague.

132   A mask of the mythical bird Garuda of
the *wayang wong* dance drama. Bali,
Indonesia; now in Náprstek Museum,
Prague. Height 20 cm.

▷
133   The face mask of a supernatural being
of the *barong* plays, made of painted wood.
Bali, Indonesia; now in Náprstek Museum,
Prague. Height 17.3 cm.

134   *Barong* mask of the witch Rangda,
made of painted wood. Bali, Indonesia; now
in Náprstek Museum, Prague. Height 25 cm.

135 *Wayang topeng* mask of an old man, made of wood with vestiges of paint and animal hair. Bali, Indonesia; now in Náprstek Museum, Prague. Height 19 cm.

wooden peg attached to the inner side of the mask on a level with his mouth. It was only in the present century that the masks began to be tied to the face. The characteristic style of the Javanese dance masks is also identical with that of all three forms of Javanese puppet theatre, i.e. the *wayang kulit* using shadow puppets made of leather, the *wayang kerucil* with its flat wooden puppets, and the *wayang golek* with three-dimensional puppets. A specialist is able to discern slight regional differences in them, but the style of all of these masks is uniform in principle. They are carved from pale wood, light in weight and painted in many colours. They taper from the forehead to the chin, this tendency being so pronounced in Java that their shape is almost triangular (Plate 125). Slots enabling the dancer to see out are placed under the eyes or, in exceptional cases, above them. The Javanese masks are always earless. The mouth is small and half-open, giving the impression of a stiffened grin. The most striking feature is a small and slightly upturned nose with a sharp ridge (Plate 126), endowing the mask with a supernatural bird's mien, emphasised during the performance by jerky movements of the dancer's head and a slight backward tilt of the head made necessary by the low position of the slots for seeing out (Fig. 57).

The older masks are characterised by a deeper relief carving of diadems and various jewels, beard, etc.; in more recent masks, these details are often only simulated by painting (Plate 128). Exceptionally, other materials such as beards made of goat-hair occur in Javanese masks.

185

The masks of Madura are more closely related to the style of the ancient Javanese religious sculpture; unlike the Javanese masks, their chins do not taper off and their painted decoration is even less pronounced.

The Javanese *wayang topeng* originally had only nine different masks, but their number gradually increased to 80 types.

The Balinese *wayang topeng* is somewhat different in character. Its contents are secular, the subjects being drawn from the history of the island and some of them treating events which took place in the Javanese empire of Majapahit, the province of which was Bali, in the fourteenth century. However, attention is not focused on these events, but on the represented persons acting under various circumstances. The *topeng* is no sophisticated court entertainment in Bali, but a lively popular spectacle for the villagers. There are

Fig. 59
The mask of Banaspati, 'Lord of Forests', in which two dancers perform in the temple drama, *barong keket*.

a large number of folk characters and many farcial elements. The entire ensemble usually consists of between 20 and 30 masks. Those of the main characters such as the king, prince or princess (Plate 131) are established in type, but the masks of folk characters and clowns are not so constant, their features depending rather on the carver's individual inventiveness, and their number is not restricted in any way.

Compared to the Javanese masks, those of Bali are more realistic and independent in terms of style. Their colours are more lively, the shape is basically oval, ears are carved in them, the eyes are almond-shaped or rounded, and the size of the mouth is not reduced but realistically adapted to the proportions of the rest of the mask. More frequent than in the Javanese masks is the use of different materials, especially for making hair and beards, and the teeth are also inlaid with mother of pearl. The masks of the main characters, whose performance is pantomimic, cover the entire face, whereas those of comic characters often cover only the upper part of the face. These half-masks are characterised by bristly hair and moustaches (Plate 135) and a knob-shaped nose; in some of them an eye is missing, replaced by a hole (Plate 136), through which the actor's own eye may be seen, others have the teeth knocked out, a harelip, etc.

The main roles, including those of women, are usually played by two or three older men who change their masks several times during the performance. When the main female role is played by a girl, she performs unmasked. Each main character is accompanied by two servants of comic appearance, commenting upon the pantomimic performance of their masters in a dialogue.

Although the contents of the Balinese *topeng* are entirely secular, the masks are considered sacred. This again points to their original religious and magic function. They are kept in a village temple, each of them separately and carefully wrapped up in a scarf. Before the actor puts the mask over his face, he offers a small sacrifice to it. This ritualised act is particularly apparent in the Balinese form called *topeng pajegan,* in which all the roles are performed in a pantomimic way by a single man who may change his mask 40 times during his performance

186

136 A folk-type mask with a disfigured face, for the *wayang topeng,* made of wood with vestiges of paint. Bali, Indonesia; now in Náprstek Museum, Prague. Height 21.5 cm.

(Fig. 58). These changes take place in a small, improvised shed placed directly on the stage. The actor is hidden from the sight of the spectators, but all ritual prescriptions are maintained during his dealings with the masks, which are not meant to be a spectacle for the audience, but an expression of real devotion towards a sacred object.

The dance drama *wayang wong,* mentioned in connection with Javanese theatre masks, has its Balinese parallel, albeit somewhat different. Whereas the Javanese *wayang wong* draws from both the *Mahabharata* and the *Ramayana,* its Balinese version is exclusively based on the *Ramayana.* Originally all of the dancers performed in masks in this drama, except Ravana's sister, Shurpanakha. Unlike the Indian original, Balinese tradition presents her as a beautiful woman, which is why an unmasked girl dances in her role. In the present century, the main characters also perform without masks, including Rama, his brother Lakshmana and Ravana's brother Vibhishana. Rama's wife Sita carries a dance crown on her head, similar to that adorning the dancers in the temple dance *legong.* The original masks of the heroes were derived from the iconography of ancient Hindu sculpture and the Balinese shadow-play *wayang ku-*

137 A funeral mask made of painted papier-mâché. Jehol, Manchuria; now in Etnografiska museet, Stockholm. Height 22 cm.

lit. Most expressive are the masks worn by Hanuman's army of monkeys. These are provided with richly carved crowns (Plate 130), elongated on both sides of the face into wide wings. The faces of all masks of the *wayang wong* are characterised by deeper carving (Plate 132) than those of the Balinese *topeng* and the conception of the monkey masks of this dance drama corresponds to the general conception of animal masks of the *barong* plays, the third and probably the best-

known genre of Balinese dances performed in masks.

The Balinese Hindu exegesis of today connects the *barong* plays with the Shi-vaistic deities of the Hindu pantheon, but the dominating magic element of these plays suggests their pre-Hindu origin. The animal masks of the *barong* type are many in number, such as that of boar, elephant, tiger or cow, but some of them have already lost their importance and have ceased to be used entirely. The most significant and best-known among them is the mask called *barong keket*, which does not represent any actual animal, but is a wild beast par excellence (Fig. 59). This is suggested by its Bali-Sanskrit denomination 'Banaspati', i.e. 'Lord of the Forest'. Its face combines the stylised features of a lion, tiger, goat, elephant and also perhaps other animals in an anthropomorphised form. Attached to a wooden, many-coloured face with a movable lower jaw are 'wings' made of gilded leather, decoratively carved and ornamentally cut through, reminiscent of elephant ears. The chin is provided with a long beard made of human hair intertwined with flowers. The mask is attached to a construction consisting of bamboo and strings, covered with a cloth to which are attached mirrors, feathers and other decorations made of gilded leather and forming a sort of lion's mane. Two dancers are hidden under the construction, animating the mask.

The performance of the masks of the *barong* type is accompanied by a number of anthropomorphic masks, both comic and terrible in their demonic features (Plate 133). Outstanding among them is the mask of the witch Rangda (Plate 134). This is a mask provided with a demonic anthropomorphic face. Under the large semi-globular eyes, a prominent nose is to be seen with widely flaring nostrils, out of which tufts of animal hair protrude. Long curved tusks are set into the upper and lower jaws of the open mouth and a red tongue, with stylised flames made of gilded leather, hangs down on to the chest. This mask, carved from pale wood and painted in many colours, is attached to a helmet-shaped construction which covers the dancer's head. This is provided with a white 'mane' of goat-hair, flowing in long tresses around the dancer's entire body. The dancer is clad in a cloth costume, to which are sewn limp cloth breasts stuffed with sawdust. The hands are covered with gloves provided with long nails which are carved from horn.

Rangda devouring little children is an embodiment of black magic and all evil: the forces which threaten human society. Hindu tradition connects her with the Indian goddess Durga. The *barong* plays culminate in a fight, in which Rangda measures her strength against *barong keket* and is defeated at the end. However, the mask of *barong keket* is not an embodiment of the principle of good, as is sometimes explained in a simplified way, but only another demonic force which the villagers have succeeded in winning over to their side by sacrifices and magic rites.

Japan

In terms of development and history of masks, Japan, situated at the easternmost end of Asia, occupies an extraordinarily important position among the Asian countries. Because of a deep esteem for tradition, specific forms of dramatic art, maintained over the centuries, still flourish here and many old masks have been preserved in active use. The masks which date back to early times probably rank among the oldest extant masks in the world. Among those which have survived, we may admire a number of outstanding artefacts, both anonymous and sometimes signed with the names of outstanding artists.

Before we turn our attention to the unique carved works of Japan, we must mention the remarkable clay masks which originated in the middle and late periods of the prehistoric Jōmon culture, i.e. around 3000—300 BC. In spite of considerable stylisation, these miniature faces, about 10 cm in width, are reminiscent, with their closed eyes, a closed or half-open mouth and a projecting nose, of a person who has fallen into a trance (Fig. 60). Some archaeologists think that the purpose of these masks was to enable those who put them on to gain the magic abilities of a shaman.

GIGAKU MASKS

The oldest masks of the historic period, mostly made of wood, were connected with cult functions, but in this particular case they were used within the framework of the developed religious system of Buddhism which began to spread over all Japan from the first half of the sixth century onwards. The masks were used at pantomimic and dance performances called *gigaku*, which took place in open areas within the complex of a Buddhist temple, and obviously served not only to

Fig. 60
A clay mask from Asō in the Akita Prefecture of Japan. Dated as the late Jōmon period, *c.* 300 BC. Now in Tokyo University.

190

138   Mask of the King of Go for the *gigaku* dances, made of camphor wood with vestiges of paint. The diadem is made of gilded bronze. Japan, second half of the seventh century; now in Tokyo National Museum, formerly Hōryūji temple. Height 29.9 cm.

enlighten but also to amuse the audience. Due to the fact that the new religion was supported by the Emperor for reasons of prestige, the *gigaku* dances were closely linked with the imperial court and its ceremonies. However, more favour was gradually won by the more grandiose *bugaku* dances, and in the Heian period (784—1185), the *gigaku* was pushed out of the court milieu entirely.

Tradition has it that in the mid-sixth century a relative of the ruler of the Wu Empire (Go in Japanese) of southern China brought not only Buddhist books and statues, but also masks, musical instruments, and costumes for *gigaku* performances to Japan. In actual fact, however, the *gigaku* performances proper were learned by the Japanese only in 612, from a man named Mimashi, a dancer from the Korean Paekche kingdom. Mimashi, who travelled widely in China, be-

came acquainted with the *gigaku* in the Go kingdom. This origin of the dances is also suggested by two masks belonging to the *gigaku* repertory: the 'King of Go' (Plate 138) and the 'Lady or Princess of Go'.

A complete set of *gigaku* masks comprises various bizarre faces testifying to a more remote source of inspiration for these dances. We may find among them, for example, 'Konron', a half-animal barbarian from South-East Asia, 'Baramon', the Indian 'Brahmin' (Fig. 61), and also the Persian 'Drunken Barbarian King' and his body of retainers.

Little can be said today about the music which accompanied the *gigaku* dances and consisted, besides singers, of small *dōbatsu* cymbals and hour-glass-shaped drums. The more valuable testimonies to this perished art, therefore, besides fragments of the musicians' and dancers' cos-

191

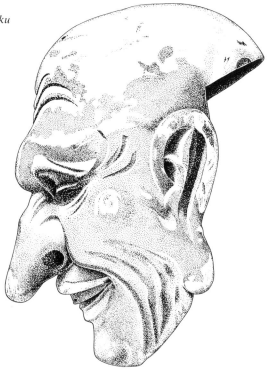

Fig. 61
Baramon mask from the *gigaku* dances. From Shōsōin, Nara, Japan. Dated AD 752.

tumes, are the masks. Altogether 251 of them have been preserved, which is an astonishingly high number. The largest collection, of 161 pieces from the eighth century, is kept in Shōsōin, the imperial treasure house at the Tōdaiji temple in Nara. A further 23 masks from the same period are in the care of the monastery there.

Even older in origin are the masks from the Hōryūji monastery near Nara, the major part of which originated in the seventh century. The monastery lost part of its treasure, including many *gigaku* masks, during the Meiji period (1868—1912), when it became so poor that it had to hand them over to the Imperial Household Office, in exchange for a subsidy for repairing the shabby temple buildings. The artistic objects, *gigaku* masks among them, were taken into the custody of the Imperial Museum, now the Tokyo National Museum.

The overwhelming majority of the *gigaku* masks are carved from wood; 19 masks were made from camphor wood *(Cinnamomum camphora)* and nine pieces from paulownia wood *(Paulownia tomentosa)*, as was the only mask which remained in the temple (apparently by mistake). The masks preserved in Shōsōin and Tōdaiji are mostly carved from pau-

lownia wood, although in the Nara period (710—784) the wood of the Japanese cypress *(Chamaecyparis obtusa)* began to be generally used in carving. Paulownia wood is more fragile, but very light in weight and is better suited for making massive masks.

For the same reason the masks were also made by another sculptural technique, i.e. the dry lacquer method. Lacquer was brought to Japan from China and was, besides clay, the material most favoured in sculpture in the Nara period. A rough form of the sculpture or mask was first made of clay and then covered with multiple layers of hemp cloth soaked in natural liquid lacquer. After drying, the clay foundation was removed and the surface was finished; it was modelled from a mixture of flour, sawdust and powdered incense, bound together by means of liquid lacquer, and covered with lacquer, pigment or a sheet of gold.

Except for the masks made for the religious processions called *gyōdō*, the *gigaku* masks are the largest among the Japanese masks. Their width is usually 20 to 30 cm, their height 30—40 cm and their depth 18—35 cm. Thus they cover not only the face, but also the top of the head, sometimes reaching down to the nape of the neck. The mask is carved from a single piece of wood, but the back part is usually joined to the part forming the face and the top of the head. The masks are provided with ears, the only exception being some examples of the 'Lady from Go'. Konron and Karura have pointed animal ears, otherwise the earlobes of the masks are mostly elongated in the same manner as in Buddhist statues, and are sometimes perforated.

The *gigaku* masks have holes for the eyes and the nostrils, and mostly have half-open mouths. Exceptions are the masks of the 'Lady from Go' who has the lips of her graceful mouth closed, and that of the athlete Rikishi whose stiffly closed mouth expresses aversion to evil and resolution to fight against it. Variants of some other masks, for instance the servants of the Drunken King, also have their mouths closed. The effectiveness of the *gigaku* masks which, except for the lion mask, had no movable parts, was based on their static form and was attained by deep carving, emphasising certain features of the face, almost crossing the borderline of caricature, and by their varied painted decoration.

Before the paints were applied, wooden masks were hardened with lacquer and coated with kaolin. The features of the face were sometimes emphasised with Chinese ink, also used by the carver for drawing the hair, eyebrows and beard. Some masks have short hair made of plant fibres which are glued on to the skull and also fixed in place with a minute tin disc. The eyebrows, the moustache and the beard were also formed by tufts of animal hair or plant fibres, but these have disappeared, only tiny and regularly distributed holes remaining.

All of the *gigaku* dancers performed in masks and altogether 14 types of masks were necessary for the entire performance; some of them, such as the mask of the lion, bird Karura and barbarian Konron, are fantastic in appearance, others are lifelike. Particularly resembling actual human faces are the masks of the 'Lady from Go', those of the children attending upon the lion, and the mask of the old man Taikofu.

For the sparsely bearded inhabitants of the Far East, a dense beard was the mark of an alien, and one is not surprised to find the masks of the 'Brahmin' or the bellicose guardians of the 'Beauty from Go', Kongō and Rikishi, adorned with beards. Remnants of a glued-on beard also heighten the exotic appearance of the mask of the Drunken King from Shōsōin, made by the carver Sutemeshi, in which an elongated cap with a flower ornament is, at the same time, a unique example of the original colouring of the eighth century.

A similar cap, reminiscent of a fez, and the same eagle's nose are also characteristisc of the mask of the old foreign man Taikofu. The long-nosed masks of Chidō (Plate 139), who introduces a *gigaku* performance, are easy to mistake for the masks of the attendants of the Drunken

139   Chidō mask of the *gigaku* dances, made of dry lacquer and painted, plus a decoration of plant fibres and a sheet metal disc. Japan, Edo period (1600—1868). This is a replica of a mask from the eighth century. Now in Náprstek Museum, Prague. Height 31.5 cm.

140 Chikyū mask for a *bugaku* performance, made of painted hinoki wood. Japan, carver Inshō, dated 1185; now in Kasuga shrine, Nara. Height 21.3 cm.

King, and the same is true of the smiling children's masks of the lion's attendants, on the one hand, and that of Taikofu's grandson Taikoji on the other. The identification of the mask of the 'King of Go' is sometimes helped by a diadem or crown made of sheet-metal and open-worked in a flower-like pattern.

Confusion between the functions of the individual masks is also prevented by their denominations, or the names of the respective dances, inscribed on the back of the mask or on the pouch in which it is kept. In the same place, the signature of the carver or even the date of the festival for which the mask was made may be found.

The oldest extant *gigaku* masks, i.e. the set of camphor-wood masks from the Hōryūji monastery, are neither signed nor dated, but they are supposed to have been made for a festival organised on the occasion of rebuilding Hōryūji which was destroyed in a fire in 670. Somewhat later in date are the masks made of paulownia wood, preserved in Hōryūji. These are linked with the construction of the eastern precinct of the temple, finished in 739. No date is borne by the three masks, made of dry lacquer, from the set which belonged to Hōryūji, and they cannot even be said definitely to have originated in the seventh century, like the masks made of camphor wood. On the ground of the dry-lacquer technique used in their production, however, they seem to be older in origin than the masks from Tōdaiji, which are dated 752.

In a relatively large percentage of the masks preserved in Shōsōin and Tōdaiji, the name of the carver, or the date and name of the dance are given. Most of them bear the date of 'the ninth day of the fourth month of the fourth year of the Tempyō-Shōhō era' (i.e. AD 752), when a grandiose temple ceremony of 'opening

194

the eyes' of a new giant statue of Buddha Vairochana, made of bronze, was performed in the Tōdaiji temple. The masks used in that occasion were deposited in Shōsōin, along with the other ritual equipment.

BUGAKU MASKS

The cultural and historic value of the *gigaku* masks must be assessed from several viewpoints — those of aesthetics, artistry, religious iconography and antiquity. First of all, however, they are significant relics of the sculpture of the Nara period, standing on a dividing line between the sacred and profane arts; some of them may even be ranked among the early examples of Japanese portrait carving. The *gigaku* masks are also testimonies to contacts with remote cultures, along the so-called Silk Road connecting China with the Mediterranean, as well as being the most significant relics of the dances they were used at.

The golden age of the *gigaku* dances was the Nara period; in the subsequent Heian period, their popularity strongly decreased, and in the Kamakura period (1185—1332) their performances became sporadic. The last report of a *gigaku* performance dates from the Genroku era (1688—1704). Even in the Nara period,

however, the *gigaku* dances with masks were not the only type of musical and dance performances accompanying temple or court ceremonies and entertainments. From the fifth century onwards, various musical and dance forms penetrated Japan, at first from Korea and then directly from China. At the beginning of the Heian period, in the ninth century, these varied musical traditions were gradually consolidated into two fundamental genres — the Chinese *tōgaku* and the Korean *komagaku*. When the music was played in a concert-like way without any dance, in the Chinese style, it was called *kangen*, while a performance with dances, partly performed in masks, was called *bugaku*, irrespective of whether it was a composition in the Chinese or Korean style. Unlike the orchestra of the *kangen*, in which all main instrumental groups were represented, the *bugaku* was accompanied by wind and percussion instruments.

The *bugaku* dances became an indispensable part of the programme of various festivities at the court and at large temples such as banquets, audiences, festivals or wrestling matches. Music and dance were part of the education of every courtier and their practice was a much favoured pastime. The Japanese court was modelled on the example of the T'ang

Fig. 62
The mask of the drunken baron for the Kotokuraku dances. From Tamukeyama shrine, Nara, Japan. Dated 1160.

195

court, with its government divided into left and right sides. Each side had not only its own ministers and officials, but also music and dances of its own. The *bugaku* of both sides differed in characteristic dance movements, musical instruments and the colour of the robes. The dances of the two groups usually alternated in a single performance according to the harmonious system of 'pair dances', the second dance being a parody of the first. The cut of the robe and the composition of its parts were derived from the contemporary fashion of civil and military dignitaries, according to the character of the music and mask.

The grandiose spectacle offered by the *bugaku* performances became ever rarer during the Kamakura period. After the government of the military shōguns was introduced in Kamakura, the political and financial power of the Kyoto court decreased and the organisation of festivities and dance performances was beyond its means. The *bugaku* musicians and dancers departed to large temples in Nara, Kyoto and Osaka. Many masks, preserved in shrines and temples all over Japan, bear witness to their spread throughout the provinces.

During the restless time of wars, lasting from the fourteenth to the sixteenth centuries, the *bugaku* did not thrive. New

types of dramatic art, especially the *nō* plays, began to be preferred. It was only the government of the shōguns of the Tokugawa dynasty, in the peaceful Edo period (1600—1868), which brought forth a revival of the *bugaku* dances, among other old arts. A desire for the truest possible record of the original form of music and dances is shown by the book called *Gakkaroku* (Notes of a Musician) written by Abe Suenao in 1690. Until today this has served the *bugaku* artists as a handbook covering all aspects of music, costumes and masks.

The *bugaku* dances, as performed today, thus correspond to the form of this art as reconstituted at the beginning of the Edo period. Nowadays the *bugaku* is performed at court by musicians who are mostly descendants of the court orchestra musicians of the eighth century. *Bugaku* performances in which amateur artists participate also take place in Buddhist temples and Shintō shrines several times a year.

A performance today may thus give us an idea of what the *bugaku* looked like in the Heian period. Numerous mentions to be found in old literature are also of help, particularly chronicles and diaries, special sources, such as *Kyōkunshō* (Books of Instructions) by Koma Chikazane, a member of an old dancing family, from 1233,

Fig. 63
A Genjōraku dance from the twelfth century. According to *Illustrations of Ancient Music,* Tokyo University of Fine Arts.

Fig. 64
A paper mask for the Soriko dance. Shitennōji temple, Osaka.

196

141 Ryōō mask for a *bugaku* performance, made of wood with painted decoration, plus yellow sheet metal and horsehair. Japan, signed 'Uzumasa Sukune Toshinaga', dated 1856. Now in Náprstek Museum, Prague. Height 39 cm.

various works of art, and especially the *Illustrations of Ancient Music* by Shinsei from the first half of the twelfth century, as well, of course, as the old masks worn at the *bugaku* dances.

Unlike the *gigaku* dances, whose performance was monopolised by masked dancers, some of the *bugaku* dances were performed without masks. According to old records, 32 out of more than a hundred dances required a mask; 24 of these have so far been identified, along with the corresponding number of masks. Each type of dance required a special mask and in some cases the dancers played various roles, therefore using more than one mask.

Apart from a single mask made of dry lacquer, the *bugaku* masks were carved from wood. An exception was a special type of paper mask, which will be discussed later. The oldest extant wooden masks are dated approximately to the beginning of the eleventh century and like the other masks from the Heian period they are carved from the light wood of the Japanese cypress, *hinoki* or *kiri*. The carvers of later masks, coming from areas more remote from the cultural centres of Kyoto and Nara, used various kinds of wood, both hard and soft.

Generally we may state that the *bugaku* masks are smaller in size than those of *gigaku*, but considerably larger than the masks used in the *nō* plays. The *bugaku* masks are 20—25 cm high, 15—20 cm wide and 10—15 cm deep. They mostly cover only the face, some of them being earless. The holes for the eyes are of different sizes and are modelled according to the character of the mask. Well-executed masks are carved deeply, with very thin walls. The later and provincial masks are more massive, whereas in the perfectly executed replicas of old masks from the Edo period, which are very thinly carved, the date of origin is very difficult to assess. The Edo carvers worked in the same way as those of the Heian period while processing the mask's surface, the latter having taken over this technique from sculpture. Various materials were used for the impregnation and hardening of the mask's natural wood, most frequent being *sabi urushi*, which was a mixture of fine flour and lacquer, with *tonoko*, or powder made of unrefined clay, added. Before the application of *sabi urushi*, the surface of both sides of the mask was sometimes covered with hemp cloth saturated in lacquer. In the next phase, a kaolin background was laid in several layers on the outer side, and black or brown lacquer on the inner side. Lastly the carver painted the mask with colourful clays or drew a hairstyle, beard and eyebrows with black Chinese ink. In a few types of mask, which were covered with red lacquer, the kaolin background was not found necessary.

In later masks and those of poorer quality, simpler processes may be observed. Sometimes the paints were even applied directly to untreated wood.

Some *bugaku* masks have long, soft hair, eyebrows and a beard made of animal hair inserted into tiny apertures and fastened by means of wooden or bamboo pegs. Only the Batō mask, covered with red lacquer, is supplemented with very effective dark blue hair made of silk cords.

The *bugaku* masks are also unique among the Japanese masks in that a relatively high percentage of their types are provided with movable parts, especially the chin and the eyes. Those *bugaku* dances which were more amusing and dramatic in character spread from the cultural centres to the countryside, for example the Ryōō, Nasori and Genjōraku dances. In the provincial masks worn at these dances, however, we often do not find any movable parts. Instead, the carvers sometimes emphasised the eyes and teeth with gilded pieces of copper or gold lacquer.

The *bugaku* dances were based on very different sources of inspiration and this is why a complete extant set of the types of masks used at these dances comprises works varied in character, starting with the sweet female Ayakiri and ending with the wild Nasori, endowed with an intentionally exaggerated expression of ferocity and strength. Generally, however, the *bugaku* masks are characterised by their efforts to enhance the significance of the dance they are used in. The masks of 'calm' dances usually excel in their mild, smiling expression, and those of 'military' or 'swift' dances are dramatic in character, emphasising the rhythm of dance with its movements and sound effects.

The carvers of the *bugaku* masks were not so much interested in portraying an actual human face, as in expressing a symbol, a state of mind or a mood. This was achieved by the way of carving, which was summary rather than detailed in character, but also by a style which brings the art of the *bugaku* masks close to the Buddhist sculpture of the late Heian period. The oldest extant masks originated in 1042, but the oldest among those which also bear the signature of the carver date only from the end of the twelfth century. Almost all of these artists were the *busshi*, or carvers of Buddhist sculptures, employed at the workshops of the individual monasteries.

The most suitable classification of the *bugaku* masks is offered by the programme of a performance, during which three basic types of dances were performed: first, the graceful *hiramai*, i.e. 'calm and peaceful dances' also called *bunnomai* or 'literary dances', executed in a slow or medium quick tempo and performed by dancers clad in civil court costumes; secondly, the *bunomai*, i.e. 'military dances', manly and heroic in character, performed by dancers in military dress, armed with swords and halberds and wearing larger masks personifying energy; thirdly, *hashirimai*, swift 'dances in running', danced by individual dancers wearing grotesque masks.

The introductory dance of a *bugaku* performance and one of the 'calm' dances, is the relatively lively Shintoriso, performed by four or six dancers wearing large caps and carrying sticks like those used for playing polo in their hands. All of them are provided with the same smiling and strongly stylised egg-shaped mask with slot-like eyes, the elegant arch of which is repeated and emphasised by the painted eyebrows. The comic expression of the face is stressed by little red discs with black dots on the cheeks and a caligraphic moustache and beard. Similar to some other types of the *bugaku* masks, that of Shintoriso also has a hair-style suggested by means of a black and slightly protruding bow bordering the forehead.

Altogether ten examples of this type have been preserved, the oldest of which is dated 1042. Another mask from the Kasuga shrine in Nara, signed by the carver of Buddhist statues, Inshō, in 1185, is a perfect piece of carving.

Inshō was also the maker of one of about 40 masks made for the next item of the programme, the felicitation dance,

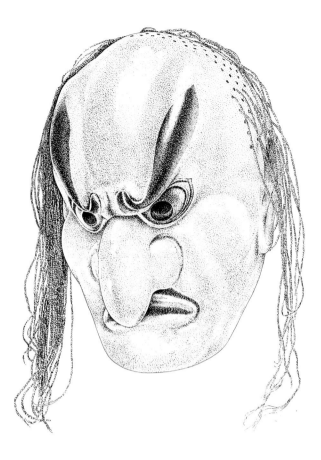

Fig. 65
Batō mask for a *bugaku*
performance. Made of wood,
red lacquer and silk strings.
Carver Gyōmyō, Itsukushima
shrine, Japan. Dated 1173.

was allegedly performed by the scholar Wani from the Korean Paekche state at the coronation ceremony of the Japanese ruler Nintoku. The dance later became part of a ceremony held at the time when a prince attained maturity.

The Ōnintei mask, with the eye-slots elongated upwards and sidewards and a tightly closed mouth, gives an impression of nobility. Similar to the Chikyū and Taishōtoku, this mask also has a protuberance over the top of the nose, which points to a common origin for all of them. One of the 17 preserved masks of the Ōnintei type, from 1185, is signed by the carver Inshō.

The number of extant bird masks of the Korobase type is larger. These masks are decorated with little bells which symbolise the voice of a crane. Four of them date from 1142. They originally belonged to the ancient temple of Tōdaiji, and represent several styles. Some of them have large, deeply carved beaks, others are flatter and their carving is shallow.

The Ayakiri is the only female mask of the *bugaku*, except for the repellent Haremen solo mask for the Ninomai dance. Since the dance had already vanished in the Middle Ages, only a few Ayakiri masks have been preserved. However, four examples from the Sumiyoshi shrine in Osaka represent this type which is the most eloquent testimony to the close connection of *bugaku*-mask carving with Buddhist sculpture. The calm face, with the crescents of the eyebrows arching above the half-closed eyes and the tiny closed mouth, is closely related both to the bōdhisattva masks used at *gyōdō* processions, and to their statues.

The Kotokuraku is the only *bugaku* dance representing a sort of short episode, which is why it requires three kinds of masks. A group of four tipsy young barbarians, Kotokuraku, wear masks with a cheerfully smiling mouth, slot-like eyes and an especially long nose which swings merrily from side to side during the lively dance (Fig. 62). Only one of them is provided with an immovable nose, because he drank very little wine. This is because the inn-keeper, who served the young men, stole the wine for himself. His own mask expresses exhilaration caused by the amount of wine he has drunk.

Especially suggestive is the Heishitori mask from the Tamukeyama shrine in

Chikyū. In contrast with the graphic effect of the Shintoriso mask, the Chikyū mask excels in its sculptural qualities. Typical is an expressive and beautifully modelled nose and a smiling, as if talking, mouth. A medallion with a triple protuberance is set between the three-dimensional arching eyebrows of the Chikyū mask, as well as on a few types of those worn at 'calm' dances.

The word *chikyū* means 'eternal land' and this dance is a eulogy about the endless existence of heaven and earth. The mask expresses pleasure in this fact, increased by the performance of between four and six dancers, wearing huge caps surmounted by figures of birds (Plate 140).

Thirty-two masks for the Taishōtoku dance have been preserved. The oldest among them is dated 1042 and belonged to the famous Shintō shrine in Ise; the latest is from 1498. Common features of the masks are a large nose and bulging, squinting eyes.

An ancient tradition is connected with the mask of the Ōnintei dance, performed by a group of four dancers wearing beautiful crowns on their heads. The dance

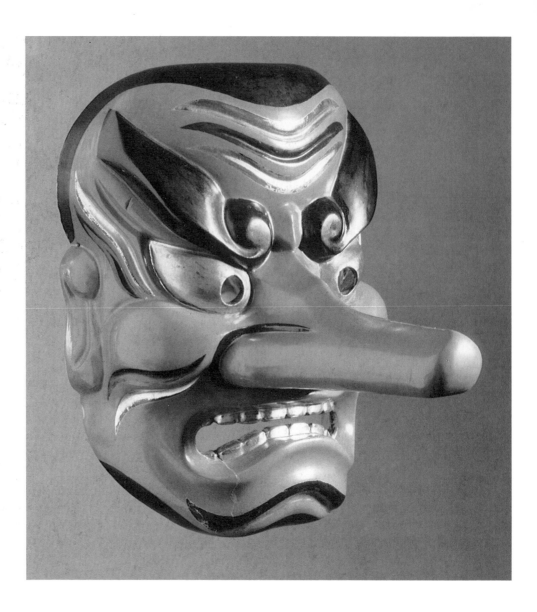

142 Tengu mask used at Shintō festivals, made of painted, lacquered wood. Japan; now in Náprstek Museum, Prague. Height 25 cm.

Nara, dated to the beginning of the thirteenth century. The smiling, rather vulgar face, with many wrinkles and gappy teeth, gives the impression of spritely laughter. In the same shrine a beautiful wooden jug or wine bottle has been preserved, with a lacquer decoration of a *kiri* tree in flower. It is an outstanding example of the lacquer art of the Kamakura period.

Similarly to the Heishitori is the noble Kempai of the Kotokuraku dance. The court cap *(kammuri),* with little fans at the sides, makes it impossible for the dancer to fasten a wooden mask to his face, and he therefore uses an oblong cloth or paper mask called *zōmen.* In the Hōryūji temple, nine wooden masks for the Kotokuraku dance have been preserved, among which two, dating to the middle or even early Heian period, are

among those very oldest *bugaku* masks.

Two dancers of the next slow Ama dance, performing in ancient court robes, wear a *kammuri* cap on their heads and their faces are covered with an oblong mask made of cloth or paper. The features of the face are painted on its surface with Chinese ink in an entirely schematised form. The prototype of this mask, the two oldest extant examples of which are dated 1693 and 1695, respectively, was probably a mask of the Nara period, made of hemp cloth, and now kept in Shōsōin.

A very similar mask is used at a dance of the 'right hand' called Soriko, the purpose of which is to secure a rich distillation of *sake* rice wine (Fig. 64). By contrast, the Ama dance was probably connected with the ancient Indian groundbreaking ceremony.

143   A dragon mask for New Year folk
dances, made of painted papier-mâché on
a wooden frame. China; now in Náprstek
Museum, Prague. Height 46 cm.

144 *Shishigashira* mask of a lion dance, made of painted, lacquered wood. Japan, nineteenth century; now in Náprstek Museum, Prague. Height 33 cm.

▷
145 A male mask of the *kagura* dances, made of painted wood. Japan, nineteenth century; now in Náprstek Museum, Prague.

203

146 A male mask of the *kagura* dances, made of painted wood and horsehair. Japan, nineteenth century; now in Náprstek Museum, Prague. Height 21.1 cm.

147   A boy's mask for the *kagura* dances,
made of painted wood. Japan, nineteenth
century; now in Náprstek Museum, Prague.

148 Kasshiki. A boys' mask for the *nō*
plays, made of painted wood. Japan, Edo
period; now in Náprstek Museum, Prague.
Height 21.3 cm.

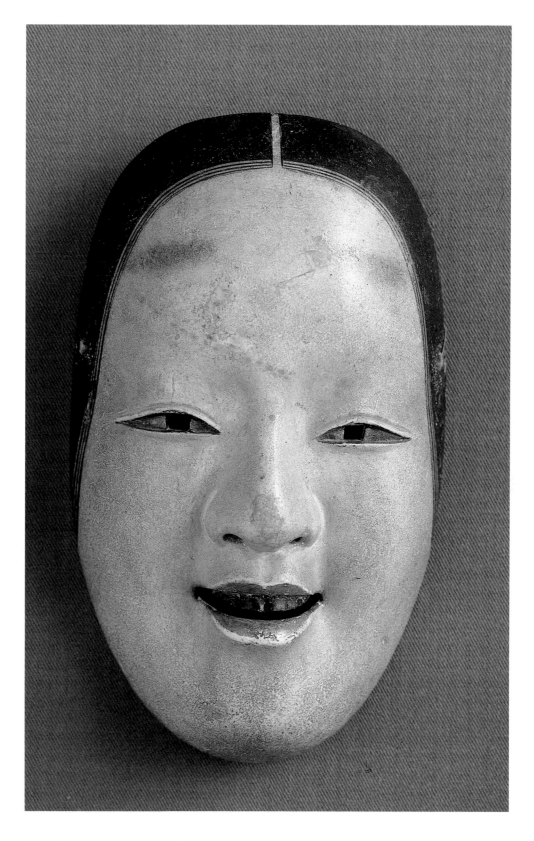

149   *Ko-omote* female mask for the *nō*
plays, made of painted wood. Japan, Edo
period, signed 'Deme Tohaku'. Now in
Náprstek Museum, Prague. Height 21.4 cm.

150 Obeshimi demon mask for the *nō*
plays, made of painted wood. Japan, Edo
period, signed 'Shojuken'. Now in Náprstek
Museum, Prague. Height 22.6 cm.

The dancers have not yet left the stage, when another pair appears to perform the pair dance, Ninomai. The dancers, one wearing the mask of Emimen, a smiling and wrinkled old man, and the other that of Haremen, a bloated old woman disfigured by leprosy, ask for one of the sceptres with which the Ama dancers are provided, and when they are refused they perform a comic parody of the preceding dance.

The oldest extant examples of Ninomai masks, from 1173, the property of the Itsukushima shrine in Miyajima, are the most perfect pieces of artistry among masks preserved today. Their author was a carver of Buddhist statues called Gyōmyō. The widely smiling and semi-toothless mouth of the old man and the fans of wrinkles around his slot-like little eyes are in sharp contrast to the ugly face of the old woman whose eyelids are swollen and whose mouth is contorted in a painful grin.

For the next Saisōrō solo dance, an older parallel may be found among the *gigaku* dances, namely the Taikofu dance. This is because the Saisōrō is a dance of death; it was always performed by an old man who was supposed to die within a year. Nowadays it does not form part of the *bugaku* programme any more, but it was performed as such in the Edo period, as attested to by the preserved masks. In terms of typology, the Taikofu mask forms a link with the famous Saisōrō mask from 1249, which also belongs to the Itsukushima shrine. In spite of an almost graphically conceived stylisation of the wrinkles, this white face, at one time supplemented with a dense beard and eyebrows and provided with movable eyes and a movable chin, makes a very vivid impression, which corresponds to the realistic art of the Kamakura period.

Masks worn at the 'military' dances have been preserved in a smaller number than those of the 'calm' ones. We have a single example, from the Sumiyoshi shrine in Osaka, of the Shinnō dance mask used at a celebration commemorating the founding of the T'ang dynasty and the memory of soldiers of merit. The inscription to be seen on the mask, also containing the date 1287, shows that this was one of the four pieces used at the dance. The mask is comparatively small and shallow. The energetic wavy line of its eyebrows, steadfast look and firmly closed mouth express strength and resolve.

A couple of legends are connected with the significance of the Sanju dance. One of them says that the dance was created and danced by the father of Shākyamuni, who was to become Lord Buddha, at the latter's birth. According to another version, the dance is an expression of the joy experienced by the guardian deity Isakawa Myōjin at the defeat of the army of the Korean Silla state. The resolute heroic dance is performed by the helmeted main dancer wearing a sword at his waist and carrying a halberd in his hands. The face is covered with a red, elongated mask provided with closed, fleshy lips, pronounced nostrils and thick eybrows. The slightly converging eyes look stern. The majority of the extant examples follows this type, only one of them, preserved at the Kasuga shrine and made by the famous sculptor Jōkei in 1184, being different. This particular mask is large, with a huge forehead, half-closed mouth and strongly converging eyes. Unlike most masks of this type, it is provided with ears.

Kitoku is the Japanese form of the Chinese name of a character represented in the next military dance by the main dancer, Marquis Kuei Te. The dancer performed wearing a helmet surmounted by a dragon, and carrying a sword at his waist and a halberd in his hands. Either a mask with a human face or one with a carp-like O-shaped mouth may be used at the dance. In the latter case, six masked attendants take part in it.

The extant Kitoku masks with human faces belong to different styles. Some of them are oblong, only differing from the Sanju masks by being green in colour. Others are squarer, their ferocious squinting eyes reminding one of the statues of the guardian deities from the Kamakura period. The 'carp-mouthed' masks were also of different types, although preserved in only a few examples. A mask in the Hachiman shrine in Kamakura, dated from the thirteenth century, has a pouting mouth, whereas the mask of Kitoku Koikuchi, kept in the Kasuga shrine and dated 1537, is reminiscent of a fish not only because of its rounded mouth but also because of its bulging eyes. Rounded holes for the eyes can also be found in the only authentic mask of the attendant Kitoku Banko, which has been preserved in the

Sumiyoshi shrine in Osaka and was made in 1163.

The first of the masks used at the 'dances in running' is Konju, representing a drunken barbarian. Before putting on the costume, the dancer drinks *sake,* and during the dance he brandishes a stick symbolising a rice-wine ladle. Only one old mask of the Konju dance is extant today. It is kept in the Tamukeyama shrine in Nara, and is supposed to originate from the end of the thirteenth or the beginning of the fourteenth century. Three-dimensional eyes bulge under a huge and bony forehead with eyebrows, a short, but prominently hooked nose and a wide mouth confirming the image of a drunken foreigner.

According to Shinsei's *Illustrations of Ancient Music,* the masks of the Konju dance had long, loose hair, similar to the mask worn at the next Batō dance, at which the dancer runs around the stage, kneels down, brandishes the blue mane adorning his red mask and combs it passionately with his fingers. The dance represents either the joy of a barbarian over the killing of a wild animal which devoured his father, or the sorrow of a man looking for the corpse of his father

who was killed in the mountains by a tiger. Another version even quotes an ancient Indian narrative, according to which the dancer represents a white horse killing a venomous snake.

The Batō mask is very similar to the Konju, but is provided with an even angrier and more ferocious expression, enhanced by the squinting and bulging eyes and two rows of bared teeth. The oldest of the 20 extant examples is preserved in the Hōryūji temple and dated 1144. Another somewhat later mask, owned by the Itsukushima shrine and made by Gyōmyō in 1173, is one of the most impressive Japanese masks (Fig. 65). A recently discovered Batō mask from 1219, the author of which was one of the most renowned Japanese sculptors, Unkei, is preserved in the Seto shrine in Yokohama.

A pair dance of Batō is the Genjōraku festive dance performed by a dancer wearing a fierce red mask and carrying a stick in one hand and a wooden model of a coiled snake in the other (Fig. 63). This dance dates from the Nara period, and is mentioned in an inventory of the Saidaiji temple dated 780. Today we know of around 20 extant pieces, the most perfect in artistry being the mask from Hōryūji, dated 1144, and one from the Itsukushima shrine, which was made by Gyōmyō in 1173. Similar to the Konju and Batō masks, that of Genjōraku is also covered with red lacquer, but is even less like a human face than the preceding two examples. On a furrowed skull, swollen veins are seen; a massive nose sticks out of the face which is creased up into a victorious grin. The chin and the lower teeth form a small cup which is tied to the mask. The eyes, nose, cheeks and upper lip are carved separately, and shake and rattle during the dance.

No less exacting in terms of carving is the Ryōō mask surmounted by the figure of a dragon (Plate 141). This was worn at a 'swift' dance, originally expressing the joy of victory. The Ryōō mask became very popular in Japan as a mask of one of the eight Dragon Kings of the Buddhist iconography. The inhabitants of the Far East consider the dragon to be a giver of rain, and the Ryōō dance has been expressing man's entreaty for this life-giving moisture since time immemorial. This is probably why this dance, already performed in the Nara period, was the most

Fig. 66
Bōdhisattva mask from 1201. Jōdoji temple, Hyōgo Prefecture.

favoured *bugaku* dance and why such a large number (64 masks) have been preserved. The Ryōō mask is extraordinarily decorative. The winged dragon forms a kind of crown on the top, giving it a dynamic appearance. The forehead, nose and cheeks around the eyes, which are placed rather close together, are wrinkled, and long teeth protrude above a loosely hanging chin which was carved separately.

A short time ago a Ryōō mask from the Nara period was discovered in the Fujita Museum in Osaka. Although the mask is defective and its movable eyes and chin were made of *kiri* wood, it is unique among the *bugaku* masks in having been made by the dry-lacquer method.

The Nasori, which is a pair dance of the Ryōō, only reached Japan in the Nara period. The content of the dance, usually performed by two dancers, is not known, but it is explained as a 'merriment of dragons', which might account for its extraordinary popularity. Sixty-three Nasori masks have been preserved in various areas of Japan. With its snub nose, bulging movable eyes, graphically stylised wrinkles and tufts of hair, moustache and beard, the Nasori mask is strongly reminiscent of the Ryōō mask. It is not decorated with a dragon, however, being provided with huge, upraised tusks. The loose chin, with its large teeth, is semicircular, perfectly fitting the upper part when closed. The mask is covered with green or blue paint; the eyes and teeth are white or gold. Particularly well preserved is the painted decoration of a Nasori mask kept in the Kasuga shrine, and dating from the mid-twelfth century. No less interesting are some provincial masks, among which an example preserved in Chiryu, in the Aichi Prefecture, bears the date of 1256.

CEREMONIAL MASKS

One of the most common masks, and also one of the oldest, not only of the Far East but also of South and South-East Asia, is the lion mask. The lion, as a stately animal and a symbol of strength and majesty, carrying both Hindu and Buddhist gods on its back and guarding the sacred precincts, has long served as a guardian against evil spirits and a bringer of happiness and prosperity. As elsewhere in Asia, in Japan the lion mask and the lion dance have always been exorcist and beneficial in character. In areas famous for fairground entertainments near Shintoist shrines and Buddhist temples, on New Year's Day you may still meet a man wearing a large wooden lion mask covered with red, black and golden lacquer and provided with a wide movable lower jaw bearing many teeth and two protruding tusks.

The popularity of various forms of the *shishimai* lion dance, performed at countless folk festivals all over Japan, is confirmed by literature and both dramatic and art records. The *shishimai* inspired the much-favoured type of dances which became a permanent part of the repertory of the middle-class *kabuki* theatre in the Edo period (1603—1868). A lion's head, or dancers wearing lion masks, are often depicted in miniature carvings of ivory or wood, called *netsuke*, which date from the same time. The movable lower jaw of the mask and the decorative wavy mane offered the *netsuke* carvers an opportunity to demonstrate their skill, wit and precision.

In their basic forms, innumerable lion masks of a more recent provenance (Plate 144) are direct descendants of a very old tradition, the prototypes of which are represented by a group of nine masks from the Nara period, preserved in Shōsōin. Most of them were carved from paulownia wood, one from that of the camphor tree, and one was produced by the dry-lacquer method, supported with an inner wooden construction. All of them are masterly pieces, made for the ceremony of 'opening of the eyes' of the Great Buddha, held in the Tōdaiji temple in Nara in AD 752. The lion masks differ from the other *gigaku* masks, to which group they belong, by having the lower jaw carved separately, as well as the ears and tongue. In one case the eyes of the mask are movable and can be turned sideways.

Within this group, as well as in other lion masks or the *shishigashira* 'lion's heads', preserved, for example, in Hōryūji and other temples and shrines, we may notice a number of variants of the details of carving and painting, but in principle, the lion masks are characterised by bulging, rounded eyes placed under three-dimensional and angrily frowning eyebrows, an upturned nose with widely

procession was headed by Chidō and a lion with two 'cubs' or 'lion's children'. This custom was maintained in processions of later times. The masks of these children, as well as of the man heading the procession and leading the lion, have been preserved, but in small numbers. That man was given different names, but was always characterised by a strikingly long nose, protruding from the face in an almost obscene way. Descendants of this mask are the masks of the long-nosed forest spirit Tengu, until recently much favoured as playthings and talismans (Plate 142).

A pleasing contrast to this comic or even bizarre mask of the procession's leader and the ferocious lion mask was formed by the sweet masks of the children accompanying the lion. The skull part is disproportionately high which emphasises the innocence of the small smiling faces of the little children. The head is either bare or covered with upright tufts of hair, as for instance in the mask of a boy from the Kyoto Tōji temple, probably originating from 1334. This mask is almost unpleasantly realistic in its perfect painted decoration; under the eyebrows arching from the base of the nose, a pair of eyes, placed close together, stare at the spectator. The small half-open mouth shows a row of upper teeth and has stiffened in an ingratiating smile.

This mask was not used at the *gigaku* performances, but worn to lead a procession at the *gyōdō* ceremonies. This term originally referred to various rituals, such as common prayers or recitals of the *sutras*, which were performed by Buddhist monks along the lines of Chinese and maybe even Indian practice, while walking round the individual buildings of the monastery and along its verandas and corridors. In the course of time, masks began to be used at some of these ceremonies. One of the oldest is the Shōryōe ceremony held in the Hōryūji temple, where, once a year, Prince Shōtoku is commemorated by a procession including a decorative palanquin which contains the prince's remains and a statue. This valuable burden could not have been entrusted to ordinary mortals and this is why the heads of the bearers were covered with large masks of some of the *bushu*, Buddha's attendants, or some of the Twelve Guardian Deva Kings.

151   An actor wearing a Hakushikijō mask at an Okina dance. *Netsuke* made of ivory. Japan, nineteenth century; now in Náprstek Museum, Prague. Height 5.5 cm.

flared nostrils and the wavy edges of a wide muzzle, the opening of which must have dramatically enhanced the overall impression of the supernatural power of this mythical animal, at the same time making possible an imitation of its majestic voice.

In the Shinsei's scroll from the twelfth century, a *shishi* is also recorded. This is an impressive mask with a widely opened muzzle. The mask is worn by two dancers whose legs show under the shaggy 'hair'. The lion is lead on a rope by another dancer and attended by two boys. As stated in the section on the *gigaku* masks, the

A very important set of *gyōdō* masks, comprising representatives of both groups, was once owned by the Tōji temple, the main Kyoto centre of the esoteric Shingon sect. Part of the set is now kept at the Kyoto National Museum. The masks form a varied group, including an almost portrait-like mask of the god of fire, Katen, wearing a winged cap, the charming feminine face of the sun god, Nitten, the bizarre Kendatsuba with two pairs of eyes placed one above the other and wearing a lion-mask head-cover, or the ferocious Karura whose dramatic appearance is completed with a winged diadem surmounted by the figure of a mythical bird.

Some of these beautifully painted masks are dated to 1086 and others to 1334. The latter were made for a ceremony held on finishing the reconstruction of the Tōji temple pagoda. They well represent the sculpture of the late Heian and Kamakura periods and the iconographic orientation of the Shingon sect.

The purpose of the festive processions, in which relics or a god's statue were carried around the temple (the relics usually being hidden from the public) was to offer the believers an opportunity to 'meet' the god and to come closer to his virtues. Apart from these commemorative ceremonies, a special type of masked procession developed, the aim of which was to teach the believers the fundamental truths of the doctrine or religious practice. According to an old record, in AD 861, after the head of the Great Buddha in the Tōdaiji temple of Nara had been repaired, dozens of dancers played the role of various deities worshipping Buddha and offering him gifts. We may suppose that they were masked, as was and still is the case with a ceremony of a similar character called Raigōe. In a Raigōe procession figures may be seen looking like statues which have come alive because their heads are covered with masks of godly beings. The believer is shown what his death will be like if he dilligently invokes Buddha. He will be met at the last moment by Buddha the Merciful and the entire celestial court, who will take him to heaven.

It is not surprising to find that as this simple and comprehensible doctrine spread quickly among the people the Raigōe processions also became a popular spectacle, and for this reason a relatively large number of bōdhisattva masks have been preserved. The oldest known example, bearing the date of 1086, is now preserved at the Honolulu Academy of Arts. Until recently, a beautiful mask of a bōdhisattva from 1102, one of the eight preserved in the Hōryūji temple, was considered to be the oldest specimen of this genre. Its author was obviously an outstanding carver of Buddhist statues. The mask is characterised by the perfect proportions of the face which is rather feminine in spite of the usual moustache and beard indicated by the drawing, and by the tender expression of the eyes, the compassionate look of which is directed downwards, as is usual in icons. Twenty-five bōdhisattva masks are kept in the Jōdoji temple in the Hyōgo Prefecture. Some of them have perforations in the crescents of the eyebrows (Fig. 66). In other respects, the bōdhisattva masks maintain the iconographic pattern of the face, which is rather wide, bordered by a hair-style divided into regular tresses and usually ending in a low diadem or perhaps only an incision into which a diadem made of an openwork metal was usually set. Only in rare cases is the hair carved in the form of a knot on the top of the head, which is usual in the bōdhisattva statues.

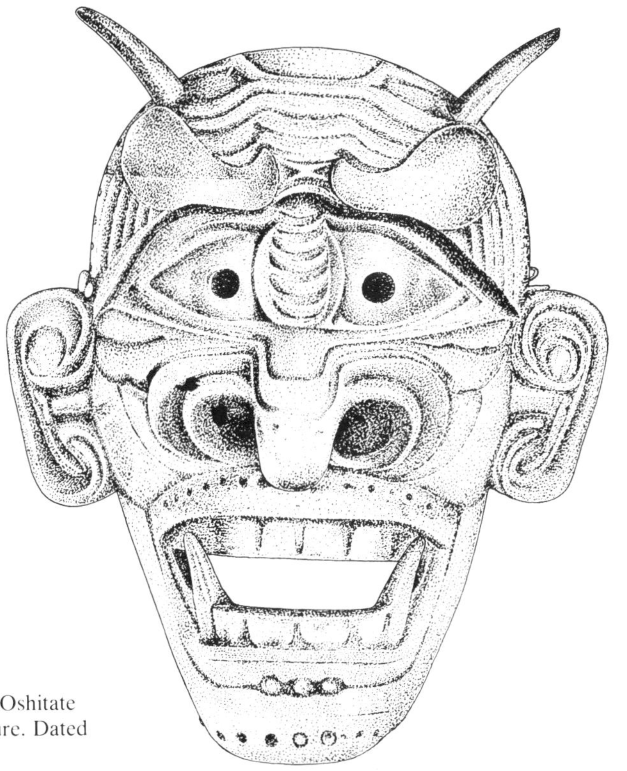

Fig. 67
A demon mask from Oshitate shrine, Shiga Prefecture. Dated to sixteenth century.

213

The group of bōdhisattvas welcoming the dying man to the Western Paradise was accompanied by Tendō, the Children of the Paradise. Their masks, which originated in the Kamakura period and were provided with a smooth hairstyle or rings of hair instead of ears, are strongly reminiscent of the well-known statue of the seven-year-old Prince Shōtoku from Hōryūji.

The call of 'Oni wa soto, fuku wa uchi' ('Off with the devils, happiness into the house!') may still be heard at the beginning of February in Japanese households. Its purpose is to drive off evil spirits. For the same reason fried beans, mostly soya, were scattered within and around the house. This custom was originally practised in temples, where it began some time in the Muromachi period (1333-1568), and was turned into a household custom later on. It linked up the *tsuina* ceremony of exorcising demons, which had come from China and, since the ninth century, had been part of the annual customs maintained at the imperial court. The spread of this ceremony over the whole country is confirmed by numerous extant masks of demons, used on this occasion.

At early times, a mask was worn by a master of ceremonies, called Hososhi, who exorcised demons. Gradually the demons themselves began to be personified, naturally in masks. Sometimes a devil family, consisting of a father, mother and son, was embodied by masked men.

Some demon masks, such as the thirteenth-century devil-father mask from the Hōryūji, are close to the Konron of the *gigaku*. Others are comic rather than fearsome in character, which accords with the little-defined character of the demon or *oni*, to whom positive traits are also assigned in the Far East. The *oni* from Chōyūji temple in the Shiga Prefecture is almost good natured; he has small horns protruding from the top of his head, curly eyebrows, a flat nose and a small grinning muzzle full of teeth. Entirely peculiar in character is the mask of an *oni* from 1295, which once belonged to the Hōryūji, but is now kept in the Tokyo National Museum. This mask consists of three separately carved parts — the forehead adorned with imposing horns, the nose with the eyes, and the ears connected with the cheeks and the chin. In spite of its considerable stylisation, the mask makes a more suggestive impression than the almost pitiable *oni* from the Oshitate shrine in the Shiga Prefecture, which originated in the sixteenth century (Fig. 67).

The Japanese ritual masks also include a large number of folk masks used at the *kagura* dances connected with the Shintō cult. The *mikagura*, performed at the imperial court and at shrines connected with it, is performed without masks, whereas dances and ceremonials in masks are part of the majority of the *kagura* taking place in the provincial countryside. Thus at the Ise *kagura* a masked man becomes a deity temporarily, blessing the villagers and holding a dialogue with their representatives. A the Izumo *kagura*, dances actualising mythical narratives are performed.

The central point of the *shishi kagura* is a procession with a sacred lion mask which is the seat of deity. Within the framework of the same *kagura*, a large number of other dances in masks have developed, enhancing the interest in, and the attraction of, the ceremonies.

Ceremonial folk masks (Plates 145, 146 and 147) made of various materials, particularly paper and wood, bear testimony to the imagination, skill and humour of their makers. However, types

Fig. 68
Nasori mask for a *bugaku* performance. Made of painted wood and animal hair. From Kasuga shrine, Japan. Dated from the mid-twelfth century.

152 Miniature fox mask with a movable lower jaw for the *kyōgen* plays. *Netsuke* made of wood. Japan, nineteenth century. Signed by Deme Sukemitsu Tenka ichi; now in Náprstek Museum, Prague. Height 5 cm.

which are nothing other than degenerated replicas of the masks used at *nō* and *kyōgen* plays are far from rare.

MASKS OF *NŌ* AND *KYŌGEN* PLAYS

The wonderful masks which are used at the musical and dance *nō* plays are closest to the Japanese spirit and facial characteristics and, at the same time, are the masks best known outside Japan. These plays, formerly called *sarugaku* and now

representing the oldest extant professional theatre, crystallised into their supreme form in the Muromachi period (1333—1568), towards the end of the fourteenth century. The ideology which defined the way of thinking and art creation of the time was the teaching of the meditative Buddhist Zen sect. Its artistic and moral principles of self-restraint, sober expression and suggestion influenced the art of *nō* in a decisive way, and were reflected in the aesthetics of the mask as an essential component of this theatrical genre.

Rarely more than two actors move on the simple stage of the *nō* theatre, the only permanent decoration of which is the painting of an old pine tree at the back of the stage. The protagonist *shite* may be joined there either by his attendant *tsure* or his opponent *waki*, but in principle the *nō* is the theatre of a soloist, i.e. the *shite*; the *waki* only offers him an opportunity to present his dance.

The *waki* always represents a living male human being and thus does not need any mask. By contrast, the *shite*, or even his *tsure*, mostly uses a mask. Only in plays in which the hero is a middle-aged man can he do without a mask. Since the mask is then replaced by his face, the actor keeps it absolutely unmoving, without the slightest suggestion of any sentiment, as do all the other persons performing in the play, i.e. his co-actors, the eight members of the chorus, the three- or four-member orchestra and the stage assistant *kōken*. However, the *shite* usually does need a mask because he has to personify many varied characters of the rich *nō* repertory: handsome young heroes, old men, both old and young women, deities, spirits, madmen and demons. All of these roles have their respective masks, each with a number of variants. Except for a few masks which only suit a single character, such as the One-horned Sennin, the old, blind Kagekiyo or the gaunt Shunkan, the *nō* masks generally represent a human or demonic type and not an individual hero. The actor therefore selects his mask, within the framework of tradition and the custom of his school, choosing also the costume which suits it.

The *waki*'s costume usually shows him in an unambiguous way as a member of a well-defined social group, so that the audience understands whether he is an aristocrat, a monk or a simple man. The gorgeous costume of the *shite*, on the other hand, is often socially neutral and the character is defined by the mask he is wearing. Moreover, experienced spectators know as soon as the protagonist enters the open corridor leading to the stage, how he has conceived his role and how he will play it, on the basis of his choice of costume and mask. The right choice of mask is considered by the actor to be of utmost importance and his care for it reflects this. Before he puts the mask on, he greets it and looks at it for a long time

to let its life force touch him. At the moment when the mask is fastened to the head with a decorative ribbon, the actor's own personality vanishes and he becomes possessed by the spirit of the mask.

Except for the ferocious extrovert demon masks, with wildly rolling eyes and a grinning mouth, the *nō* masks, otherwise very close to a real human face (Plate 148), are characterised by a peculiar lack of any expression. This neutral expression is especially typical of the numerous masks of beautiful girls and women, called *waka-onna*, *ko-omote* or *manbi*, respectively. Both these masks and three further types of female ones, although seeming identical to a layman, differ from each other in the number and position of the hair strands parting from the black area of the hairstyle.

On the other hand, the neutrality of the mask's expression incites the actor to make it expressive by the movements of his head. His art also involves the ability to make the mask 'shining' by merely raising his head, and to make it 'gloomy' by bowing it.

The heroes of the *nō* plays are often victims of a tragedy, but the drama usually ends in a conciliatory way, in tune with their general Buddhist tone which, albeit melancholy, resounds with the hope of salvation. On the other hand, the connection of the *nō* plays with Shintō ritual is shown by the play, or three-part dance, Okina, which precedes the *nō* performance on a festive occasion. This dance is of an explicitly sacred character, its purpose being a prayer for the blessing of the gods, happiness and a rich harvest. All performers prepare themselves by a ritual purgation and the *shite* receives the white mask directly on the stage in a ceremonial way. His dance, called Okina, is majestic and the *shite* performs it with a fan in his hand and the high *eboshi* headgear on his head (Plate 151). The subsequent Sambasō dance is performed by an actor wearing a black mask and similar headgear, holding little bells in his right hand and a fan in his left. Except for the colour, their masks are almost identical. This is the considerably stylised face of a kindly, smiling old man, composed of regular wrinkles and provided with holes for the eyes shaped like the letter *he* of the Japanese *kana* script. The ancient masks of the 'white and black old man' are entirely different in character from the other *nō* masks, being close to the Taikofu mask of the *gigaku*, and especially the mask of the old Saisōrō from the *bugaku* dances; they are also linked to the latter by a separately carved chin.

As well as the other musical and dance forms, the *nō* plays uphold the *jo-ha-kyū* principle, i.e. the division into an introduction, exposition and a speedy finale, both in the individual phases and the entire composition and programme. This consists of five plays, the first of which forms the introduction, a further three the exposition and the last one the finale. The performance is introduced with a play about gods, in the first part of which the god appears as an ordinary man and in the second reveals his true identity. In such a way the goddess Benten, the Dragon King or even the spirit of an old plum tree may appear. This is why the masks of the deities are different, their majesty sometimes being mixed with fearsomeness, as is the case with the mask of the spirit of the Arashiyama mountain; in other instances, the mask manifests happiness and a caring attitude, promised by the deity in the concluding dance, such as the Sumiyoshi spirit in the famous play *Takasago*.

The *shite* of the plays of the second category represents an unreconciled and unhappy spirit of a warrior who meets a monk and is delivered from suffering by his prayers. These plays usually treat well-known stories taken over from the war-romances of *Heike monogatari* and *Gempei seisuiki*. In these dramas the *shite*, usually in the second part when he appears in his true form, also performs in masks of various types, corresponding to the age and sex of the deceased. For example, in the play *Tomoe* the main character is the spirit of a woman who accompanied her husband in a battle but was not able to die with him. This is why the actor's face is covered by the mask of a beautiful young woman.

However, female masks are mostly used only in a play of the third category, one of the 'wig-plays', the protagonists of which are women pursued by love (Plate 149). A well-known instance of this group is the play *Matsukaze*, introducing the spirits of two village girls who remember the love of the nobleman and poet Yukihira.

The next group of plays, designated as 'plays from the life' or 'various plays', is most numerous. Out of the 240 extant *nō* plays, which mostly originated in the fifteenth century, 97 belong to this particular group. Since mad women often appear in them, they are also called 'plays about mad women' (Fig. 69). Their characters include, for example, the 'emaciated woman' whose mask with sunken cheeks is worn by her representative in the play *Kinuta*, in which a deserted woman dies of longing for her distant husband. One of the famous masks of female demons is the horned Hannya mask with a fearsome look in the golden eyes, bearing teeth in a wide muzzle and with drawn, dishevelled hair. The mask is a personification of womanly jealousy, performing, for example, in the play *Aoi no Ue*, in which the spirit of the lady-love of Prince Genji attacks the prince's wife and is the cause of the latter's serious illness (Plate 154).

In the 'demon' plays forming the finale, various supernatural characters, both good and evil, appear, and the programme ends with their energetic dance. Particularly impressive is the dance of two lions provided with huge red and white manes, who dance amidst peonies in the

Fig. 69
An actor playing the part of a mourning mother in the *nō* play *Fujito*.

217

play *Shakkyō*, or the dance of Shōjō, a legendary man fond of strong drinks, in a play bearing the same name. Whereas the actors personifying the lions wear ferocious and demoniac masks, the mask of the happy drunkard is youthfully innocent; he wears a gigantic red wig and knows how to cast a spell on a jar of wine in such a way that it is always full.

The *nō* theatre needs about 80 types of masks for its repertory, but in actual fact more than 200 are used. Compared to the *gigaku* and *bugaku* masks, those of *nō* are smaller in size and shallow, often not covering the entire face. Their average height is 21 cm and their width 13 cm. Whereas the *gigaku* and *bugaku* masks were made by the carvers of Buddhist statues, and therefore often attaining a high level of artistry, the perfection of the *nō* masks is due to the fact that their production was participated in by specialists well versed in the aesthetics of the *nō* plays and capable of penetrating the spirit of every role for which a mask was made.

Several schools of mask carvers developed, but from the seventeenth century onwards, only copies of old pieces have been made. Like the actors of the *nō* theatre, the carvers of the masks worked under the patronage, and according to the wishes, of the members of the ruling Tokugawa family and individual feudal lords. The most outstanding makers of *nō* masks in the Edo period were the Izeki and Deme families, descendants of the famous sculptor Sankōbō.

Although the masks are often signed, the authenticity of these signatures is very problematic, particularly as far as the names of the masters of the oldest periods are concerned. Apart from the name of the maker, we may find on a mask's back its name, the history relating to it, its purpose, especially whether it was made as a votive donation to some temple or shrine, the date of the production and the name of, and comments by, the person who evaluated the mask.

For centuries the carvers of the *nō* masks have maintained the shapes of the classic prototypes, and have continued to work in the same way as their predecessors. They usually carve the mask from the wood of the Japanese *hinoki* cypress, which is durable, soft and light in colour. They use implements of various sizes and shapes, made of a special mixture of soft iron and steel. The surface of the mask is sanded with several types of rough paper. Then the mask is covered with a number of layers of *gofun*, the main component of which is powdered shell. The painting is done with Chinese ink and natural pigments such as powdered crystal, vermilion and ultramarine. In order to obtain special effects in the masks of demons and gods, the details, especially the eyes and teeth of the mask, are gilded or covered with silver-grey mica. The hair and beard of the smiling, troubled and evil-minded old men consist of light and dark horsehair, set into regularly distributed little holes.

The *nō* plays have developed from a number of dances, plays and other entertainments, some of which contained many comic elements. By separating out these funny parts, a new dramatic genre, the farce called *kyōgen* ('crazy words') was created as early as the Muromachi period. The programme usually consisted of five *nō* and three *kyōgen* plays, the latter refreshing the spectator, wearied by the slow tempo of the *nō* plays, with their wit and liveliness. The realistic character of the *kyōgen* is reflected also by the fact that only in 50 plays, out of the entire extant repertory formed by 260 plays, do the ac-

Fig. 70
An actor performing the title character in the *kyōgen* Octopus (Tako).

218

153 Usobuki mask for the *kyōgen* plays, made of painted wood and plant fibres. Japan; now in Tokyo National Museum.

tors appear in masks. However, since the masks are used for various roles, as in the *nō* plays, the number of types of *kyōgen* mask is much smaller, being not more than 20.

The *kyōgen* masks may be divided into three categories: the masks in which gods and demons perform, the masks of animals, plants and their spirits, and the masks of human beings (Fig. 70). The first group includes the masks used for the 'beneficial' *kyōgen*, which is performed after a beneficial *nō* play in a special formal performance introduced by the Okina dance. In a beneficial *kyōgen*, gods appear just as they do in a *nō* play. These are some of the seven gods of happiness and longevity, especially the most popular among them, the god of wealth, Daikoku, the patron of fishermen and merchants, Ebisu, and the god of happiness, Fuku no kami. Their anthropomorphic masks represent the faces of happily smiling corpulent men, corresponding to the play which

219

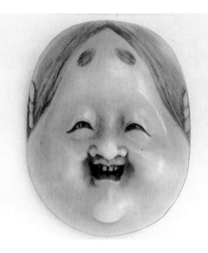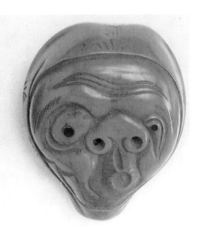

154 Three miniature *netsuke* masks. From the left: a Hannya female demon mask for the *nō* plays, made of ivory. Signed by Shungetsu. Japan, nineteenth century; now in Náprstek Museum, Prague. Height 3.5 cm.
Oto or Okame mask for the *kyōgen* plays, made of ivory. Signed by Mitsuyuki. Japan, nineteenth century; now in Náprstek Museum, Prague. Height 3.8 cm.
Hyottoko mask for the *kyōgen* plays. Signed by Gyokuzan. Japan, nineteenth century; now in Náprstek Museum, Prague. Height 3.3 cm.

is not a farce in the proper sense of the term.

The masks of demons are comic rather than fearsome. Perhaps the most popular of all *kyōgen* masks is that of Buaku, which is a universal mask representing demons of all kinds and is, in principle, a variant of the common demonic Beshi-mi mask of the *nō* plays (Plate 150).

The second group comprises animal masks and more or less anthropomorphic masks, in actual fact representing animals, and plants and their spirits. In a play on the monkey son-in-law, many actors wearing monkey masks appear. The mask of the intriguing *tanuki,* or raccoon dog, and the mask of a fox with teeth in a movable jaw are also popular (Plate 152). The mask called Kentoku is in the form of a stylised face with regular wrinkles on the forehead, large, hollow pupils squinting upwards and sidewards, and a sunken area around the nose and upper teeth. It was named after a Buddhist monk who allegedly made such a face once when an icy wind struck him. Nevertheless the mask is used by the representatives of animals of varied size and character, i.e. cow, horse, dog. tortoise, sparrow and crab.

No less frequent is the use of the mask called Usobuki, which is usually a wrinkled face with the lips pursed as in whistling. The mask may equally well represent the spirit of a mosquito, bogey, octopus and locust, or the spirit of pine resin or a mushroom (Plate 153). A very similar comic mask with pouting and turned up lips is very popular in the *kagura* dances, too, but is here called Hyottoko.

As was the case with the *gigaku, buga-ku* and *nō* masks, we also find among those of the *kyōgen* a special mask of an old man called Oji. The emaciated face of the old man, with regularly carved wavy wrinkles, irregularly modelled eyeholes placed on different levels, and a dried-up, almost toothless mouth, is tragic rather than comic. There is also a very lively, hairless mask of an old, wrinkled nun.

The female characters of the *kyōgen,* represented by men, are usually characterised by a white turban provided with flowing streamers. Only in the case of a nice, but not particularly beautiful woman does the actor use a mask called Oto or Okame. This comic, female, pear-shaped face, with plump cheeks emphasised by dimples, is provided with smiling eyes and a small mouth, by which it differs from the very similar Fukuro mask which has a cold look and a wide mouth with drooping corners. This is because the latter represents an older and always angry woman, whereas the Oto mask is used in plays the point of which is that a husband finally finds out that he has not married a beauty but an ugly woman. Nowadays one may find the popular Okame mask not only among paper playthings sold at fairs, but also in every large collection of *netsuke* (Plate 154).

The *kyōgen* masks are not signed and nothing is known about their makers. It is supposed, however, that they were made by the same carvers as the *nō* masks. Old *kyōgen* masks are now kept in various temples, shrines and museums, but most of them have remained the property of the families in which this unique art of acting has been hereditary for centuries.

Korea

The oldest masks of the Korean Peninsula were found in a heap of shells in the city of Pusan in 1969—71. They are mainly *pecten Jacoboeus* shells, mostly 11.6 cm in diameter, with holes for the eyes and a mouth drilled in a rough way. Some archaeologists presume that they are pictures of children's faces or even playthings, but it is more probable that these primitive masks were cultic in purpose, as is the case with Korean masks of all ages until contemporary times.

Few old masks have been preserved, but their existence and functions are documented in various literary and historical records. The main reason why old pieces, and even those from the relatively recent past, have not survived is the fact that each of them was used only once. The performance began in the evening and continued throughout the night in the light of torches. At dawn the masks were burned because they were believed to have been infected by evil spirits. Although the connection of present-day masks with their older prototypes is highly problematic, the very forms of them, sometimes very bizarre, allow us to suppose a connection with animism, the concepts of which shaped the life of Korean society since prehistory and are alive there even today.

The masks were originally purely ritual objects, serving the shamans of both sexes at their invocations and often connected with dances. In the course of time, these dances got mixed up with secular elements and social satire, but their connection with the cult has never vanished, even though the dances were turned into a folk entertainment performed by professional dancers or actors.

Probably the oldest of the masks were those which served the cult of certain animals, especially the dragon, tiger and bear. As in other countries of the Far East, the dragon was worshipped in Korea as a bringer of rain, while Tangun, the mythical ancestor of the Koreans, was believed to have been born of a god and a she-bear. Tigers once lived in the mountains of Korea in large numbers and the tiger dance, intended to honour them, has been performed since ancient times. By contrast, the lion dance, which is of Central Asian origin, came to Korea only around the sixth century. A dance with a lion mask also introduced a *gigaku* performance which, as stated in the preceding chapter, the Japanese learned through the work of the Korean dancer Mimashi. In Korea, however, not a single *gigaku* mask, or *kiak* as it is called here, has been preserved. On the other hand, the tradition of folk 'lion plays' is extant in the city of Pukch'ŏng in the southern part of Hamgyŏng Province in south-eastern Korea. Originally the lion dance was of an explicitly exorcist character; besides taking part in the performance proper, which lasted all night, the lion mask went round visiting individual houses and expelling evil spirits.

In the lion dance of Pukch'ŏng, ten persons perform altogether, wearing five different masks. Apart from two lion masks, each worn by two men, the dance is participated in by the mask of a noble official, his servant, a hunch-backed woman and a messenger. These secondary masks are made from gourds, but the most important lion mask is carved from lime wood. This mask is circular in shape and painted red, black and yellow. A rich mane and shaggy coat are formed by numerous strips of red, yellow, black, blue and white cloth, attached to a fisherman's net. These colours symbolise the four cardinal points of the compass and the centre of the world.

In 1946 archaeologists discovered a

Another type of masks, which gave rise to the later dance theatre with masks, are medicinal masks used for expelling the spirits of illnesses. Thus in Cheju Island, south of the Korean Peninsula, a ceremony is still organised today, at which two female shamans sing and dance, wearing the masks of old brothers, in order to lure the spirit of the illness from the bodies of young women. Local folk belief ascribes their illness to the lechery of old men.

Among the masks repudiating the spirits of illnesses, the most favoured one was that of Ch'ŏyong, used both at a dance and as a protection against illness, for which purpose it was hung on the door. The name of this mask is derived from a son of the Dragon King of the Eastern Sea, who allegedly lived at the time of the Silla dynasty. The mask is connected with a humorous story. Ch'ŏyong once came home and found his wife being embraced by another man. Instead of attacking the pair, he turned and went away, dancing and singing about what he had just seen. The philanderer, who was in fact a spirit of an illness, was so moved by Ch'ŏyong's magnanimity that he bowed low to him and disappeared. This dance then became one of the main dances performed in masks, called *sandae,* its performance being maintained until recently.

The fact that the mask very often served as a protection against an illness or some other disaster is indicated by the most current Korean term for it, the word *t'al,* originally meaning a calamity or illness.

Also of ancient origin are the shamanistic ceremonies, the purpose of which was to placate the spirits who, according to animistic concepts, dwell in all material objects. At these ceremonies, the masks of the respective spirits were used. For example, ten masks, the purpose of which was to placate the spirits of the earth, appeared at an ancient ceremony organised at the beginning of the lunar year. King Hŏn'gang (875—885) is known to have ordered a 'mask with a white beard' of the spirit of the mountains to be made, in order to conciliate him.

Commemorative masks connected with historic personalities may be found in Korea, as among Japanese masks. Thus, as early as the time of the united Silla kingdom (668—918), a male sabre dance in masks was performed in memory of the

155 The mask of an old man for dance plays, made of painted paper and plant fibres. Pongsan, Hwanghaedo Province, Korea, mid-twentieth century; now in Náprstek Museum, Prague. Height 27 cm.

wooden mask covered with lacquer in one of the graves of the kings of the Silla kingdom, dating from the fifth to the sixth century AD in Kyŏngju. This mask is reminiscent of the Chinese mask of Fang Siang ssi, a four-eyed guardian demon, used four times a year to exorcise evil spirits. Another extant group of old masks probably originated in the period of the Koryŏ dynasty (918—1392). They are preserved in the Chong-gye-dang shrine in Kesong, which is the present-day name of the former capital of the Koryŏ kingdom. These masks are carved from wood, representing the spirits of foolishness, evil, the god of theatrical art, and laughter, respectively. Except for laughter, all of these masks have an intimidating expression.

young hero Hwang Ch'ang who perished during a battle against the Paekche kingdom. Sabre dances have been preserved until today, but they are now danced exclusively by unmasked women.

The Silla period is also probably the time of the rise of the *muwae-mu* mask dance, although its origin is ascribed to the Buddhist monk Wonhyo. According to the *Chronicle of Three Kingdoms,* from the end of the thirteenth century, its style as well as its music pointed to a Central Asian provenance. The monk propagated Buddhism in villages, dancing a mask dance, which deals with the highest goal to be attained in Buddhism. (*Muwae* means 'no obstacles'.)

The end of the Koryŏ dynasty (around the eleventh to the twelfth century) is the time of the appearance of a set of wooden masks which were used at the *py-*

ŏlsinkut New Year's sacrifices in the Hahoe and Pyŏngsan villages of the Andong district of Kyongsangpukto Province, situated in the south-eastern part of Korea.

The masks are carved in a considerably schematic way, but in spite of their primitiveness, they display an obvious effort by the carver to characterise different male and female types. Some of them are, or originally were, provided with a movable and separately carved chin, attached to the face by a string passing through holes drilled in both parts. In this respect, they are reminiscent of some Japanese *bugaku* and *okina* masks. Almost all the main characters of the later *sandae* mask plays are represented: the monk, concubine, nobleman and his servant, high dignitary and young girl or female shaman.

The purpose of the *pyŏlsinkut* sacrifice was to conciliate the female guardian

156 A monkey mask for dance plays, made of painted paper with rabbit fur. Pongsan, Hwanghaedo Province, Korea, mid-twentieth century; now in Náprstek Museum, Prague. Height 28 cm.

deity of the village. The masks used at it were considered pure and sacred and were therefore exempted from being burned. The new masks, nowadays used at ceremonial performances in Hahoe and Pyŏngsan, are modern replicas of old examples from the Koryŏ period, and this is the reason why they are utterly different from the masks which are now used in the ceremonial plays of other regions. The latter may generally be said to be very remote from an actual human face, the fantastic aspects of their form and colour sometimes verging on ugliness.

Under King Sŏngjong (982—997) of the Koryŏ dynasty (918—1392), who turned Confucianism into the state doctrine, shamanistic and Buddhist ceremonies were repressed, but they were revived in the eleventh century and the royal gardens once again became the theatres of various colourful spectacles.

After the conclusion of a *narye* exorcist ritual, held towards the end of a lunar year, at which masked shamans brandishing swords expelled evil spirits, a secular performance took place, consisting of musical and dance items and a drama was performed in masks by professional musicians and actors. These performances were later called *nahŭi* (i.e. *na* plays).

During the subsequent period of the Yi (Chosŏn) dynasty, founded in 1392, Confucianism became the state religion and society was graded in a strictly hierarchical way. In the mid-sixteenth century, the Sandae Togam office was instituted in order to take care of theatre performances which took place on various official occasions such as the visit of a foreign delegation. The actors of the mask theatre (called *sandae*, literally a 'raised platform') came under the auspices of this institution. However, the office was abolished towards the end of the seventeenth century, the actors scattered all over the country and it was only itinerant groups which maintained the tradition of mask plays during subsequent centuries.

The *sandae* theatre always retained its ritual character. The performance proper was preceded by a ceremony in which the shamans summoned gods and dead actors and invited them to join the audience. The actors begged for their protection during the performance. On the other hand, the *sandae* plays were closely connected with the reality of everyday life, to which they were offering the mirror of satire. The objects of criticism and ridicule were morally corrupt Buddhist monks, hypocritical Confucian scholars, immoral female shamans and greedy old men.

Except for the sacrificial ceremonies in the Hahoe and Pyŏngsan villages, where masked performances have been preserved from the eleventh century until today, the tradition of plays performed in masks cannot be traced back further than the nineteenth century in other regions. Nevertheless around 15 types of *sandae* theatre are still extant.

There is a long tradition of *ogwangdae*, plays performed in masks in T'ongyŏng and Kosŏng in the Kyongsangnamdo Province situated in the south-eastern part of the country. They are obviously connected with the plays which arose in the large market-town of Pammŏri on the Naktong River. A legend has it that once upon a time this river flooded and brought to Pammŏri a large box full of masks and other requisites as well as written instructions on how to use them at a performance. As soon as the performance was held, the flood receded.

Old *ogwangdae* masks made of paulownia wood were destroyed in a large fire in 1909 and none of the other wooden masks, which were said to have replaced the original ones, have been preserved. Those which are used in *ogwangdae* plays at some places now are made of dried gourds, paper, bamboo splinters and other materials. For example the masks from Kosŏng are exclusively made of paper, but the majority of the masks from T'ongyŏng consist of dried gourds.

Among the masks worn in the *ogwangdae* plays, several types of the mask of a *yangban*, i.e. a Confucian aristocratic scholar, occur. The white mask of an old *yangban* is provided with a long beard, dense eyebrows and moustache and sparse teeth in a half-open mouth. The mask of a scholar afflicted with leprosy makes a humorous and at the same time repulsive impression. The convex area of the gourd is covered with dark brown paint and many protuberances are meant to evoke the impression of an ulcerated face. The rings of the eyes are plastic in treatment and the mouth is curved sideways. The nose, which consists of a glued-on piece of wood, is split in some masks.

The *yangban* mask, with its cheeks

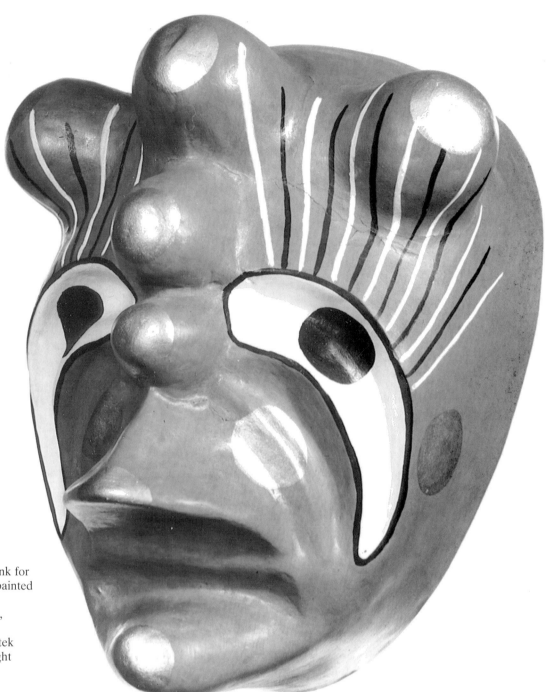

157 A mask of a monk for dance plays, made of painted paper. Pongsan, Hwanghaedo Province, Korea, mid-twentieth century; now in Náprstek Museum, Prague. Height 28.5 cm.

spotted by small-pox, is painted white and covered with a large number of dark spots. In other respects, this mask, provided with oblong seed-shaped holes for the eyes and mouth and with the eyebrows painted black, does not differ from another *yangban* mask, one half of the face of which is painted white and the other red, because he is a 'son of two fathers, Mr White and Mr Red', as he is ridiculed in the play by a shrewd servant. The latter's mask is comic in character, with shaggy eyebrows, white rings around the eyes and a large, sparsely toothed mouth which sticks out from the dark face. The mask is made of bamboo splinters and paper and framed in string, nooses of which form striking ears.

The white mask of an old woman in the *ogwangdae* plays also has large ears, her age being suggested by wavy wrinkles on her forehead and cheeks. By contrast, the

158　A monkey mask for dance plays, made of painted paper and grass. Pongsan, Hwanghaedo Province, Korea, mid-twentieth century; now in Náprstek Museum, Prague. Height 22 cm.

mask of a concubine is smooth, oval and has a pleasant mouth.

Rabbit fur was sometimes used for the masks, for instance a *yangban* mask with a face disfigured by paralysis, or a monkey mask. Other animals also appear in the *ogwangdae* plays, namely a lion who devours a monkey at the end, and the bird-monster *yŏngno* who fights the hated *yangban* and, of course, wins.

In terms of both geography and charac-ter, very close to the *ogwangdae* plays are the mask plays *suyŏng yayu*, which flour-ished east of the Naktong River until the beginning of the present century, whereas the *ogwangdae* plays were common in the area to the west. Unlike the 26 masks of the *ogwangdae*, only 11 are needed for a *yayu* play. Besides eight human charac-ters, a lion, a tiger and a mythical bird-monster appear. The majority of the anthropomorphic masks are made from gourds, but the masks of the lion and tiger consist of bamboo frames covered with paper. The simple white mask of a concubine is entirely made of paper, the ears being painted with Chinese ink and the cheeks provided with two red discs. Worth attention is the mask of an old *yangban* with a long beard and a movable lower jaw, and the red mask of the shrewd servant which is covered with ball-shaped protrusions is most bizarre. The large rounded eyeholes and the grinning mouth are framed in white and this raw caricature of an ordinary man is complemented with a long nose and huge ears in the shape of elongated figures of eight.

The *ogwangdae* and *yayu* mask plays are exorcist in purpose, the *ogwangdae* also summoning beneficial rain. Also connected with the exorcism of evil spirits were the masks plays of Pongsan in the Central Korean province of Hwanghaedo. These are supposed to have been performed for over 200 years. The masks from Pongsan (Plates 155—158) are all made of paper, painted in many colours and usually provided with rounded eyes emphasised by variously modelled white backgrounds. Among other characters, morally corrupt Buddhist monks appear in the plays, whose masks are deformed by bumps and covered with many spots and lines. The mask of a butcher and even that of a monkey, framed in rabbit fur, are closer to a human face than the ugly mask of the monk. Even more fantastic, however, is the mask of a debauched man with a high, wrinkled forehead crowned with three horns.

Selected Bibliography

General

Bihalji-Merin, Oto, *Masks of the World*, London, 1971
Het Masker, Alle volken—Alle tijden, Antwerp, 1956
Lommel, Andreas, *Masks, Their Meaning and Function*, New York, 1972
Mylius, Norbert, *Antlitz und Geheimnis der überseeischen Maske. Eine Einführung in das Maskenwesen der Übersee*, Vienna, 1961
Riley, Olive L., *Masks and Magic*, New York, 1955

Africa

Bleakly, Robert, *African Masks*, London, 1978
Fagg, William, *Masques d'Afrique*, Paris, 1981
Herold, Erich, *The Art of Africa, Tribal Masks*, London, 1967
Himmelheber, Hans, *Les Masques Africains*, Paris, 1960
Huet, Michel — Laude, Jean — Paudrat, Jean Louis, *Danses d'Afrique*, Paris, 1978
Krieger, Kurt — Kutscher, Gerdt, *Westafrikanische Masken*, Berlin, 1960
Monti, Franco, *African Masks*, London, 1969
Underwood, Leon, *Masks of West Africa*, London, 1950

Oceania

Bodrogi, Tibor, *Art in North East New Guinea*, Budapest, 1961
Guiart, Jean, *The Arts of the South Pacific*, London, 1963
Kelm, Heinz *Kunst vom Sepik*, Vols. I—III, Berlin, 1966—8
Newton, Douglas, *Art Styles of the Papuan Gulf*, New York, 1961
Parkinson, Richard, *Dreissig Jahre in der Südsee*, Stuttgart, 1907
Schmitz, Carl, *Oceanic Art: Myth, Man and Image in the South Seas*, New York, 1969
Stöhr, Waldemar, *Melanesien. Schwarze Inseln der Südsee*, Cologne, 1971

The American Continent

Cordry, Donald, *Mexican Masks*, London, 1980
Crumrina, N. Rose — Halpin, Marjorie, *The Power of Symbols*, Vancouver, 1983
Frías, F. J. — Rodriguez, B. P., *Masken aus Mexiko*, Vienna, s. a.

Hartmann, Günter, *Masken südamerikanischer Naturvölker*, Berlin, 1967

Kıng, J. C. H., *Portrait Masks from the Northwest Coast of America*, London, 1979

Krusche, Rolf, 'Zur Genese des Maskenwesens im östlichen Waldland Nordamerikas', in *Jahrbuch des Museums für Völkerkunde*, Leipzig, Vol. XXX, Berlin, 1975

Mora, Joseph, *The Year of the Hopi*, New York, 1979

Mose, José, *Maskaras Animistas*, Buenos Aires, 1979

Vastokas, Joan M., 'The Relation of Form to Iconography in Eskimo Masks', in *The Beaver*, Autumn (Eskimo Art), 26—31, 1967

White, Leslie A., 'The Pueblo of San Felipe', in *Memoirs of the American Anthropological Association*, No. 38, 1932

India

Bhattacharyya, Asutosh, *Chhau Dance of Purulia*, Calcutta, 1972

Bhattacharyya, Asutosh, *Folklore of Bengal*, New Delhi, 1978

Burney, A. C., *Devil Worship of Tuluvas*, 1872

Datta, G.S., *The Folk Dances of Bengal*, Calcutta, 1954

Devi, Ragini, *Dance Dialects of India*, New Delhi, 1972

Elwin, Verrier, *The Tribal Art of Middle India*, London, 1951

Elwin, Verrier, *The Art of the North-east Frontier of India*, Shillong, 1959

Iyer, K. Bharatha, *Dance Dramas of India and the East*, Bombay, 1980

Mathur, J. C., *Drama in Rural India*, Bombay, 1964

The Performing Arts, Marg Publications, New Delhi, 1982

Sarkar, Dr Sabita, 'Chho Masks of Dumurdi', in *Indian Museum Bulletin*, Vol. XVII, 1983

Thurston, Edgar, *Castes and Tribes of Southern India*, 7 vols., Madras, 1909

Sri Lanka

Callaway, John, *Yakkun Nattanawā and Kōlam Nattanawā*, London, 1829

Goonatilleka, M. H., *Masks of Sri Lanka*, Colombo, 1976

Grünwedel, Albert, 'Singhalesische Masken', in *Internationales Archiv für Ethnographie*, Vol. 6, 1893

Höpfner, Gerd, *Masken aus Ceylon*, Berlin, 1969

Lucas, Heinz, *Ceylon-Masken*, Kassel, 1958

Pertold, Otakar, 'Foreign Demons: A Study in the Sinhalese Demon-Worship', in *Archiv Orientální*, Vol. I, 1929

Pertold, Otakar, 'A Singular Sinhalese Mask in the Collection of Náprstek Museum in Prague', in *Archiv Orientální*, Vol. I, 1929

Pertold, Otakar, 'The Ceremonial Dances of the Sinhalese', Parts I—III, in *Archiv Orientální*, Vol. II, 1930

Sarathchandra, E. R., *The Sinhalese Folk Plays and the Modern Stage*, Colombo, 1953

South-East Asia

Covarrubias, Miguel, *Island of Bali*, New York, 1938

Holt, Claire, *Art in Indonesia*, New York, 1967

Höpfner, Gerd, *Südostasiatische Schattenspiele*, Berlin, 1967

Zoete Beryl de — Spies, Walter, *Dance and Drama in Bali*, London, 1938

Japan

Kaneko, Yoshikazu, 'Nō kyōgen men', *Nihon no bijutsu*, Vol. 108, Tokyo, 1975

Maruoka, Daiji — Tatsu, Yoshikoshi, *Noh*, Osaka, 1969

Nakanishi, Toru — Komma, Kiyonori, *Noh Masks*, Tokyo, 1983

Nishikawa, Kyōtarō, *Bugaku Masks*, Tokyo, New York and San Francisco, 1978

Noma, Seiroku, *Masks*, Rutland, Vermont, Tokyo, 1957

Tanabe, Saburōsuke, 'Gyōdō men to shishigashira', *Nihon no bijutsu*, Vol. 185, Tokyo, 1981

Uehara, Shōichi, 'Gigaku men', *Nihon no bijutsu*, Vol. 233, Tokyo, 1985

Korea

Eikemeier, Dieter, *Getanzte Karikaturen. Traditionelle Maskenspiele in Korea*, Stuttgart, 1988

Lee, Du-Hyun, *Les Masques Coréens*, Seoul, 1981

Masks of Korea, The National Folklore Museum, Seoul, 1982

List of Plates

1 A face mask made of wood and sheet brass. Marka, Mali; now in a private collection in Prague. Height 32 cm.

2 A face mask of the *lo* society, made of wood stained black with vestiges of red pigment. Senufo (Siena), Ivory Coast; now in Náprstek Museum, Prague. Height 27 cm.

3 A face mask of black-stained wood. Kulango, Ivory Coast; now in Náprstek Museum, Prague. Height 37 cm.

4 A face mask of painted wood. Shira/Bapunu, Gabon; now in Náprstek Museum, Prague. Height 27 cm.

5 A ceremonial mask for *bedu* dances, made of wood with a painted surface. Nafana, Ivory Coast; now in Náprstek Museum, Prague. Height 121 cm.

6 A face mask of wood with a brownish-black-stained surface and tree bark. Bete, Ivory Coast; now in Náprstek Museum, Prague. Height 27 cm.

7 A male face mask of wood with vestiges of paint, iron nails and sheet iron strips. Ibo, Nigeria; now in Náprstek Museum, Prague. Height 59.5 cm.

8 A face mask of painted wood. Teke, People's Republic of Congo; now in a private collection in Prague. Height 33.2 cm.

9 An elephant mask of stained wood and white clay pigment. Baule-Yaure, Ivory Coast; now in Náprstek Museum, Prague. Height 44.5 cm.

10 Mask of the *gelede* society, made of wood with traces of paint. Yoruba, Nigeria; now in Náprstek Museum, Prague. Height 30 cm.

11 A helmet-shaped initiation mask of the *bundu* female secret society, made of stained wood. Mende, Sierra Leone; now in Náprstek Museum, Prague. Height 40 cm.

12 *Kebe-kebe* dance head-dress of painted wood. Kuyu, People's Republic of Congo; now in Náprstek Museum, Prague. Height 50.5 cm.

13 *Yoké* head-dress made of wood with a black-stained surface. Baga or Nalu, Guinea; now in Náprstek Museum, Prague. Height 78 cm.

14 A buffalo mask of stained wood and white clay pigment. Bamileke, Cameroon; now in Náprstek Museum, Prague. Height 43.5 cm.

15 A miniature mask of stained wood covered with cotton fabric and cowrie shells. Gerze, Liberia; now in Náprstek Museum, Prague. Height 9.5 cm.

16 A buffalo mask of wood with a stained and painted surface. Guro, Ivory Coast; now in Náprstek Museum, Prague. Height 54.5 cm.

17 A dance head-dress of wood, antelope skin, sheet aluminium, bone (teeth) and a basketwork base. Ekoi (Ejagham), Nigeria; now in Náprstek Museum, Prague. Height 44 cm.

18 A face mask of wood decorated with synthetic paints, sheet iron, string, tow, horsehair and brass cartridge cases. Ngere, Ivory Coast; now in Náprstek Museum, Prague. Height 32 cm.

19 A face mask of black-stained wood, sheet aluminium, red factory-made cloth, plant fibres (coloured blue) and an iron nail. Dan or Tura, Ivory Coast; now in Náprstek Museum, Prague. Height (without beard) 23.7 cm.

20 A mask with a figure superstructure, made of brass cast by the lost-wax method. Bamum, Cameroon; now in Náprstek Museum, Prague. Height 43.6 cm.

21 The mask of a guardian of an initiation camp, made of rod construction, sackcloth, resin and textile cuttings, with an extension made of strings. Chokwe, Zaire; now in Náprstek Museum, Prague. Height 51 cm.

22 *M'kishi* mask made of rod construction and bark cloth painted with latex paints. Luvale, Zambia; now in Náprstek Museum, Prague. Height 41 cm.

23 Initiation helmet mask of painted wood with a basketwork construction, fabric and raffia fringes. Yaka, Zaire; now in Náprstek Museum, Prague. Height 52 cm.

24 A face mask of the *ekpo* society, made of painted wood. Bini, Nigeria; now in Náprstek Museum, Prague. Height 27 cm.

25 Miniature replicas of face masks, badges of initiation, made of bone. Pende, Zaire; now in Náprstek Museum, Prague. Height 4.7 and 5.2 cm.

26 *Koruru* mask made of wood inlaid with mother of pearl. Northern New Zealand; now in Museo Nazionale Preistorico e Etnografico 'L. Pigorini', Rome.

27 A miniature mask of pale wood and lime. Sepik, northern New Guinea; now in Náprstek Museum, Prague. Height 17 cm.

28 A miniature mask of pale wood and lime. Sepik, northern New Guinea; now in Náprstek Museum, Prague. Height 20.4 cm.

29 *Jipai* mask of basketwork in bark and wood. Asmat, Irian Jaya; now in Náprstek Museum, Prague. Height (without fringes) 85 cm.

30 Painted *eharo* mask of bark cloth on a wicker construction. Elema, Papuan Gulf, southern New Guinea; now in Náprstek Museum, Prague. Height (without fringes) 90.5 cm.

31 A helmet mask of bark cloth on a bamboo construction. Baining, New Britain; now in Museum für Völkerkunde und Vorgeschichte, Hamburg.

32 *Lor* mask. The facial part of the skull is complemented with black mastic. Tolai, Gazelle Peninsula, New Britain; now in Náprstek Museum, Prague. Height 24 cm.

33 *Sisu* mask made of basketwork from strips of tree bark. Sulka, New Britain; now in Überseemuseum, Bremen.

34 A face mask of wood stained black and white. Baule, Ivory Coast; now in Náprstek Museum, Prague. Height 23.5 cm.

35 A face mask representing female beauty, made of painted wood. Ibo, Nigeria; now in Náprstek Museum, Prague. Height 33 cm.

36 A face mask of painted wood. Fang, Gabon; now in Náprstek Museum, Prague. Height 33.5 cm.

37 A helmet mask with a figure superstructure for the *epa* ceremony, made of painted wood. Ekiti-Yoruba, Nigeria; now in Náprstek Museum, Prague. Height 106.5 cm.

38 A face mask of black-stained wood with white clay pigment and strings. Dan, Ivory Coast; now in Náprstek Museum, Prague. Height 24.5 cm.

39 A face mask of painted wood. Guro/ Bete, Ivory Coast; now in Náprstek Museum, Prague. Height 29.5 cm.

40 *Mwana pwo* face mask of painted wood with a knitted extension of strings and glass beads. Chokwe, Zaire; now in Náprstek Museum, Prague. Height 25 cm.

41 Initiation face mask of painted wood, raffia cloth and fringes. Pende, Zaire; now in Náprstek Museum, Prague. Height 46 cm.

42 A face mask of painted wood. Vuvi, Gabon; now in Náprstek Museum, Prague. Height 33.5 cm.

43 A face mask of painted wood. Aitape, northern coast of New Guinea; now in Náprstek Museum, Prague. Height 46 cm.

44 A helmet mask of painted wood. Bismarck Archipelago, Witu Island; now in Rautenstrauch-Joest Museum, Cologne.

45 *Kulapteine* mask of painted wood and plant fibres. Northern New Ireland; now in Náprstek Museum, Prague. Width 58 cm.

46 *Nit* mask of painted wood and plant fibres. Northern New Ireland; now in Náprstek Museum, Prague. Height 105.5 cm.

47 Mask of stained wood and plant fibres. Northern New Caledonia; now in Náprstek Museum, Prague. Height 39 cm.

48 A mask of the False Face society, made of wood. Onondaga, USA; now in Deutsches Ledermuseum, Offenbach a.M. Height 32 cm.

49 'Suffering Moor' mask for the scenes 'Moros y Cristianos', Nahua, Mexico; now in Náprstek Museum, Prague. Height 29 cm.

50 Mask of Pedro Alvarado for the dance 'La Conquista', made of painted wood. Chichicastenango, Guatemala; now in a private collection in Prague. Height 19 cm.

51 A face mask of painted wood. Sepik, northern New Guinea; now in Náprstek Museum, Prague. Height 53 cm.

52 A *kani* mask of painted wood. Tami Island, northern New Guinea; now in Náprstek Museum, Prague. Height 44.5 cm.

53 Painted *eharo* mask of bark cloth on a wicker construction. Elema, Papuan Gulf, southern New Guinea; now in Náprstek Museum, Prague. Height (without fringes) 58 cm.

54 *Kepong* mask of painted wood. Northern New Ireland; now in Náprstek Museum, Prague. Height (without fringes) 62 cm.

55 *Tatanua* mask of painted wood and bark cloth on a bamboo frame. Northern New Ireland; now in Náprstek Museum, Prague. Height 32 cm.

56 Painted mask of the *quat* secret society, made from the wood of a fern-tree and clay. New Hebrides; now in Náprstek Museum, Prague. Height 65 cm.

57 A painted face mask made of driftwood. Nunivak, Alaska; now in St Museum für Völkerkunde, Munich. Perimeter 55 cm.

58 A dance mask of a wolf made of painted wood. Kwakiutl, British Columbia, Canada; now in Náprstek Museum, Prague. Length 63 cm.

59 A dance mask made of wood coloured with graphite. Kwakiutl, British Columbia, Canada; now in a private collection in Prague. Height 27 cm.

60 Tecum Uman mask for the dance 'La Conquista', made of painted wood. Chichicastenango, Guatemala; now in a private collection in Prague. Height 16 cm.

61 Mask of a young bull for the dance 'La Conquista', made of painted wood. The mask is used along with those of Nos. 50 and 60. Chichicastenango, Guatemala; now in a private collection in Prague. Height 16 cm.

62 A dance mask of sheep skin and horsehair, with horns made of wood covered with leather. Mapuche, Chile; now in Náprstek Museum, Prague. Height 46 cm.

63 A dance mask of sheep skin with horns made of wood covered with leather. Mapuche, Chile; now in Náprstek Museum, Prague. Height 41 cm.

64 A bat mask for an animal dance, made of painted wood. Nahua, Mexico; now in Náprstek Museum, Prague. Height 67 cm.

65 A butterfly mask for an animal dance, made of painted wood. Nahua, Mexico; now in Náprstek Museum, Prague. Height 63 cm.

66 'Fariseo' mask for Easter plays, helmet-shaped and made of untanned skin. Yaki, Mexico; now in Náprstek Museum, Prague. Height 27 cm.

67 A dance mask of wood, with glass eyes and painted. Mexico; now in Náprstek Museum, Prague. Height 19 cm.

68 A helmet-shaped dance mask of painted wood with leather ears, hart antlers and a hart's hooves. Nahua, Mexico; now in Náprstek Museum, Prague. Height 85 cm.

69 The mask of a spirit, made of tree bark painted with white clay. Yaghan, Argentine; now in Museum of the American Indians, Heye Foundation. Height 61 cm.

70 A dance mask of fired clay. Mexico; now in a private collection in Prague. Height 13 cm.

71 The mask of a giant, made of calabashes and bark cloth. Kobéua, Brazil; now in Museum für Völkerkunde, Berlin. Height 33 cm.

72 Mask worn in tiger plays, made of painted wood. Oaxaca, Mexico; now in Náprstek Museum, Prague. Height 26 cm.

73 Mask used at the 'Diablo Macho' dance, made of painted wood. Nahua, Mexico; now in Náprstek Museum, Prague. Height 71 cm.

74 The mask of the leading dancer at a devils' dance, made of textile, plaster and paste-board and painted. Bolivia; now in Náprstek Museum, Prague. Height 57 cm.

75 Mask of a Spaniard for the dance 'La Conquista', made of painted wood. Guatemala; now in Náprstek Museum, Prague. Height 19 cm.

76 The mask of an ordinary dancer at a devils' dance, made of painted papier-mâché. Bolivia; now in Náprstek Museum, Prague. Height 26 cm.

77 A dance mask of painted leather. Mexico; now in Náprstek Museum, Prague. Height 23 cm.

78 A wooden mask with decoration derived from the painting of the face. Huichol, Mexico; now in Náprstek Museum, Prague. Height 25 cm.

79 A bark cloth mask, covered with a layer of resin with yellow and white decoration. Central Brazil; now in Náprstek Museum, Prague. Height 33 cm.

80 A hood-shaped mask of bark cloth, resin and white clay. Tucuna, Brazil; now in Náprstek Museum, Prague. Height 35 cm.

81 Mask of the sun demon, made of wood painted black. Kágaba, Colombia; now in Museum für Völkerkunde, Berlin. Height 17 cm.

82 Mask of the sun demon, made of wood painted brown with feathers. Chiriguano, Bolivia; now in Museum für Völkerkunde, Berlin. Height 21 cm.

83 The god Ganesha's ceremonial dance mask, made of layered painted paper covered with transparent varnish. Orissa, India; now in Náprstek Museum, Prague. Height 39.5 cm.

84 Rakshasa, a demon of the *Ramayana.* Mask of the dance drama *Ramlila,* made of cloth on a stiff paper base, silver tinsel, textile appliqué, sewn-on glass beads, bullions and pailletes, by the so-called *zari* technique; beard made of strings and cotton yarn. Varanasi, Uttarpradesh, India; now in Náprstek Museum, Prague. Height 36 cm.

85 Mask of Ganesha with a Shivaist trident carved in relief on the forehead and the sacred syllable 'om' at the top of the trunk, made of wood stained dark brown and oiled, decorated with white dots. Nepal; now in a private collection in Prague. Height 65 cm.

86 Mahakala, king of the kingdom of the dead. Note the third eye on the forehead. Nepal; now in a private collection in Prague. Height 37 cm.

87 Jatayu. A bird mask of the dance drama *Ramlila,* made of painted lacquered paper. Allahabad, Uttarpradesh, India; now in a private collection in Prague. Height 30 cm.

88 Animal masks of the dance drama *Ramlila* (from left to right): Sugriva, tiger, bear, Jatayu, and Hanuman; made of painted lacquered paper. Allahabad, Uttarpradesh, India; now in a private collection in Prague. Height *c.* 30—40 cm.

89 Rakshasa. The mask of a demon of the dance drama *Ramlila,* made of painted layered paper. Jaynagar, West Bengal, India; now in Náprstek Museum, Prague. Height 28 cm.

90 A horse mask of dance dramas dealing with legends of Rajput aristocracy, made of textile with bamboo frame, sewn-on bullions, fringes, ribbons etc. Rajasthan, India; now in Náprstek Museum Prague. Height (including the skirt) 190 cm.

91 The mask of a mythical bird from a lamas' dance, made of painted and lacquered wood. Bhutan; now in Náprstek Museum, Prague. Height (without horns) 22.5 cm.

92 Dushana, a general of Ravana's army. A wooden, painted and lacquered mask for a dance drama of the Deshi-Polia, inspired by the *Ramayana.* Dinajpur, West Bengal, India; now in the Indian Museum, Calcutta. Height 32 cm.

93 The black goddess Kali. A mask of a ritual *gambhira* drama, made of painted sola (*Aeschynomene indica*). Maldah district, West Bengal, India; photo from field research. Height *c.* 40 cm.

94 The mask of a wife of a British colonial official, used in a comic scene filling up an interval of a puppet theatre performance; made of painted and lacquered wood. Jodhpur district, Rajasthan, India; now in Rupayan Sansthan (Institute of Folklore), Borunda, Rajasthan. Height 40 cm.

95 A mask of Shiva for the *chau* dance drama, executed in the Dumurdi style, made of painted and lacquered paper covered with a layer of clay and fabric. Purulia district, West Bengal, India; now in the Indian Museum, Calcutta. Height 35 cm.

96 Kariraya, and attendant deity of local village goddesses, of painted and lacquered wood. Mandya district, Karnataka, India; photo from field research. Height 40 cm.

97 A hero of noble origin with a shivaistic mark on his forehead, made of wood carved with paste called *putuni* and a layer of textile, decorated with paint. Orissa, India; now in Náprstek Museum, Prague. Height 36 cm.

98 The goddess Durga. A mask for the *chau* dance dramas, executed in the Charida style, made of layered paper covered with a layer of clay and textile and decorated with coloured varnish. Ornaments are made of synthetic materials, glass beads, gold-foil, wool tassels, etc. Purulia district, West Bengal, India; now in a private collection in Prague. Height 91 cm.

99 The tribal deity Buriya. A mask for a dance drama of the Bhil tribe, named Gauri; made of wood lacquered in orange with many-coloured tinsel. The hair and moustache are made of black fibres and the teeth of peacock quills. Udaipur district, Rajasthan, India; now in a private collection in Prague. Height 32.5 cm.

100 Masks of a man and a woman of comic

interludes of religious dance dramas, made of dark brown stained wood. Borderland of India and Nepal; now in a private collection in Prague. Height 35 and 32 cm.

101 Mahakali. A mask of religious dances performed during the Mahakali Pyakhan festival, made of papier-mâché, covered with polychrome and transparent lacquer. Kathmandu, Nepal; now in Náprstek Museum, Prague. Height 65 cm.

102 The monkey god Hanuman, attendant of the hero Rama, with the mark of Vishnu on his forehead. Wood with a dark brown stained surface. Puri, Orissa, India; now in a private collection in Prague. Height 41 cm.

103 A mask of the Nagaraj mythical being which performed at masquerades. It has a pair of arms and two lion figures with a lion-tail handle. The arms are made of painted layered paper; lions made of painted layered paper are glued to the layer of clay covering the straw core. Raghurajpur, Puri district, Orissa, India; now in Náprstek Museum, Prague. Length of the arms 62 and 61 cm, length of the lions 91 and 89 cm.

104 The demon Taraka. A mask for a masquerade at the spring festival, made of layered painted paper, silver tinsel (jewels) and sola (teeth). Radasahi, Bhuvaneshvar district, Orissa, India; now in Náprstek Museum, Prague. Height 30 cm.

105 A tiger with a Vishnuist mark on his forehead. A mask for local dance dramas, inspired by the epic *Ramayana.* Vishnupur, West Bengal, India; now in Náprstek Museum, Prague. Height 25 cm.

106 Mask of the god Shiva, made of painted layered paper. Midnapore district, West Bengal, India; now in Náprstek Museum, Prague. Height 21 cm.

107 The demon king Hiranyakashipu. A mask for the dance drama *Prahladacharitam,* made of lacquered papier-mâché and painted. Jodhpur district, Rajasthan, India; now in a private collection in Prague. Height 23 cm.

108 An icon of Shiva-Khandoba in the form of a metal face mask, made of brass. Bangalore district, Karnataka, India; now in Náprstek Museum, Prague. Height 18.5 cm.

109 The mask of an ascetic for a satirical dance scene of the Muria tribe, made from a gourd (*Lagenaria vulgaris*) with details burned in with a red-hot poker. The nose is carved from wood. Jagdalpur district, Madhyapradesh, India; now in Náprstek Museum, Prague. Height 34.5 cm.

110 The mask of a *bhuta,* made of painted leaf-sheaths of the areca palm (*Areca catechu*), coconut leaves and plant fibres. Kerala, India; photo from field research. Height *c.* 45 cm.

111 Maha-kola Sanniya, leader of the Sanni-demons. Eighteen spirits of illnesses stand at both sides of the main figure. A mask made of painted wood. Sri Lanka; now in Náprstek Museum, Prague. Size 110 × 78 cm.

112 Rukdeviya, a tree-deity identified by O. Pertold, which, according to E. R. Sarathchandra, appears in a *kolam* drama entitled 'Gothayimbara Katava'; made of painted wood. Sri Lanka; now in Náprstek Museum, Prague. Height 23.8 cm.

113 Sandakinduru. A mask of one of the main *kolam* dramas entitled 'Sandakinduru Katava'. Identified by Gamini Wijesuriya. Colombo, Sri Lanka; now in Náprstek Museum, Prague. Height 22.5 cm.

114 The mask of a king of the *kolam* dramas, made of painted wood. It is helmet-shaped, and consists of three individual parts. Sri Lanka; now in Náprstek Museum, Prague. Height 115 cm.

115 The mask of Totsakan (Ravana) of the *khon* plays, made of painted and gilded papier-mâché, leather, mother of pearl, wood and mirrors. Thailand; now in Museum für Völkerkunde, Berlin. Height 70.5 cm.

116 The mask of the demon Bilua, made of painted papier-mâché. Mandalay, Burma; now in Náprstek Museum, Prague. Height 29 cm.

117 The second queen or princess mask of a *kolam* drama, made of painted wood, with the basic colour being yellow. Sri Lanka; now in Náprstek Museum, Prague. Height 34.5 cm.

118 Hevaya, a soldier disfigured by wounds suffered in fierce battles. A mask introducing a *kolam* drama, made of painted wood with a basic colour of yellowish-brown. Sri Lanka; now in Náprstek Museum, Prague. Height 27 cm.

119 A lion with its mane stylised into a ridge. A mask of a *kolam* drama, made of painted wood, with the basic colour being yellow. Sri Lanka; now in Náprstek Museum, Prague. Height 42 cm.

120 A serpent-demon mask of the *kolam* dramas, made of painted wood, with a base colour of green. Sri Lanka; now in Náprstek Museum, Prague. Height 49 cm.

121 *Topeng* mask personifying a dead only son, made of wood. Toba-Batak, Sumatra, Indonesia; now in Rijkmuseum voor Volkenkunde, Leiden. Height 31 cm.

122 A fanciful dance mask of wood, bone, tortoise-shell and glass beads. Leti Island, Indonesia; now in Koninklijk Instituut voor de Tropen, Amsterdam. Height 14 cm.

123 A half-mask, probably used in the *kuda kepang* plays, made of painted wood. Madura, Indonesia; now in Náprstek Museum, Prague. Height 13.7 cm.

124 *Wayang topeng* face mask, made of painted wood. Madura, Indonesia; now in Náprstek Museum, Prague. Height 20 cm.

125 *Wayang topeng* face mask, made of painted wood. Java, Indonesia; now in Náprstek Museum, Prague.

126 *Wayang topeng* face mask, made of painted wood. Java, Indonesia; now in Náprstek Museum, Prague.

127 A warrior's mask made of palm-leaf-sheath, coconut fibres, wood and red cotton strips. Nias, Indonesia; now in Náprstek Museum, Prague. Height *c.* 50 cm.

128 *Wayang topeng* face mask made of painted wood. Java, Indonesia; now in Náprstek Museum, Prague. Height 20 cm.

129 *Hodo-apah* mask of painted wood and mirrors. Kajan or Bahau, Kalimantan, Indonesia; now in Koninklijk Instituut voor de Tropen, Amsterdam. Height 30 cm.

130 *Wayang wong* mask of a monkey, made of painted wood. Bali, Indonesia; now in Náprstek Museum, Prague. Height 19 cm.

131 *Wayang topeng* masks of a prince and a princess, made of painted wood, mother of pearl and animal hair. Bali, Indonesia; now in Náprstek Museum, Prague.

132 A mask of the mythical bird Garuda of the *wayang wong* dance drama. Bali, Indonesia; now in Náprstek Museum, Prague. Height 20 cm.

133 The face mask of a supernatural being of the *barong* plays, made of painted wood. Bali, Indonesia; now in Náprstek Museum, Prague. Height 17.3 cm.

134 *Barong* mask of the witch Rangda, made of painted wood. Bali, Indonesia; now in Náprstek Museum, Prague. Height 25 cm.

135 *Wayang topeng* mask of an old man, made of wood with vestiges of paint and animal hair. Bali, Indonesia; now in Náprstek Museum, Prague. Height 19 cm.

136 A folk-type mask with a disfigured face, for the *wayang topeng,* made of wood with vestiges of paint. Bali, Indonesia; now in Náprstek Museum, Prague. Height 21.5 cm.

137 A funeral mask made of painted papier-mâché. Jehol, Manchuria; now in Etnografiska museet, Stockholm. Height 22 cm.

138 Mask of the King of Go for the *gigaku* dances, made of camphor wood with vestiges of paint. The diadem is made of gilded bronze. Japan, second half of the seventh century; now in Tokyo National Museum, formerly Hōryūji temple! Height 29.9 cm.

139 Chidō mask of the *gigaku* dances, made of dry lacquer and painted, plus a decoration of plant fibres and a sheet metal disc. Japan, Edo period (1600-1868). This is a replica of a mask from the eighth century. Now in Náprstek Museum, Prague. Height 31.5 cm.

140 Chikyū mask for a *bugaku* performance. made of painted hinoki wood. Japan, carver Inshō, dated 1185; now in Kasuga shrine, Nara. Height 21.3 cm.

141 Ryōō mask for a *bugaku* performance, made of wood with painted decoration, plus yellow sheet metal and horsehair. Japan, signed 'Uzumasa Sukune Toshinaga', dated 1856. Now in Náprstek Museum, Prague. Height 39 cm.

142 Tengu mask used at Shintō festivals, made of painted, lacquered wood. Japan; now in Náprstek Museum, Prague. Height 25 cm.

143 A dragon mask for New Year folk dances, made of painted papier-mâché on a wooden frame. China; now in Náprstek Museum, Prague. Height 46 cm.

144 *Shishigashira* mask of a lion dance, made of painted, lacquered wood. Japan, nineteenth century; now in Náprstek Museum, Prague. Height 33 cm.

145 A male mask of the *kagura* dances, made of painted wood. Japan, nineteenth century; now in Náprstek Museum, Prague.

146 A male mask of the *kagura* dances, made of painted wood and horsehair. Japan,

nineteenth century; now in Náprstek Museum, Prague. Height 21.1 cm.

147 A boy's mask for the *kagura* dances, made of painted wood. Japan, nineteenth century; now in Náprstek Museum, Prague.

148 Kasshiki. A boy's mask for the *nō* plays, made of painted wood. Japan, Edo period; now in Náprstek Museum, Prague. Height 21.3 cm.

149 *Ko-omote* female mask for the *nō* plays made of painted wood. Japan, Edo period, signed 'Deme Tohaku'. Now in Náprstek Museum, Prague. Height 21.4 cm.

150 Ōbeshimi demon mask for the *nō* plays made of painted wood. Japan, Edo period, signed 'Shojuken'. Now in Náprstek Museum, Prague. Height 22.6 cm.

151 An actor wearing a Hakushikijō mask at an Okina dance. *Netsuke* made of ivory. Japan, nineteenth century; now in Náprstek Museum, Prague. Height 5.5 cm.

152 Miniature fox mask with a movable lower jaw for the *kyōgen* plays. *Netsuke* made of wood. Japan, nineteenth century. Signed by Deme Sukemitsu Tenka ichi; now in Náprstek Museum, Prague. Height 5 cm.

153 Usobuki mask for the *kyōgen* plays, made of painted wood and plant fibres. Japan; now in Tokyo National Museum.

154 Three miniature *netsuke* masks. From the left: a Hannya female demon mask for the *nō* plays, made of ivory. Signed by Shungetsu. Japan, nineteenth century; now in Náprstek Museum, Prague. Height 3.5 cm.
Oto or Okame mask for the *kyōgen* plays, made of ivory. Signed by Mitsuyuki. Japan, nineteenth century; now in Náprstek Museum, Prague. Height 3.8 cm.
Hyottoko mask for the *kyōgen* plays. Signed by Gyokuzan. Japan, nineteenth century; now in Náprstek Museum, Prague. Height 3.3 cm.

155 The mask of an old man for dance plays, made of painted paper and plant fibres. Pongsan, Hwanghaedo Province, Korea, mid-twentieth century; now in Náprstek Museum, Prague. Height 27 cm.

156 A monkey mask for dance plays, made of painted paper with rabbit fur. Pongsan, Hwanghaedo Province, Korea, mid-twentieth century; now in Náprstek Museum, Prague. Height 28 cm.

157 A mask of a monk for dance plays, made of painted paper. Pongsan, Hwanghaedo Province, Korea, mid-twentieth century; now in Náprstek Museum, Prague. Height 28.5 cm.

158 A monkey mask for dance plays, made of painted paper and grass. Pongsan, Hwanghaedo Province, Korea, mid-twentieth century; now in Náprstek Museum, Prague. Height 22 cm.

Index

Page numbers in italics refer to illustrations